# The Council of Ministers

# The Council of Ministers

*Political Authority in the European Union*

Philippa Sherrington

**PINTER**

London and New York

Pinter
*A Continuum Imprint*
Wellington House, 125 Strand, London WC2R 0BB
370 Lexington Avenue, New York, NY 10017–6550
First published 2000

**British Library Cataloguing in Publication Data**
A catalogue record for this book is available from the British Library.

ISBN    1-85567-594-3 (hardback)
        1-85567-721-0 (paperback)

**Library of Congress Cataloging-in-Publication Data**
Sherrington, Philippa, 1968–
    The Council of Ministers: political authority in the European Union / Philippa
    Sherrington.
        p. cm.
    Includes bibliographical references and index.
    ISBN 1-85567-594-3 (HB) — ISBN 1-85567-721-0 (PB)
    1. Council of the European Union. I. Title.

JN34.S54 2000
341.24'24—dc21                                                          99-048962

Designed and typeset by Ben Cracknell Studios
Printed and bound in Great Britain by CPD (Wales),
Ebbw Vale.

# Contents

# Figures

# Tables

# *Acknowledgements*

The Council of Ministers was and remains a challenging EU institution to research, and without the help of many people the task would have been much harder and less pleasurable. I would like to thank all the national Ministers, members of the General Secretariat of the Council, officials of the Commission, and numerous MEPs who gave up their time to assist me. Some spoke freely about the Council, so they shall remain anonymous. A special thank you must go to the UK Permanent Representation in Brussels for enabling me to attend some Council meetings, Sir William Nicoll for some enlightening conversations, Lutz Goebel, Head of the Library of the Council, for his invaluable assistance, and Jean Thompson of the Council's Press Service for her patience. I remain grateful to Helen Wallace, Peter Anderson and Richard Luther for all their support and guidance in my research, to Petra Recter for the opportunity to write this book, and Caroline Wintersgill at Cassell for her patience and assistance in preparing the manuscript. Peter and Susie kindly provided some practical help which was much appreciated in times of technological frustration. Acknowledgements can become rather tedious for the reader if they are too personal but those who know me will understand that I must say a huge thank you to everyone at St Georges, to family and friends who were great in putting up with me, and to my sister Becky for always being there.

# *Abbreviations*

| | |
|---|---|
| Cedefop | European Centre for the Development of Vocational Training |
| CFSP | Common Foreign and Security Policy |
| COCOR | Comité de Coordination de la Communauté du Charbon et de l'Acier |
| Coreper | Committee of Permanent Representatives |
| Crest | Committee on Scientific and Technical Research |
| DTEU | Draft Treaty on European Union |
| EC | European Community |
| EcoFin | Economic & Financial Affairs Council |
| ECJ | European Court of Justice |
| ECSC | European Coal and Steel Community |
| ECU | European Currency Unit |
| EEA | European Economic Area |
| EFTA | European Free Trade Association |
| EMU | Economic and Monetary Union |
| EP | European Parliament |
| EPC | European Political Cooperation |
| ERM | Exchange Rate Mechanism |
| ESC | Economic and Social Committee |
| EU | European Union |
| Eurydice | European Community Education Information Network |
| GATT | General Agreement on Tariffs and Trade |
| IGC | Intergovernmental Conference |
| MEP | Member of the European Parliament |
| Naric | National Academic Recognition Information Centre |
| SEA | Single European Act |
| TEU | Treaty on European Union |
| UK | United Kingdom |
| VAT | Value Added Tax |

# *Author's note*

The most appropriate use of European Community and European Union is guided by institutional structures, but for simplicity the term European Union is used as much as possible. There are however references to the European Community where it is historically appropriate, and in particular in the case studies where research was carried out prior to implementation of the Treaty on European Union.

# Introduction

## Why the Council?

The Council of Ministers (hereafter referred to as 'the Council')[1] occupies the most important position in the institutional structure of the European Union (EU), having the final power of decision upon all matters of EU policy-making. The Council is a Community institution, but it also embraces fifteen member-state governments. It is the forum in which member-state representatives with diverse policy objectives come together and negotiate. These interactions and subsequent outputs define the nature of EU policies, and consequently the direction of European integration.

The significance and impact of EU policy-making activity is ever-increasing. Whilst attempts exist to explain and demystify the processes of EU policy-making, they cannot be complete without a detailed investigation of the Council. Until now, most debate concentrated upon the 'closed' nature of the Council, and its lack of direct accountability. However, until the operation of the Council is clearly understood, such debate is being conducted within a vacuum. Presently, academic research is re-examining the institutional debate in the light of the treaty revisions, as well as considering the future prospects of the EU. To achieve a better understanding of EU policy-making and the dynamics of European integration, the Council's role and operational mechanisms must take a central place in such research. This study addresses this need by examining the work of some of the technical councils that constitute the Council, between 1988 and 1992. Whilst there have been numerous developments since then, the Council is slow to change and the results of this analysis provide some useful insights into the workings of the Council, and contribute to a deeper appreciation of how member states conduct EU policy-making within the Council.

The Council is the powerhouse of the EU yet its day-to-day workings are under-investigated. This study analyses the operation of the Council, by examining its role within the EU policy network, its structure and organizational procedures, its policy-making mechanisms, and assesses its importance for the efficacy of EU policy-making. This will provide a better understanding about the precise role of the Council, and the dynamics of EU policy-making.

The main contention of this book is that detailed analysis of the Council's structure and current operational patterns are essential to an understanding of EU policy-making, yet this is one of the least studied aspects of EU affairs. Until now, academic analyses have tended to concentrate upon certain aspects of the Council.[2] There are only two published works which deal exclusively with the Council as a whole. Westlake's (1995) contribution is a valuable reference source on the structures and procedures of the Council, but does not delve deeper into the actual workings of the Council. Hayes-Renshaw and Wallace (1997) provide an incisive and stimulating analysis of the Council, treating it as a unitary body.

Most research on the Council has concentrated upon the role of the Presidency.[3] All of this is valuable, yet it only partly evaluates the structure and operation of the Council. Edwards and Wallace (1977: i) promise to provide information about the Council's 'obscure and criticised operations'. They correctly point out how the reality of Community policy-making differs from the 'blueprints' offered by the treaties and how the Council is so often portrayed as a fragmented policy-maker:

> Critics of the Council frequently point to the backlog of unfinished business, the hand-to-mouth organisation of meetings and the late circulation of papers as evidence of its deficiencies. Some of these criticisms seek to find scapegoats for political failures. (Edwards and Wallace, 1977: 14)

However, they devote only one chapter to a consideration of the Council as a whole unit. The remainder of their work analyses the role of the Presidency, and in particular that of the then-immanent UK Presidency. Despite the value of Edwards and Wallace's observations, the Council's structure and operation have altered significantly since 1977, and therefore they need updating.

Furthermore, analysis of the Presidency in isolation is misleading; it gives the reader the impression that the office of the Presidency of the Council is all-powerful. Although it is important, it is wrong to assume that the Presidency totally controls Council policy-making. Kirchner's (1992) contribution to the literature fails in exactly this respect. He adopts a useful methodology to analyse the operation of the Presidency; however, his assessment only centres on the impact of the Presidency on EU policy-making. He rightly concludes that it is necessary to distinguish between the role of the Presidency as a manager and its role as initiator, but offers little analysis of the actual work of the Presidency. There is also an inherent danger in focusing purely upon the national perspectives of the Presidency. O'Nuallain's edited collection (1985) does precisely this by showing how the Council consists of twelve distinct national structures, and failing to analyse how the Presidency of the Council functions. A purely Presidential focus can create a rather disjointed portrait of Council policy-making. Other literature proves that the office of the Presidency is an integral part of the Council's operational mechanisms. However, it is essential to recognize that it is only a part of the structure of the Council.

The European Council is part of the Council's sub-structure although its policy-making processes differ from the Council. The European Council is strictly intergovernmental in nature, and consequently, is seen as being 'above' the Council.[4] Bulmer and Wessels (1987) show how the establishment of the European Council was a necessary consequence of the deepening of the Community. Whether its establishment is a positive development is often a source of debate. Problematic issues are often 'pushed up' to the level of the European Council for discussion and hopefully solution. However, the Treaty of Rome did not provide for the establishment of the European Council (although the Single European Act (SEA) recognized its existence). This process of referral to the Heads of State or Government adds further weight to the argument that a democratic deficit inhibits EU policy-making.

The recent work by Werts (1992) is typical of the tendency to portray the European Council as a separate part of the EU's institutional structure. Although Werts provides a useful summary of the work of the European Council, he fails to place it within the context of the wider Council. Troy Johnston's (1994) contribution is rather narrative in its analysis of the European Council, and fails to examine the position of the European Council within EU policy-making. None of the literature emphasizes that the European Council constitutes a tier of the Council's overall structure, rather than a separate EU institution. It may operate according to different decision rules, but it is still an essential part of Council policy-making. Therefore, it is important to analyse the European Council from the perspective of its role in Council policy-making.

As an institution, Coreper (the Committee of Permanent Representatives) sits between the Council and member-state governments. All contributions dealing with Coreper agree that it is essential to the EU policy-making process.[5] However, the role of Coreper has increased in significance over the past two decades with the widening and deepening of the EU. Noël and Etienne's (1971) argument that the existence of Coreper has not affected the institutional balance needs reviewing. Hayes demonstrates that Coreper has speeded up policy-making, and her later contribution to the literature stresses this further by emphasizing Coreper's 'vital role for the conduct of Community affairs' (Hayes-Renshaw et al., 1989: 136). Analyses of Coreper also consider how each member-state organizes its permanent delegation according to its own criteria. The structure of Coreper differs according to geographical position and national approaches to EU policy-making, which can have an effect both on Coreper, and on the work of the Council.

The input of Coreper is often viewed from a national, rather than European perspective, either by assessing national approaches to EU policy-making (Bulmer, 1983; Evans, 1981; Feld and Wildgen, 1975; Niblock, 1971; Wallace, 1973) or by focusing upon the impact of the EU on national policy-making (Almarcha Barbado, 1993; Bulmer et al., 1992; Dreyfus et al., 1993; Francioni, 1992; Kazakos and Ioakimidis, 1994; Keatinge, 1991; Lyck, 1992; Schweitzer and Karsten, 1990; van Meerhaeghe, 1992; Wolters and Coffey, 1990). The recent research by Beyers and Dierickx (1998) on Coreper working groups is a most welcome analysis of Coreper operating methods, demonstrating the centrality of informal processes and national practices. Yet, there remains a lack of empirical research into the precise role of Coreper from a policy perspective, and in particular whether this differs between the various technical councils that constitute the Council.

Most academic works on the EU provide some information and analysis of the Council. Some are rather brief and restrictive, as they deal with EU policies as well as policy-making. The best general contributions are those by Nicoll and Salmon (1994) and Nugent (1994). Nicoll and Salmon analyse the structure of the EU institutions and provide good insight into the development of EU policy-making (after all, Nicoll is a former practitioner). However, there is little analysis of the policy-making processes. Nugent considers the processes but selects only agriculture for empirical consideration. Obviously, agricultural policy is important, being the most established EU policy area. However, agriculture is a special case. Other aspects of EU policy-making have established themselves as important areas and require investigation. There has also been a recent increase in edited publications which do contain essential chapters on institutional developments, and obviously books that deal with the Treaty on European

Union (TEU).[6] However, none of these sufficiently analyses the operation of the Council, although a certain amount of literature does deal specifically with the issue of voting in the Council (Brams, 1985; Deniau 1984; Dewost 1988; Hayes-Renshaw 1990; Hosli, 1996; Nicoll, 1984, 1986c).

Further analysis of the Council as a unitary body is still needed, which assesses its workings, policy-making mechanisms, and day-to-day operation. De Mesquita and Stokman's (1994) collection recognized the pivotal role of the Council, but failed to analyse its operation adequately. The volume rigorously tests a number of policy-making models, but only shows how these may be useful methodological tools for analysing EU policy-making as a whole. What is needed is comparative analysis of the work of the different technical councils, not only to explain and understand how the Council operates, but to enhance existing knowledge of EU policy-making processes. If the various technical councils do work differently, this could have a profound impact upon the future of EU policy-making.

## Methodological considerations

The Council meets in camera, making investigation of its operation the more difficult. The availability of sources is limited and may be one reason why little academic analysis exists on the operation of the Council. How is it possible to investigate the internal decision-making processes of the Council when discussion is kept secret? Examination of the Council's operation through application of the framework is based upon documentary analysis, Brussels-based fieldwork, and implication analysis. This three-fold approach partly overcomes the problem of limited available sources.

Council minutes were still subject to a thirty-year law of restriction when the case studies were researched. However, the contents of Council minutes are fairly comparable to Council press releases which are used, together with Commission and EP official documentation and reports from *Agence Europe* (the Brussels-based press agency whose daily reports on EU events are valuable sources for practitioners and scholars alike). To give the most accurate interpretation of these sources, a meticulous and precise cross-referencing has been carried out. All that is excluded from Council press releases are those areas of severe disagreement. Such disputes and conflicts can be deduced from *Agence Europe*, whose work is highly praised by both Brussels officials and academics.

Along with these sources, the author conducted fifty-nine in-depth interviews with officials from the three key EU institutions. These included interviews with former Foreign Ministers, as well as serving Directors-

General and Heads of Division from the General Secretariat, and other officials in the Council. Commission representatives and MEPs were also interviewed. The author was also extremely fortunate to be invited to attend three Council sessions, which enabled her to appreciate the mechanics of Council meetings.

Although the Brussels-based fieldwork and analysis of available documentation provide direct evidence of the work of the Council, these sources cannot offer a definitive account of the dynamics of Council negotiations. They do not always give sufficient detail about member-state positions on particular proposals. Therefore, it is also necessary to apply implication analysis when examining the Council. Implication analysis refers to the process whereby the positions of member states on a proposal can be inferred from their general approach to that particular policy area. Consequently, this provides a further layer of detail about Council negotiations on the proposal. This requires analysis of the political, economic, and ideological positions of each member state at a given moment. General EU literature and specialized policy literature on member states can be used as sources for such implication analysis. However, it is extremely important to stress that this approach does not give a causal analysis. It is only possible to *suggest* the likely member-state positions on EU policy proposals through examination of their general approach; their positions cannot be deduced from the available evidence. In addition, this approach is not able to identify the positions of all the 'indians' involved in Council negotiations, although it can analyse the likely approach of most of the 'chiefs'. Consideration of the context in which the Council negotiated on a proposal will also help to analyse the probable position of member states. Implication analysis partly addresses the limitations of available sources on the work of the Council, adding a further layer of detail, providing that it is applied carefully.

To achieve a better understanding of the dynamics of EU policy-making, there is a need for a multi-dimensional analysis of the structure and operational mechanisms of the Council. This is done by moving from the general to the particular, from an overall portrait of the Council's operation, to detailed cases of its work. Chapter 1 identifies the position of the Council within the EU policy network. Analysis will concentrate upon the development of EU policy-making since the Treaty of Rome, showing how the Council has remained the final decision-maker. The relevance of integration theories to the position of the Council will be examined, as will the Council's relationship with the Commission and the EP. This will enable conclusions to be made about the nature of the EU policy network and the position of the Council within it. The operation of the Council is then contextualized by surveying EU policy-making activity between 1982 and 1992, focusing in particular on the years 1988–92. This provides essential details about the environment that the Council worked within, so that the case studies can be better understood.

Chapters 2 and 3 examine the internal structure and organizational procedures of the Council as a whole so as to identify operational factors which vary between its sub-units, and its methods of decision-making. Chapter 4 proposes a new theoretical framework with which to analyse the actual operation of the Council, drawing upon various approaches to policy analysis and negotiation theory. Applying the analytical framework, the fortunes of specific policy proposals are then considered in Chapters 5–8.

The cases used to characterize the operation of the Council involve the work of the following technical councils: Economic and Financial Affairs (EcoFin); Environment; Labour & Social Affairs; and Education. Although this choice represents only four of the composite twenty technical councils, it provides a representative sample of the many and varied councils and policy areas of the EU. The role of EcoFin has increased in significance since SEA implementation. Completion of the internal market programme, and the agreement on a timetable for EMU (Economic and Monetary Union) resulted in a greater workload for the EcoFin Council. It is also considered to be in a strong position within the Council's hierarchy, meeting approximately ten times per year. Although EMU is of great importance, Chapter 5 concentrates entirely upon fiscal matters dealt with by EcoFin, as it was felt that the attention and priority given to EMU during the period under consideration could distort analysis. The SEA also made the Environment Council's competence much clearer as, although the Community had been involved in environmental policy-making since the mid-1970s, its role was not formalized until the SEA. This newly acquired legal base considerably affected the workload of the Council. Furthermore, the environment is a policy area in which an international cooperative approach is often preferred, precisely because of the nature of environmental problems. The extent to which either, or both of these factors impacts upon the work of the Council, could be an important variable in characterizing the Council overall. The Environment Council meets regularly, normally five times per year. Thus, the Environment Council can be termed a 'middle' council. The work of the Labour & Social Affairs Council has also increased in significance, especially since the Commission proposed the Social Charter in 1988. Social policy became a high priority for the EC during the period 1988–92. Therefore, it is important to ascertain whether the operation of the Labour & Social Affairs Council altered in line with the increase in policy-making activity in this area, and shifted from being a 'small' council.

In addition, the work of the Labour & Social Affairs Council is interesting from an Anglo-centric point of view because of the policy position taken by the Thatcher government and the negotiated opt-out from the Social Chapter of the TEU. Education is also a 'small' council. Its competence was not very clear under the SEA, although the TEU has enhanced the role of education policy in the EU. In its initial stages of development, education policy was the cause of institutional conflict between the Council and Commission and this clearly affected working patterns. To what extent there are still inter-institutional tensions could be a significant variable on the Council's operation, given the relative success of educational programmes such as Erasmus. In addition, the Education Council often convenes under the title 'Ministers of Education meeting within the Education Council'. This emphasizes how it often discusses educational policy issues that are outside the remit of the treaties. This situation may therefore affect the manner in which the Education Council conducts its work. It could be argued that EU education policy should be excluded from analysis because it is under-developed and different in character to other policy areas. However, analysis of the Education Council may provide some indication of Council characteristics in an evolving policy area.

For the four selected councils, the focus is upon the years 1988–92 inclusive. This period covers five years of SEA implementation so that an assessment can be made of the impact of SEA provisions on the operation of the Council. This involves ten Presidencies that clearly represent nearly all the member-state configurations and interests. This includes five of the 'Original Six' (but not Belgium), and five of the six 'new' members (but not Denmark). Larger member states (France, Germany and the UK), smaller member states (Eire, Luxembourg and the Netherlands), and the southern members (Greece, Spain, Italy, and Portugal) are all represented in this sample. Criticism could be made that the period should have been extended to cover the first two years of TEU implementation. However, there were difficulties in obtaining up-to-date Council documentation at the time of researching in Brussels, hence the choice of a cut-off point of 1992.

For each technical council, the fortunes of two policy proposals is traced and assessed using the analytical framework constructed in Chapter 4. Each of the eight case studies includes a full explanation of the aims and background of the proposal and analysis of its passage through the entire Council process using the variables set out in the framework. It is important to recognize that external pressures do cement or alter member-state positions when negotiating in the Council. Such pressures are alluded to where possible in order to account for difficulties in the Council's policy-making process. It would be easy in that case to become side-tracked and concentrate upon such issues. However, that is not the aim here: it is the art of decision-making within the Council's structure that is under scrutiny.

The findings of Chapters 5 to 8 are drawn together in a comparative analysis in Chapter 9. The justification for taking such an approach, rather than adopting a thematic basis from the outset is simply that the latter would require too many qualifiers. If comparisons were made before establishing exactly what differences, if any, exist in the operation of certain councils, then analysis would become clouded by these particular practices or peculiarities. The results provide valuable insights into the operation of the Council, and are comparatively assessed in Chapter 9 to determine what are the key characteristics of the Council.

Given that the case studies focus upon the years prior to TEU implementation, the final chapter assesses developments since 1992, examining the future of the Council of the EU. Due to the enlargement to fifteen, and the likelihood of further increases in membership, attention has concentrated upon the reform of existing policy-making procedures. Chapter 10 considers the debate over qualified majority voting, increased powers for the EP in EU policy-making, openness and transparency, and analyses whether these issues have any relevance or pose any threat to the Council's working methods or its dominant institutional position in the EU.

# CHAPTER ONE

# *The institutional and policy context of the Council*

To understand the Council, it must be placed in its institutional context. There are many influences and actors in the EU policy network, including technical experts, national and transnational interest groups, as well as other EU and national institutions. The principal concern here lies with the *institutionalized* aspects of EU policy-making, and focuses upon the three key institutions (Council, Commission, and EP), analysing their role and power in the various policy-making procedures, and examining the specific relationship between the Council and the Commission, and the Council and the EP. The second concern is to contextualize the work of the Council, thus providing crucial background information on the conditions that the Council has operated under generally, and for the case analyses that follow in particular.

## The institutional triangle

Article 145 of the Treaty of Rome gave the Council the final power of decision. Since 1958, there have been numerous changes to these procedures which altered the role and powers of the three key institutions. Nevertheless, these developments have had little effect upon the overall political position of the Council in EU policy-making. Originally, most EC policies were adopted according to the consultation procedure depicted in Figure 1.1.[1] The Commission drafts the proposal, the EP and ESC (Economic and Social Committee) give their opinions, and the Council examines and finally adopts. The Council is under no treaty obligation to accept EP or ESC opinions, and therefore has the ultimate decision in those areas covered by the consultation procedure.[2]

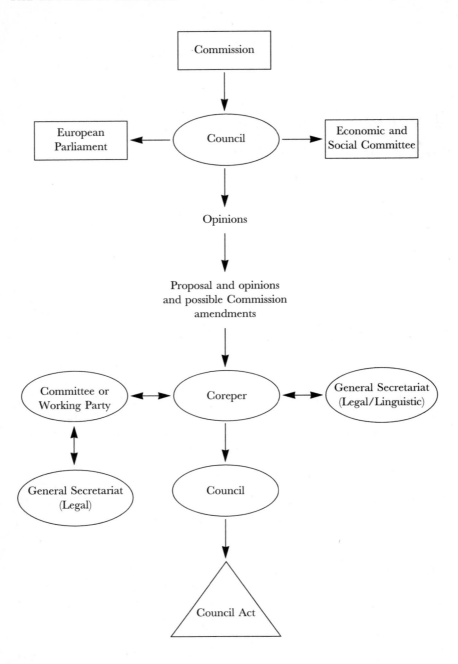

**Figure 1.1** The consultation procedure.

The Council has no treaty power to initiate or draft proposals; this is a task specifically conferred upon the Commission. However, it has sometimes side-stepped this by using Article 152 of the EEC Treaty which states that 'the Council may request the Commission to undertake any studies which the Council considers desirable for the attainment of the common objectives, and to submit to it any appropriate proposals'. The Council can also influence the initiation of policies by adopting opinions, resolutions, agreements and recommendations which carry political (but not legal) weight, or by discussing areas outside of the treaties' competences, or areas that have no formal treaty provisions.

Article 189 defines the types of legislation adopted by the Council:

> In order to carry out their task the Council and the Commission shall, in accordance with the provisions of this Treaty, make regulations, issue directives, take decisions, make recommendations or deliver opinions.

A Regulation has 'general application' and is binding upon all member states. A Directive is also binding but only in the results to be achieved. Consequently, member states are free to choose the method to obtain such a result. A decision is binding upon whomsoever it is addressed to; it can be an individual firm, not just a member-state. Recommendations and opinions are non-binding: they are adopted to clarify views, etc. Regulations are the most common of all Council acts (see Figure 1.5). Sloot and Verschuren's analysis (1990) of decision-making speed in the EC showed that the 'kind of proposal' had the greatest effect on decision-making speed in the period 1975–86.[3] The mean time-lag for the adoption of Directives was 280 days, compared to 90 days for the adoption of Regulations. Regression analysis also proved that the kind of proposal had the strongest effect on EC policy-making. The impact of the legislative 'type' of proposal on the work of the Council may still be an important variable, and is considered in subsequent chapters.

As the EC deepened, the Council strengthened its own position in the policy network through vertical and horizontal expansion. The number of technical councils increased to cope with the EC's new-found competencies. The creation of the European Council, Coreper and the numerous working groups only served to consolidate the Council's position in the EC policy network. Consequently, from the late 1960s and throughout the 1970s, analysts questioned the ability of integration theories to explain the nature of European integration.

Advocates of the federalist model believed that the Council would be increasingly unable to cope and its input in the decision-making process would diminish (Spinelli, 1972, 1978; Burgess, 1986). By the 1980s, this was clearly not the case, due to the Council's consolidated position within the EC policy network. By contrast to the federalist approach, neofunctionalism places greater importance on the process of integration rather than the goal. Federalists insist on a supranational structure. Neofunctionalists are more cautious in their approach towards supranationality. Haas argues that it depends on political behaviour, namely that there should be a shifting of 'loyalties, expectations and political activities towards a new centre, whose institutions possess or demand jurisdiction over the pre-existing national states' (Haas, 1958: 16). Lindberg, although a follower of Haas, was more cautious in defining what he meant by supranationality: 'the development of devices and processes for arriving at collective decisions by means other than autonomous action by national governments' (Lindberg, 1963: 5). If it is accepted that neofunctionalism implies a mixture of national and supra-national decision-making, then the existence of the Council poses no barrier to accepting the applicability of neofunctionalism to the EU.

However, neofunctionalists believed that qualified majority voting would become the dominant method of decision, thus reducing the dominance of national interests. The events of 1965, that led the following year to the 'Luxembourg Compromise', resulted in unanimity becoming the norm for taking decisions (see Chapter 3). Subsequently, only the theoretical approaches of intergovernmentalism and interdependence seemed to offer any analytical value (Hoffmann 1982; Webb 1983). Intergovernmentalism may go some way to explain the nature of EC policy-making during the 1960s and 1970s, but was eventually challenged by the ratification of the SEA in 1987.

The SEA was the first major treaty revision of the EC policy-making process since 1958 in terms of policy and institutional change. The 1965 Merger Treaty, and 1970 and 1975 budgetary changes were significant, but the SEA significantly altered decision-making processes through the introduction of the cooperation procedure and the extended use of qualified majority voting in the Council. The cooperation procedure extends the input of the EP through a second reading on all legislative proposals dealing with the internal market, regional development, social policy and research (see Figure 1.2). Although this clearly increased the EP's powers, time limits for the second reading were introduced to counter possible delays in EC policy-making as a result of this procedure. The Council was also required to take decisions by qualified majority voting in those policy areas covered by the cooperation procedure.

As a result of the SEA, the debate surrounding the validity of neo-functionalism reopened. Writers such as Mutimer (1989) and Tranholm-

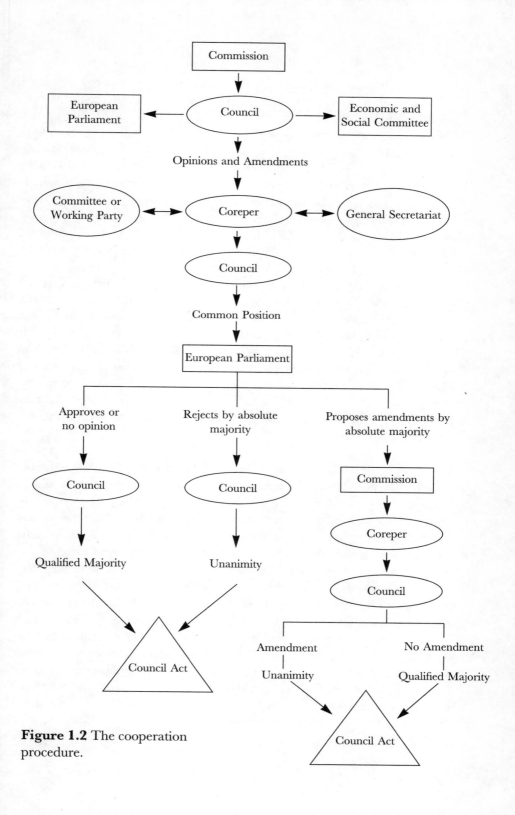

**Figure 1.2** The cooperation procedure.

Mikkelsen (1991) argued that the 1992 project witnessed the re-emergence of the logic of spillover, the central thesis behind their view of the integration process. The cooperation procedure, and the increased profile of the Commission (primarily as a result of Jacques Delors' presidency) were viewed as having potentially the most impact in achieving spillover, thus creating more centralized policy-making. However, despite SEA amendments to policy-making procedures and the so-called 'Delors effect', the Council retains the final decision-making power which undermines the neo-functionalist (and federalist) premise. EP powers were increased, but only in limited policy areas. Qualified majority voting may have been required, but evidence suggests that the Council avoided this voting method (see Chapter 3). Instead, there was simply greater coalition building, and as Ehlermann (1990) points out, the statistics omit those instances where consensus exists and minority opposition is not recorded.

The TEU built upon the aims of the cooperation procedure by extending the EP's powers through the process of co-decision, as depicted in Figure 1.3. The co-decision procedure involves up to three legislative readings for proposals concerning the internal market, consumer protection, education, health and the EU's general environmental strategy. All acts are jointly adopted by the Council and the EP. In addition, the EP has the right to reject the Council's common position (by absolute majority) and thus throw out the proposal.

However, the TEU established a Conciliation Committee to avoid such situations, in which the Council and EP try to resolve their difficulties on a particular proposal. This was clearly based on the experience of EC budgetary policy-making, where a conciliation procedure has frequently been used to facilitate agreement between the Council and the EP on the annual EC budget. The implication of the conciliation procedure, though, was that a veto should be avoided, and from the entry into force of the TEU in November 1993 until the end of March 1995 there were only two cases where negotiations failed to reach a solution – the Directives on voice telephony and biotechnology (Corbett et al., 1995). The 1997 Treaty of Amsterdam has simplified and extended the co-decision procedure and placed the EP on a more equal footing with the Council, as discussed in the final chapter. Yet, whilst there has been a gradual treaty increase in the powers of the EP, the Council is still able to assert its authority. As shown below, the culture of Council–EP relations may be shifting, but member states have been keen to ensure that procedural alterations do not threaten their freedom to protect national interests.

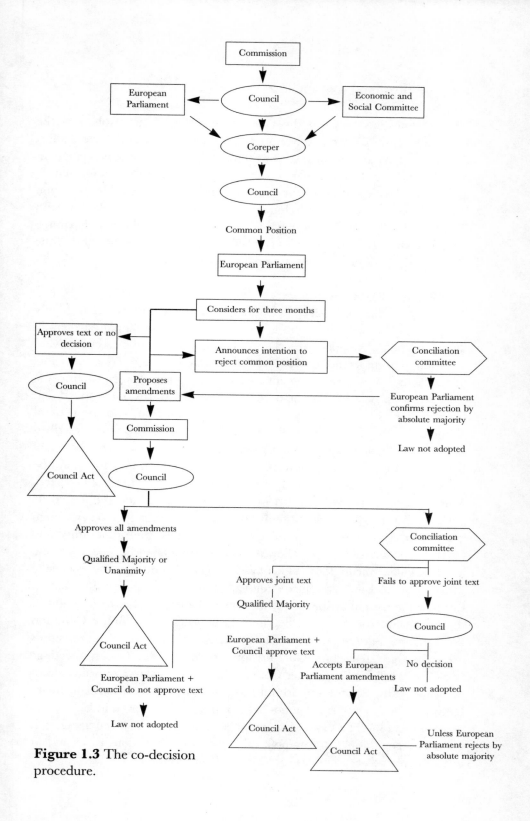

**Figure 1.3** The co-decision procedure.

## Inter-institutional relations

The relationships between the Council and the Commission, and the Council and the EP are highly complex and dynamic. Many factors affect the institutional interactions, such as the political and economic climate at a given moment, the particular concerns of a member state, Commissioner, MEP, etc., or the nature of the proposal under discussion. The intention here is to analyse the overall character of inter-institutional relations with the Council rather than engage in a lengthy examination of group dynamics. However, this general picture is crucial in assessing how the position of the Council affects these inter-institutional relationships.

### *The Council–Commission axis*

The relationship between the Council and the Commission is highly complex and sometimes contradictory. They are institutional partners in the EU, dependent upon each other. In contrast, they can be seen as rivals, promoting and defending very different interests and concerns. The relationship at any given moment is shaped by many factors, such as the aims of a proposal, the attitude of member states towards the proposal and towards the Commission, the skills of the Commission, and the general political climate. The policy-making process in the EC was often described as being implemented along the Council–Commission axis. The Treaty of Rome assumed that the Commission's role in decision-making would be enhanced as the realms of EC policy expanded, but this has not occurred. The Council expanded its own internal structure, which reinforced its position and prevented the Commission from increasing its role. Although the Commission is present at all Council meetings, the preparatory and filtering functions of Coreper allow the Council to manage its policy agenda, a task originally meant for the Commission. The Commission was essentially 'frozen out' of EPC (European Political Cooperation) policy formulation through the formalization of the European Council. SEA recognition of the European Council and EPC, and TEU articles on a future Common Foreign and Security Policy (CFSP) further restrict the Commission's input in this area. The Commission attends Antici Group meetings (see Chapter 2), which prepare Coreper II and European Council sessions, allowing both sides the opportunity to solve any conflicts between them. However, the Commission cannot be said to be truly involved in EU foreign policy initiation. The Commission's presence at summit meetings gives it political recognition, but any political weight in negotiations is dependent upon member-state attitudes towards the Commission.

Furthermore, the traditional Council–Commission axis has shifted in favour of a more triangular relationship, and the inclusion of the EP. However, the Council recognizes the expertise that the Commission can offer for policy formulation, and to a lesser extent policy negotiation. The Commission takes national interests into account at the drafting stage of a proposal, seeking support for a proposal so that the probability of acceptance in a Council session is as high as possible. The Commission attends all formal Council meetings, from *ad hoc* working group to Foreign Ministerial level (and some informal sessions). The Commission obviously aims to protect the proposal, but at the same time tr ies to adopt a flexible position depending upon the subject of the proposal, so that the piece of legislation is not rejected. This is crucial to EU policy-making processes. The Commission tries to mediate between member states, and there is often a close cooperative relationship between the Commission and the Council Presidency to find a solution to the particular problem.

Consultation and cooperation between the Commission and the General Secretariat of the Council rose dramatically after Jacques Delors took office. There are almost daily meetings between the Council and Commission Secretariats. Within the General Secretariat of the Commission, a specific *fonctionnaire* deals with Council–Commission relations. They are responsible for drafting summaries of the minutes of all Council meetings, and for preparing steering briefs for the Commission President. This helps to keep the appropriate Directorate-General in the Commission informed of Council developments in its area, and provides indications of the likely outcome of future meetings. In addition, the Commission issues reports on Council–Commission relations at the start of each new Commission.

The internal market programme and the Delors Presidency enhanced the position of the Commission within the Community policy network, but in terms of its importance within the EC for policy-making and implementation, rather than actual legislative powers. The Commission continues to play an important role as a mediator in EU policy-making, which is part of the process within the Council. However, the TEU debate showed that deep conflict between these two institutions can still occur. Examples included the difficulty in finding an acceptable definition of the principle of subsidiarity, and a common position for the Uruguay Round of the GATT (General Agreement on Tariffs and Trade) negotiations. There has to be dialogue and cooperation between the Council and the Commission so that the EU's policy-making machinery functions. It can be argued that this is helped by the fact that Council representatives from the member states are in constant dialogue with the Commission and its services. However, the inter-relationship of these two institutions can sometimes be rather fragile.

### The Council and the European Parliament

Until the SEA, the EP's input and influence in EC policy-making was rather limited (with the exception of the budgetary procedure). The introduction of the cooperation procedure increased the EP's powers, and consequently the Council found that it had to deal with the EP more regularly and in greater depth. The Council has always been legally required to consider the views of the EP. However, until the SEA, the opinions of the EP had a limited effect upon the legislative process. The cooperation procedure strengthened the EP's position by giving it the opportunity of a second reading on certain legislation, which made its voice much louder. Forty-three per cent of EP amendments at the first reading, and 23.5 per cent at second reading were accepted by the Council from 1987 to the end of 1993. Whilst these figures appear low, it should be stressed that Council acceptance of first reading EP amendments is far higher than under the consultation procedure. Furthermore, to have one-fifth of second reading amendments accepted by the Council under a 'new' procedure is substantial.

Therefore, the Council had to start taking greater notice of EP opinions, recommendations, etc. In interviews, MEPs were keen to stress how the EP is concentrating upon its relationship with the Council rather than maintaining the traditional emphasis on its partnership with the Commission. The key contact between the Council and EP is the Council Presidency. Many argue that the Presidency pays far more attention to the EP than individual member-state delegations. This is probably for reasons of agenda management. The Council cannot act without the submission of EP amendments, so the Council Presidency aims to ensure that EP amendments are on the table to avoid delays in the policy-making process. The problem lies in cases where the EP deliberately stalls submission of its opinions to gain further bargaining advantage. Consequently, the Council Presidency in particular has tried to develop the Council–EP dialogue to avoid this.

Twelve members of the General Secretariat, together with individuals from the Directorates-General of the General Secretariat, attend all EP plenary sessions in Strasbourg. Staff from the Permanent Representations have also been known to attend, particularly at the beginning and end of Council Presidency terms of office. Ministers are also invited to attend EP Committees once or twice per Presidency to explain the targets set by the Presidency work programme, and at end of Presidency to give results. At these meetings, MEPs can directly ask member-state ministers about particular proposals. In addition, representatives of the Council (but not usually ministers) speak at nearly all EP committees, and have done so since 1992. These delegates do not have the political authority to negotiate fully, thus reducing the effectiveness of this practice and perhaps reflecting the

Council's view of the EP. Nevertheless, the fact that a representative of the Council is generally attending EP committee meetings has to be viewed as positive in terms of enhancing the Council–EP dialogue.

However, there is one major complaint made by MEPs. The EP does not have the right to attend Council meetings (except in cases of conciliation), or consult Council minutes. Moreover, the EP does not have any informal internal records of Council deliberations, unlike the Commission. Although the EP can ask the Council questions, oral and written, most representatives interviewed felt that the Council does not give this procedure its full attention, and that Council responses are generally useless. At each EP plenary session, there is 'Question Time' to the Council and the Commission. Question Time, introduced in 1973, was based on the more formal Greek and UK traditions, rather than typical continental European practices. It is held at 8.45 p.m. on the Wednesday evening of each EP plenary session. Before 1989, Question Time was held in the afternoon, and this change has resulted in a poorer attendance.[4]

Most MEPs interviewed felt Question Time to be rather a pointless exercise. The Council President answers questions for a maximum of 90 minutes, 60 minutes on questions to the Council, 30 minutes on questions concerning EPC. The TEU reduced this to 60 minutes and makes no division between subject areas. The Council answers are usually inadequate, as the questions sent by MEPs can only be addressed to the President of the Council who does not have the technical expertise to give concise answers. MEPs try to pursue a response by asking supplementary questions, but again the President of the Council lacks the necessary specialist knowledge to provide an adequate response. However, it would surely be difficult to expect that all of the technical experts from the Council attend EP Question Time. Other commitments, time, and the cost of doing so prevent this at present. Consequently, most MEPs rely on written questions to the Council as shown in Figure 1.4.

Although the response to written questions is more detailed, the Council takes, on average, three months to reply. The only other method available to the EP is informal meetings with Council representatives or personal correspondence. There have been requests for MEPs to have Question Time in Brussels so that it would be easier for the appropriate Council officials to attend. However, this could enhance current pressures for a complete move from Strasbourg to Brussels, and has therefore been rejected.

The cooperation procedure may have been limited in scope, but it began the process of what can be termed a cultural shift within EU policy-making practices. Compared with pre-SEA relations, the Council was beginning to take far more notice of the EP, and to be open to dialogue and greater

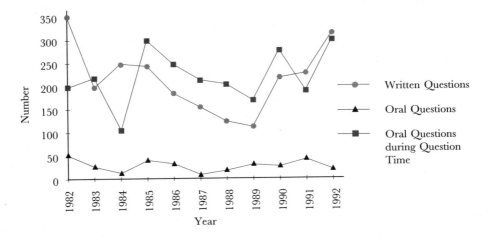

Source: *Annual Reviews of the Council's Work.*

**Figure 1.4** EP Questions to the Council 1982–92.

cooperation. More importantly, the EP seemed to be able to exert greater influence than before in areas not covered by the cooperation procedure, and especially in those areas where member states have traditionally been more favourable to EP input, such as the environment or social policy. Therefore, the significance of the cooperation procedure was not only in the formal extension of powers granted to the EP, but also the cultural shift in Council perceptions of the EP.

Fairly rapidly within the historical development of the EU came a further extension of EP powers through the co-decision procedure, introduced by the TEU in 1993. The EP saw this procedure as confirmation of its importance within EU policy-making, despite the complicated nature of the mechanisms of co-decision. By agreeing to its inclusion within the TEU, member states believed that the enhanced cooperation between the Council and EP from 1987 onwards was beneficial to the effective operation of EU policy-making. In addition, it was seen by commentators as a manoeuvre on the part of member states to try to dispel notions of the 'democratic deficit'. Whilst further empowering the EP alone is insufficient to remedy this problem of legitimacy and democracy in the EU, it was, and is, significant for generating a more positive climate of opinion towards the European endeavour.

From the entry into force of the TEU in November 1993 until the end of March 1995, 53 cases were concluded under the co-decision procedure. Of these, agreement was reached in 51 cases – 32 without conciliation, either because no amendments were made to the Council's common position

(18 cases), or because the Council accepted EP amendments (14 cases). The remaining 19 cases were resolved within the Conciliation Committee, with only two failures (see above). However, the data conceals the significance of amendments made by the EP, the nature of the conciliation negotiations, and the overall working relationship being established between the Council and EP. The experience of co-decision also countered accusations from the more sceptical that this procedure would decrease efficiency; the average time for a proposal to be translated into a legislative act was only ten months (Wessels and Diedrichs, 1997: 5).

Co-decision did not lead directly to consistent confrontation between the Council and EP. Conciliation has been a procedure of last resort, with both the Council and EP generally committed to finding a solution through negotiation rather than having to convene the Conciliation Committee. More significant, though, is the informal relationship between the Council and EP. Earnshaw and Judge's (1997) qualitative analysis of the cooperation procedure demonstrates how EP members regard the use of informal channels as more effective than formal routes for gleaning information, negotiating, and thus having an impact upon the legislative process. Peterson (1995) illustrates a similar pattern emerging under the co-decision procedure. The strategy seems to be one of promotion of informal rather than formal dialogue. Perhaps informal relations are perceived by the Council as less threatening – member states can negotiate behind closed doors with EP delegates, yet can still be seen as protecting national interests to interested observers when discussion moves to more formal surroundings.

## Policy-making activity in the Council 1982–92

Having sketched out the inter-relationships within the evolving institutional triangle of the EU, attention now turns to the policy context of the Council. The intention is to illustrate the conditions that the Council worked under between 1988 and 1992, by showing both the areas of Council policy-making activity and the political and economic environment of the period. The case studies are taken from the period 1988–92, primarily to assess the effects of SEA implementation. However, it is also necessary to analyse events, issues, etc. prior to 1988, as these will have partly shaped the environment that the Council found itself operating under from 1988 to 1992. Therefore, this section also considers the period from 1982 to provide a wider picture of the background to the Council's work.

There are numerous layers to identify and consider: the internal policy agenda focusing on the main areas of Council policy-making during the decade 1982–92; the key institutional developments from a Council perspective; and the wider context that the Council operated under during this period. Obviously, numerous aspects will be interlinked. However, this is the most appropriate method of providing the background information necessary to analyse the work of the Council, without going into excessive detail. Apart from the impossibility of identifying and discussing every relevant development over ten years, it is also the case that concentrating on only the main or 'special' events can paint a distorted picture. Attention has to focus primarily on those developments that particularly affected the Council. This can be done by looking at Council Presidency priorities and programmes.[5] However, member states can promote their own agendas during their Presidency, and taking a purely Presidential focus may distort analysis. Consequently, this section will look at the context that the EU operated under, but only deal with those developments and incidents that particularly affected the operation of the Council, or had the potential to do so.[6]

The period 1982–92 was probably the most significant and demanding in the EU's history thus far. Excluding the first two of those years, this was essentially a period of 'relance' and rejuvenation for European integration. It would be wrong to state that these years were straightforward; there were numerous policy tensions and disputes between member states. However, this period was fundamentally significant. It includes both of the key revisions to the Treaty of Rome (the SEA and the TEU), which brought about major institutional changes and the completion of the internal market. Europe also altered in shape during these years as a result of the end of the Cold War, bringing additional pressures on the development of European integration and its future course.

### The internal EC policy agenda

The period 1982–92 was extremely busy for the Council in terms of policy-making. The most important point to make is that the two treaty revisions dominated the Council's work. Discussions that led to the SEA began in 1984, and the drafting of the TEU took priority from 1989 to 1991. As Daniels et al. (1991: 17) point out, it is possible to draw a parallel between the 1985 and 1990 Italian Presidencies, as they both launched the IGCs (Intergovernmental Conferences) to prepare the treaty revisions; Milan in 1985 and Rome in 1990. However, although the treaty revisions demanded much of the Council's attention, 'normal' day-to-day Council work continued. Figure 1.5 provides an illustration of the policy outputs of the Council between 1982 and 1992.

This graph illustrates some interesting trends. Firstly, despite the increased legislative programme as a result of the SEA, the highest outputs occurred in 1986, which was before SEA ratification. This can be explained by the fact that from 1985, when the White Paper on completion of the internal market was issued, there was a concerted move to get the EC 'back on track'. This obviously involved getting rid of the backlog of legislative proposals to make way for the increased workload that would result from SEA implementation. Another observation is the relative decrease in the amount of Regulations adopted, compared with the relative increase in Directives adopted during the period 1982–92. This corresponds to earlier discussion and the relative ease with which a Directive can be adopted in

| Year | Regulations | Decisions | Directives | Total |
|------|-------------|-----------|------------|-------|
| 1982 | 393 | 128 | 42 | 563 |
| 1983 | 395 | 108 | 41 | 544 |
| 1984 | 351 | 99 | 53 | 503 |
| 1985 | 447 | 109 | 59 | 615 |
| 1986 | 473 | 184 | 74 | 731 |
| 1987 | 458 | 125 | 40 | 623 |
| 1988 | 434 | 131 | 63 | 628 |
| 1989 | 410 | 151 | 80 | 641 |
| 1990 | 402 | 127 | 71 | 600 |
| 1991 | 327 | 115 | 63 | 505 |
| 1992 | 375 | 120 | 93 | 588 |

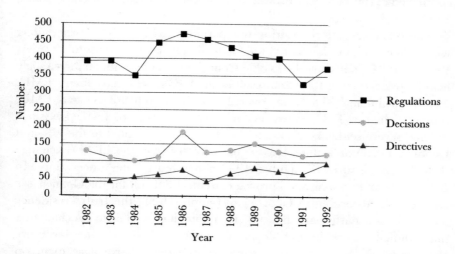

Source: *Annual Reviews of the Council's Work.*

**Figure 1.5** Legislation (by type) adopted by the Council 1982–92.

comparison to Regulations. The latter are far more precise in terms of implementation details, which member states may find difficulty with.

Three main economic themes ran through the work of the Council during the period 1982–92: economic recovery; completion of the internal market; and the development of EMU. Clearly, the economic climate was a key consideration for all member states during this period with economic recession in the early 1980s and early 1990s. Consequently, all member states supported Community policies that they felt would assist economic recovery, with emphasis upon growth and employment. In particular, the Presidency of Denmark in 1982, Germany in 1983, Italy in 1984, and the Luxembourg Presidency of 1985 made combating unemployment a priority. This resulted in an EC action programme adopted by the Council in 1987 aimed at reducing long-term unemployment, which was continued in 1988 with reform of the structural funds.

The second focus of the Council's work was the internal market. Member states were keen to promote the SEA because of the benefits that they believed a truly single market might bring to their economies. Completion of the internal market was a stated priority for all member states holding the office of the Presidency from July 1987. Germany was extremely keen to implement the SEA to the letter, especially in areas of qualified majority voting. Consequently, the 1988 German Presidency was seen as very efficient in terms of internal market policy outputs, although the UK Presidency of 1992 tries to claim the glory for ensuring that the '1992' programme was completed (Trumpf, 1988; Brewin and McAllister, 1989: 325; Garel-Jones, 1993: 261–7).

The other key priority during this period was EMU. This issue, along with political union, dominated the Council agenda from 1990 to 1992. As Wallace (1994) points out, the EcoFin Council found itself with an increasingly heavy workload from 1990 as a result of the IGC meetings to discuss EMU. The Council managed to secure overall agreement on the objective of EMU, cemented in the TEU. However, achieving the goal of EMU has since suffered severe set-backs. Not only did the opt-outs granted to the UK and Denmark create difficulties, but the partial collapse of the ERM (Exchange Rate Mechanism) in September 1992 generated greater uncertainty. In addition, fiscal harmonization proved extremely difficult for the Council (see Chapter 5). According to Geoghegan-Quinn (1990), the Irish Presidency found this issue particularly difficult. Therefore, it is possible to conclude that the Council's work in this economic policy sphere became far more challenging as the years progressed. Despite the relative agreement on economic recovery in the early 1980s, and the enthusiasm generated by the 1992 programme, the Council (and the EC) had to face increasing difficulties when these policies were developed further in the form of EMU.

Another area which had significant impact upon the operation of the Council was that of finance. Resolving the future financing problem of the EC, and in particular British difficulties with the level of contributions, was high on the Council's agenda from 1982 to 1984. Temporary agreements were reached in 1981 and 1982, but it was the French Presidency that was instrumental in resolving this issue. A final solution was reached at the Fontainebleau European Council in June 1984. After this, it seemed that internal tensions between the member states were reduced. The post-Fontainebleau environment was far more positive; even Council document-ation recognized this by stating that 1984 was 'more encouraging' than previous years in terms of policy discussions (Council, 1985: 8–9). Budgetary issues proved to be less problematic in subsequent years. The 1987 budget was successfully agreed by the Council and EP, and the Delors I package was concluded fairly easily under the Belgian and Danish Presidencies, although this meant a drastically increased workload for Coreper. In contrast, there were difficulties in reaching agreement on the Delors II package as member states tended to be preoccupied with domestic concerns, as economic recession was again beginning to affect most member states. Consequently, the issue had to be pushed up to the European Council in 1992.[7]

Spanish and Portuguese accession was also of concern in the early 1980s. The German Presidency of 1983 placed great emphasis on completing the negotiations as quickly and successfully as possible. Agreement on the Integrated Mediterranean Programmes was reached in 1985, and was seen as the 'cost of enlargement'. Indeed, agricultural policy was high on the Council agenda and list of Presidential priorities throughout this period. Agricultural prices settlements were a continual source of dispute between member states. Member states tried to use the veto on this issue in 1982, 1983, and 1988. Germany and the UK also clashed over the 1986 agricult-ural prices settlement.[8] Fisheries policy preoccupied the work of the Council in the early 1980s. There were difficult negotiations over fishing quotas between 1982 and 1983. These had to be re-negotiated in the light of future Spanish and Portuguese accession. Further alterations to fishing quotas were agreed in 1985 after two years of protracted negotiation. Denmark had been the most reluctant to reach a compromise, but a solution was event-ually found. All of these issues placed great strain on the working relationship between member states in the Council.

In looking at some other policy outputs from 1982 to 1992, it is possible to observe how both the pressure of external events and Presidential priorities can have a profound impact upon the work of the Council. For example, industrial policy became a focus of discussion during the 1986 UK Presidency, with a particular emphasis upon shipbuilding. The 1986 UK Presidency was also crucial in expanding the remit of the Trevi Group (see Chapter 2) to include judicial cooperation by making the fight against terrorism a priority. Environmental policy moved up the agenda after Chernobyl in 1986, and was also high on the list of German priorities in 1988. The key reforms to the structural funds in 1984 were in part a result of Greek Presidential pressures a year earlier. Finally, the development of social policy was promoted by France and Spain in 1989 after the introduction of the Social Charter, and by the Irish and Italian Presidencies in 1990. The Irish Presidency pushed hard for the EC to develop the social dimension, as this corresponded to Ireland's own national policy programme. The Council also managed to make great strides in the development of other policies. For example, from 1987 the Council began to introduce new programmes within EC educational policy, such as Erasmus in 1987 and Youth for Europe in 1988. Transport and research policies were also developed in the late 1980s. Obviously, these are only a few out of the many examples that could be given. However, it is possible to see from this that the work of the Council between 1982 and 1992 was wide-ranging and often difficult.

### Institutional developments

There were several institutional issues between 1982 and 1992 that affected the operation of the Council, with the issue of institutional reform remaining high on the agenda throughout. There was growing concern about the ineffectiveness of existing institutional practices, which had contributed to the feeling of stagnation in the EC during the 1970s. This even appeared to be acknowledged by the Council itself. In the introduction to its 1982 Annual Review, the Council stated that:

> the Council was able to demonstrate . . . for all the cries of alarm which are often heard, its own effectiveness in achieving the necessary compromises and finding appropriate solutions. It is true that it was not always possible to reach final conclusions, but in many areas solutions were found and substantial progress was made. (Council, 1983: 5)

Belgium responded to the calls for some institutional reform by making this a priority during its 1982 Presidency. In June 1982, the Council, Commission, and EP adopted a common declaration on various measures to improve the budgetary procedure. The aim was to increase consultation between the three institutions and avoid the use of the conciliation procedure in agreeing the EC budget. This aim was developed further by the 1988 Inter-Institutional Budgetary Agreement.

However, the primary revision to EC policy-making during this period was the cooperation procedure, enshrined in the SEA. The 1985 Milan summit considered the report of the Dooge Committee, which had been set up at Fontainebleau to review existing EC institutional structures and policy-making procedures. This report, together with the Draft Treaty on European Union, resulted in an institutional agenda for the 1985 IGC.[9] Italy was regarded as having taken quite a robust approach during its 1985 Presidency and the IGC meetings, keen to promote a more federal institutional structure as enshrined in the DTEU (Draft Treaty on European Union). Other member states, such as Greece and the UK, were less willing to allow such a radical reform of the EC. Although the SEA reformed EC policy-making procedures by introducing the cooperation procedure, and extending the use of qualified majority voting, these changes hardly met the federal aspirations of the DTEU. Consequently, Italy was extremely disappointed by what was seen as insufficient institutional reforms contained in the SEA: Italy only signed the SEA after the Danish referendum was held (Daniels *et al.*, 1991). However, the SEA was the first major revision to the Treaty of Rome since 1958.

Various institutional adjustments were needed as a result of Spanish and Portuguese accession to the EC in 1986. In terms of the Council, the qualified majority voting thresholds and the rotation of the Presidency were agreed in 1985 under the Italian Presidency. Further changes to qualified majority voting rules had to be agreed a year later in accordance with the SEA. It has long been argued that decision-making in the Council was rather too slow on occasion. As a result of the institutional debates that led to the SEA, even the Council recognized that there was a problem with the length of time taken to lay down the particular decision-making procedure. As a consequence of Article 10 of the SEA, the Council adopted the 'Comitology' decision in 1987 under the Belgian Presidency. This decision reduced the number of possible policy-making procedures from twenty to seven, with the Council stating that policy-making would be speeded-up considerably as a result. Although the next few years required that the EC concentrate upon implementing the cooperation procedure, and Comitology decision, the issue of further institutional reform remained on the agenda. There was much debate over the question of the legitimacy of the EC, particularly because of the EP's new powers, but still-limited role in EC policy-making. It could be argued that the public backlash to the TEU provided evidence that the TEU had not sufficiently addressed this issue. The 1992 UK Presidency tried to respond to the public backlash to the TEU. At the Birmingham and Edinburgh summits, the member states agreed to introduce the policies of transparency and openness. Overall, these were welcomed, although they have had little effect on the operation of the Council and the EU as a whole (discussed further in Chapter 10).

The issues of jumbo and informal councils are examined in some depth in Chapter 3. However, some interesting points need to be raised here. For example a joint EcoFin and Agricultural Council had to be convened in 1987, as the Commission complained that the various budgetary decisions taken by individual councils were coming into conflict. However, the jumbo session failed to achieve any solution to the problem. Spain attempted to solve the problem of too many informal sessions in 1989. In December 1988, member states had agreed to limit the number to seven per Presidency, and for these to be spread more logically throughout the year. In the face of general scepticism about this aim, the 1989 Spanish Presidency announced that there would be only seven informal sessions of the Council and 'refused to supply them with either an agenda or supporting documents' (Brewin and McAllister, 1990: 454). This appeared to be a concerted move by Spain to be a 'good' member state; it was Spain's first Presidency.

### The wider context

In analysing the operation of the Council, it is also important to consider the wider picture in which member states negotiated upon EC policies during this period. This requires the analyst to take into account both domestic context and priorities of individual member states and key international events and developments. These may help to explain more fully the pressures that the Council worked under at a particular time.

Electoral considerations, be they local, regional, national or European, may affect the policy approach of a member state, and thus the operation of the Council. National legislative elections occurred every year in one or more EC member state during the period 1982–92. The most significant in terms of party change were as follows: the French election of 1986 that resulted in cohabitation between the Socialists and Gaullists, and the subsequent reversal of this in 1988; the majority gained by the Socialists in the 1987 Portuguese election; the 1988 change from a centre-right to centre-left coalition in Belgium; and the victory of the Greek right-wing New Democracy party over the Socialists in 1990. These results could not fail to affect the policy direction of the above-mentioned member states. Clearly, local, regional and European elections should also be taken into account. For example, there is consensus that occupying the Council Presidency in 1989 helped the Spanish Socialists' fortunes in the EP elections of that year (Story and Grugel, 1991).

Where there has been no party change in member-state governments, such as in Germany and the UK during this period, it may still be necessary to consider any changes in policy direction. Government instability may also be a factor that affects the operation of the Council, particularly in the case of Italy, The Netherlands and Belgium. For example, a Culture Council had to be cancelled in 1987 due to disagreements between the various Belgian communities (Brewin and McAllister, 1988: 434). Government reshuffles and the establishment of new ministries also need to be taken into account. For example the Greek government set up the Ministry of the National Economy in 1986, and an Environment Ministry was introduced in Germany in 1986.

International events and political pressures also impact upon the operation of the Council. Tensions and difficulties in reaching agreement upon a particular policy proposal in the Council may be enhanced by conflicts between member states over external events. The obvious example here is in relation to the UK. Tensions between Britain and the other member states intensified from 1982. Britain held up settlement of the issue of budgetary contributions, by linking agreement to the yearly setting of agricultural prices. The other member states were rather irritated by this, especially as they had supported, with some reluctance, British military intervention in the Falklands. Margaret Thatcher's controversial Bruges speech in 1988 did little to improve EC working relations, nor did the bombing of Libya in April 1986. Unlike Britain, France and Spain refused America the use of their air bases for this operation. Consequently, relations between these EC partners were incredibly tense. The differing foreign policy objectives of EC members also strained internal EC relations when discussing sanctions against South Africa in 1985 and 1986, during the Gulf Crisis, which began in August 1990, and the Yugoslavian conflict from 1991.

Discussion of relations with EFTA (European Free Trade Association) states worked its way up the Council agenda from 1987, culminating in the EEA (European Economic Area) agreement in 1991.[10] The EEA negotiations were highly technical and increased the already heavy workload for the Council in the early 1990s. EC–US trade relations became a particularly difficult issue for the Council after a deterioration in relations from 1986. The Belgian Presidency of 1987 made great efforts to try to improve the situation, but with limited success. Pressures on the Council increased further in 1988 when the Uruguay Round of the GATT negotiations began. This took four years to be concluded under the 1992 UK Presidency.

The issue that put most pressure upon the EC during this period was that of political change in Central and Eastern Europe. Not only did the member states have to respond to the need for policy changes towards individual central and East European countries, but these changes also challenged the future direction of the EU 'since all the ideas and schemes for the organisation of the continent of Europe were now called into question' (Council, 1990: 6) Further demands were placed upon the operation of the Council after the break-up of the former Soviet Union in 1990. Member states were unsure and tentative in their responses, which meant that much time was taken up in the General Affairs Council on issues such as financial and food aid to countries of the former Soviet Union. Consequently, such issues dominated the Council policy agenda from the summer of 1989 to the end of 1992 and beyond, with all Presidential agendas giving them top priority. German unification, whilst welcomed by the EC, caused difficulties in terms of accession. Essentially, the former East Germany was incorporated into the EC without actually acceding. This went against EP wishes, but it was felt important to send out the right political signals.[11]

A special third European Council was held in 1989 under the French Presidency to discuss the issues facing the EC as a result of the political developments in Central and Eastern Europe. The issue was high on the 1990 Irish and Italian Presidency agendas as well, although little of substance was achieved. The Irish Presidency did manage to succeed in getting agreement that Central and Eastern European countries should be included in EC educational schemes, which eventually resulted in the Tempus programme. It is noteworthy that Spain was keen to emphasize other EC external relations during its 1989 Presidency, in particular the Mediterranean and Latin America. Spain hoped to ensure that other countries were not ignored, especially those with close Spanish relations. Italy opted for a similar line during 1990 by promoting the EC's Mediterranean policy.

## Conclusion

Despite treaty blueprints, member states have been able to maintain their control of EU policy-making through the Council, and it is evident that the Council remains the dominant institution. The Council does rely upon the Commission to a certain extent in helping to seek out consensus amongst member states in the initiation of policy proposals, and if need be acting as an alternative broker in formal negotiations within the Council. In this sense, they could be viewed as partner institutions. However, where vital national interests are at stake, member states are able to circumvent Commission ambitions through the framework of the Council. Relations with the EP have developed as a result of SEA implementation, and the need to seek compromises in those policy proposals governed by cooperation or co-decision. What is most interesting, though, is that this has tended to evolve informally and loosely: member states are still reluctant to formalize and acknowledge the growing input of the EP. Subsequent chapters will put these initial observations to the test, and establish whether these inter-institutional patterns of relations differ between policy areas. The purpose of providing a context to the work of the Council illustrates the demanding policy agenda that member states have to confront, and the large number of variables that have to be accounted for in any analysis of a proposal dealt with by the Council. The internal policy agenda is important, but more significant for teasing out the characteristics of the Council is the wider policy context. Internal domestic pressures within member states, electoral factors, and the external political environment can all have an impact upon the workings of the Council. Tensions between member states or domestic political difficulties can have an effect upon Council discussions, even when the particular proposal under discussion is not directly related to the surrounding political context.

# CHAPTER TWO

## *The structure of the Council*

In any analysis of an organization or institution, it is essential to paint a clear picture of its structure and procedures to appreciate its operational characteristics. Most academic analyses of the Council only deal with aspects of its structure, which can be misleading as the Council's component parts function alongside each other, and cannot be understood in isolation. There are five elements to the internal structure of the Council: the ministerial level, the European Council, the Presidency of the Council, Coreper, and the General Secretariat of the Council. These components of the Council's structure are of key importance in ensuring the effective operation of the Council. Analysis of these elements identifies the actors involved in the Council's policy-making process, as who plays can affect the way in which decisions are made, and consequently impact upon the final decision outputs.

The Council has strengthened its policy-making capacity through the development of its five component parts. As discussed in the previous chapter, the Treaty of Rome envisaged that the power of the Council would decline, yet this has not been the case. The Council has managed to retain the final power of decision through its own internal expansion and consolidation in line with the 'deepening' of EU competences. The Council's structure expanded vertically through the establishment of Coreper, and the formalization of the European Council which increased the importance of the Council Presidency. Horizontal extension also occurred as the remits for various technical councils became more clearly defined, treaty or Presidential influence established new councils, and certain technical councils began to meet more frequently. Moreover, over time there has been an increase in the number of support committees of the Council, and an amplified role for the General Secretariat.

## The ministerial level

In analysing the operation and characteristics of the Council, it is imperative to recognize that 'in constitutional theory, there is only one Council, in practice, there are many' (Butler, 1986: 73). The term Council refers to the General Affairs Council, comprising of member-state Foreign Ministers, and the technical or sectoral Councils. The overall structure of the Council is illustrated by Figure 2.1

In the initial years of the Communities, member states conducted negotiations on *all* policies within the General Affairs Council. With the rapid expansion of policy-making during the 1960s, Foreign Ministers became increasingly over-burdened. Specialist technical councils were set up to alleviate this. What is more important however is that relevant national ministers were determined to be involved in policy discussions at the

**European Council**

**General Affairs Council**

Article 113 Committee

Political Committee

| **Agriculture** | **EcoFin** | **Internal Market** |
| Special Committee on Agriculture | Monetary Committee | Internal Market Committee |

| **Budget** | **Environment** | **Fisheries** | **Industry** | **Labour & Social Affairs** | **Research** |
| Budget Committee | | | | Standing Committee on Employment | Crest |

**Transport** **Energy** **Development** **Education** **Health** **Justice & Home Affairs** **Telecommunications**

Education Committee

K4 Committee

**Consumer Protection** **Culture** **Tourism** **Others**

Coreper I & II

Working Parties

General Secretariat
(supports entire Council)

Note: Bold type refers to Councils, whilst normal type refers to permanent supporting committees. Specific named committees are part of Coreper, not distinct from it.
·········· denote the implicit hierarchical structure of the Council.

**Figure 2.1** Structure of the Council of the European Union.

supranational level, as they argued that they were better qualified to carry out discussions on their particular portfolio.

The General Affairs Council is seen as more influential and powerful than the other technical councils.[1] Although this theoretical horizontal differentiation has no legal status, an implicit hierarchy exists in the Council's structure, as depicted in Figure 2.1. This arises because the General Affairs Council often considers and takes decisions on a much wider range of issues than the other technical councils. Along with its own workload, the General Affairs Council examines proposals that the appropriate technical council negotiations have failed to resolve. These have consequently been referred up to the level of Foreign Ministers. Alternatively, proposals that have been agreed in principle are tabled for the next General Affairs Council as an 'A' point, simply for formal approval (see Appendix 1, Article 2). Furthermore, the General Affairs Council can also be regarded as more important than other technical councils due to its role as overall coordinator of Council business.

The General Affairs Council meets once a month and is by far the busiest Council. Between 1988 and 1992, it discussed 414 agenda items, excluding 'A' points.[2] This workload was over four times that of other technical councils examined in later chapters. Moreover, according to the Council's Rules of Procedure, any council can adopt an 'A' point, yet available data suggests that the General Affairs Council adopts more 'A' points than any of the other councils.[3] This may primarily be because it meets the most frequently of all the technical councils, but it does emphasize the demanding workload that faces Foreign Ministers.

The evolution of technical councils from the 1960s allowed Foreign Ministers to concentrate upon external economic affairs. Yet, difficult issues are still 'pushed up' to the General Affairs Council. Forty-four per cent of items discussed between 1988 and 1992 dealt with internal Community affairs, compared to 35 per cent for external economic issues (Cooperation Council preparations, Lomé, negotiating Directives for Association agreements, etc.). Although the European Council was not formally established until 1974, the Foreign Ministers also became responsible for preparing European Council meetings from 1972, and for discussions on EPC. Whilst EPC was a logical spillover from Community external economic policies, and the later recognition by the SEA set up a Political Secretariat, EPC discussions remained outside the official remit of the EC. Consequently, Foreign Ministers were supposed to separate EPC negotiations from their work within the framework of General Affairs meetings. However, EPC became effectively integrated into EC structures, and as one senior Council official stated, in practice there was no distinction between EPC and EC business. EPC, and now CFSP issues under the second pillar of the EU come under the General Affairs Council agenda, and in a sense the only distinction between business is the entry of the CFSP Secretary General who sits down next to the President of the Council. The two General Secretariats also became fairly integrated, primarily for greater coherence. Another reason for the merger may have been because the EPC Secretariat was so small with only six diplomats – one permanent, the other five representatives rotating as an enlarged Troika (see below). Given that both Secretariats are based in the Council's headquarters – the Justus Lipsius building in Brussels – a *de facto* merger was logical. Analysis of the subject area of General Affairs Council meetings between 1988 and 1992 shows that 21 per cent of discussion items were devoted to external political affairs (former Soviet Union, Central and Eastern Europe, South Africa, famine in Africa, Yugoslavia), namely EPC business, confirming that the distinction no longer existed between General Affairs and EPC. Council Press Releases inconsistently distinguished between EPC and other issues. Interestingly, most statements that an agenda item came under EPC were made in 1992, after the TEU had been agreed (but not implemented). Overall, examining Council Press Releases during this period leaves one with the impression that member states felt that it was pointless to pretend that EPC discussions were held separately. Soetendorp (1994: 113–19) argues that there was no institutional spillover from EC into EPC, and although there was a different Secretariat and decisions were taken by unanimity, the evidence suggests that EPC meetings did in reality become part of Community policy-making. As a result of TEU implementation, the EPC Secretariat was disbanded, and the General Secretariat expanded to support CFSP policy discussions. Nevertheless, the blurred distinction remains between pillars one and two in the context of the General Affairs Council.

The technical councils are differentiated by particular policy areas, with member-state representation varying according to ministerial portfolios. One factor that needs to be considered when analysing the characteristics of the technical councils is the differing status or policy responsibilities of the ministerial representatives. For instance, Economic and Finance Ministers, sent as representatives to the EcoFin Council, hold different hierarchical positions in the member states; the German Finance Minister can exercise a veto on any matter that incurs additional EU expenditure not accounted for in the national budget. In addition, Germany normally sends both the Finance Minister and the Economic Affairs Minister to the EcoFin Council because of the division of ministerial responsibilities in Germany. By contrast, the UK normally sends just one representative (the Chancellor of the Exchequer, whose authority embraces economic and financial matters).

An implicit hierarchy also exists in the frequency of sessions, as indicated in Table 2.1. The technical councils that meet most often are considered to be those of greater significance and importance. They include the Agriculture, EcoFin, and Internal Market Councils. Obviously, this correlates with the prominence of these areas in Community policy-making during the late 1980s and early 1990s. The EcoFin and the Internal Market Councils are relatively 'new' due to the mandate given them by the SEA, but have managed to establish their positions within the Council's structure due to the importance of these policy areas. The term 'new' refers to the different character that both these Councils have acquired since SEA implementation. In particular, the '1992' programme and EMU policy objectives have resulted in more clearly defined roles and increased workloads for the Internal Market and EcoFin Councils. The Internal Market Council could be seen as a 'model' Council; it is widely regarded as efficient and productive in terms of the amount of legislation adopted. By the end of December 1992 (the agreed completion deadline), the Internal Market Council had adopted 261 out of 282 Commission proposals, of which 75 per cent had been implemented in the member states.[4] The emphasis since SEA ratification has been upon the internal market programme. The stipulated completion deadline required the Internal Market Council to work as effectively as it could. Qualified majority voting may have helped, but as will be discussed in the next chapter, there is evidence to suggest that it was the deadline rather than the decision rule that mattered.

The frequency of meetings often affects the actual characteristics of a particular Council. On average, the Council spends 84 days each year in formal meetings, but with a significant increase in the number of meetings from the early 1980s onwards.[5] However, as Table 2.1 indicates, some Councils meet more frequently than others. Meeting on a regular basis enables ministerial representatives to 'get to know each other'. This offers all of them a greater possibility to deduce in advance the likely positions of each other on a particular policy proposal. Personal relationships – the rapport that ministers have with each other – do influence the way in which a Council conducts its negotiations. Some ministers place greater emphasis on this than others, yet the overall impression from discussions with former ministers from several member states is that a good relationship often makes agreement infinitely easier.

The Presidency can affect the frequency of sessions. Each member state naturally attaches more importance to certain policy areas than others. When occupying the Presidency of the Council, this policy preference may be reflected in the convening of more meetings of, for example, the Education Council than another member state might generally do. More often though, the frequency of meetings is affected by the immediate policy

| | 1982 | 1983 | 1984 | 1985 | 1986 | 1987 | 1988 | 1989 | 1990 | 1991 | 1992 | 1993 | 1994 |
|---|---|---|---|---|---|---|---|---|---|---|---|---|---|
| General Affairs | 13 | 12 | 20 | 14 | 12 | 12 | 12 | 14 | 13 | 13 | 15 | 18 | 16 |
| Agriculture | 15 | 14 | 16 | 14 | 11 | 16* | 12 | 12 | 16 | 13 | 13 | 12 | 11 |
| EcoFin | 10* | 8 | 8 | 7 | 8 | 8* | 7 | 8 | 10 | 13 | 11 | 11 | 11 |
| Fisheries | 7 | 9 | 5 | 3 | 5 | 3 | 5 | 4 | 3 | 4 | 5 | 5 | 5 |
| Budget | 4 | 4 | 4 | 5 | 5 | 6 | 4 | 2 | 2 | 2 | 2 | 2 | 2 |
| Labour & Social | 4* | 3* | 3 | 2 | 2 | 2 | 2 | 5* | 3 | 3* | 3 | 4 | 4 |
| Energy | 3 | 3 | 2 | 3 | 3 | 2 | 2 | 2 | 3* | 3* | 2 | 3 | 2 |
| Research | 3 | 5 | 4 | 2 | 4 | 3 | 4 | 5 | 4 | 2 | 3 | 4 | 4 |
| Development | 2 | 2 | 2 | 2 | 2 | 3 | 2 | 2 | 4 | 3 | 3* | 2 | 2 |
| Environment | 2 | 3 | 3 | 3 | 3 | 4 | 3 | 5 | 5* | 5* | 5* | 6* | 5* |
| Industry | 2 | 7 | 5 | 6 | 6 | 5 | 2 | 4 | 4 | 2 | 2 | 5* | 5* |
| Transport | 2 | 4 | 4 | 3 | 4 | 4 | 4 | 4 | 4 | 6 | 4 | 5 | 5* |
| Education | 1 | 1* | 1 | 1 | 2 | 1 | 2 | 3 | 2 | 1 | 2 | 2 | 2 |
| Justice | 1 | 0 | 0 | 0 | 0 | 2 | 0 | 1 | 1 | 1 | 1 | 1 | 4 |
| Consumer Protection | 0 | 1 | 3 | 1 | 2* | 3 | 1* | 2 | 2 | 1 | 2 | 2 | 2 |
| Culture | 0 | 0 | 2 | 2 | 1 | 0 | 1 | 1 | 2 | 2 | 2 | 2 | 2 |
| Health | 0 | 0 | 0 | 0 | 1 | 1 | 2 | 2 | 2 | 2 | 2 | 2 | 3 |
| Internal Market | 0 | 6 | 2 | 5 | 8* | 6 | 8* | 10 | 7 | 5 | 7 | 6 | 3 |
| Telecommunications | 0 | 0 | 0 | 0 | 0 | 0 | 1 | 3 | 2 | 3 | 3 | 3 | 3* |
| Tourism | 0 | 0 | 0 | 0 | 0 | 0 | 1 | 0 | 1 | 0 | 1 | 0 | 0 |
| Others | 2 | 1 | 0 | 0 | 1 | 0 | 4 | 0 | 1 | 0 | 0 | 0 | 3 |
| Total | 71 | 83 | 84 | 73 | 79 | 80 | 77 | 89 | 90 | 83 | 87 | 94 | 92 |

* Denotes a joint meeting with another technical council in that year, hence the meeting is only counted once in the totals.
Source: *Annual Reviews of the Council's Work.*

**Table 2.1** Council sessions 1982–94.

priorities of the member state holding the Presidency. For example, the Tourism Council first met in December 1988 on the Greek Presidency's initiative. Before that, tourism was simply discussed within informal Council sessions. Since then, the formal Tourism Council has only met under the Italian Presidency of 1990, and the Portuguese Presidency of 1992, reflecting the significance of tourism to the Greek, Italian and Portuguese economies in general, but also their priorities in trying to establish some policy coordination at the Community level.

From this, clearly, any analysis of the Council must identify precisely the players at ministerial level. The Council is sub-divided into policy areas, and each technical council has its own characteristics. There are differences in the status of ministers, the frequency of sessions, and the importance attached to various councils by member states. All of these affect the way in which the Council operates.

## The European Council

The European Council is distinct from the Council as it does not legislate, but it does constitute part of the Council's structure. The European Council is 'above' the Council and its policy-making methods are solely inter-governmental. However, its existence has served to strengthen the overall position of the Council in EU policy-making.

The European Council is the name given to the meetings of the Heads of State or of Government of the EU. These meetings normally take place two to three times per year, although emergency sessions are sometimes convened. Informal meetings of the Heads of State or Government occurred from the 1950s, but it was not until December 1974 that such meetings were formalized and termed the European Council. Moreover, these summits were not given treaty recognition until the SEA.

The objectives of European Council meetings are to set tasks, policy goals, and future aims for the EU as a whole. Yet the 'theatre' of the European Council is also employed if issues of political difficulty remain unresolved in the Council forum. If member states find agreement on a particular proposal difficult to reach, the matter is often pushed up to the level of European Council. However, this is not necessarily an advantage. In the words of Lord Carrington (1988: 317):

> to introduce into negotiations the top people of all is a hazardous and not always successful move . . . When detail was increasingly relegated 'on appeal' to the [European] Council it didn't mean it was dealt with more knowledgeably, or business handled more expeditiously, I'm afraid the reverse tended to be the case. One should not involve the prestige of the senior office in any country unless there is a clear advantage in so doing.

Butler (1986: 28–9) also criticizes this 'pushing up' to the European Council. Whilst analysis of the operational characteristics of the European Council is excluded here because it does not function according to the same organizational procedures as the Council, it is important to be aware of the

European Council's potential input into discussions, especially in cases where it deals with proposals that have been pushed up.[6] This often indicates that the discussion of a particular proposal involved a high level of conflict within the Council, and that ministers have exported the issue to the European Council.

## The Presidency of the Council

Each member state occupies the office of the President for six months. In theory, the aim of establishing the Presidency was to enhance coordination of EU policy-making. In practice, although the Presidency partially ensures continuity of work, it can also allow an even greater, albeit short-term, national influence upon EU policy-making than already exists within the Council.[7] The Presidential term of office is often perceived as an 'opportunity' for a particular member state to take hold of the supranational reins. The stature of this office has increased due to the rise in EU policy activity and the greater weight that decisions have upon member states. In addition, the role of the Presidency increased after the formalization of European Council sessions in 1974, and the subsequent recognition given to the European Council by the SEA.

The tasks of the Presidency are primarily to set and subsequently manage the EU agenda for the six-month period of office, and act as the external representative of the Council. In addition, although the Commission or an individual member state can call a Council session, in practice it is the Presidency that does so. Since 1989, each Presidency has presented a detailed work programme before its term of office starts in an attempt to improve the organization and coordination of Council policy-making. To a certain extent, this has resulted in more adequate preparation of Council sessions and improved continuity in the transition between Presidencies. The support of the General Secretariat enhances this continuity further.

The Permanent Representative of the member state holding the Presidency and the appropriate Director-General of the Council's Secretariat report to the Presidency before every Council session. These actors inform the Presidency of the state of discussion in Coreper, the reasons why an issue is on the agenda and the positions of the individual member states. This enables the Presidency to assess what can realistically be achieved in that particular session of the Council. Consequently, at the start of a Council session, the President will have in front of them a briefing, a steering, and a speaking note.

The office of the Presidency is also responsible for the setting of the provisional agenda for each Council session. It must sign all minutes and adopted proposals, ensuring these are accurate in form and content. Furthermore, the Presidency chairs all Council and Coreper meetings and liaises with other EU institutions. These roles are normally carried out by the national minister responsible for a particular policy area; for example the Italian Agriculture Minister will chair all Agriculture Council sessions, whilst the Italian Deputy Permanent Representative will chair meetings of the Special Committee on Agriculture, and work with the appropriate staff in the Commission and EP during the Italian Presidency. The idea of the Troika also improved continuity between Presidencies. The outgoing, present, and incoming Presidencies work closely together to inform each other of the state of discussions, particular problems, etc.

The rotation of the Presidency has been altered on two occasions, as a result of successive enlargements, and is illustrated in Figure 2.2. First, an alternating cycle was introduced with the accession of Spain and Portugal, primarily to address the imbalances in the rhythm of the Council's work. There is less EU activity in the summer months, and thus a greater concentration of business between September and December. Certain policy decisions, such as the budget, always appear on the agenda at a set time in the calendar, whilst a second semester often inherits many proposals from the first. An alternating cycle ensured that a member state does not always preside over the Council in the same half of the year. The second change resulted from the accession of Austria, Finland and Sweden in 1995. Member states agreed that the system ought to ensure that the Troika system, which had worked quite effectively, should consist of at least one larger member state. Consequently, this 'balanced' rotation began its first cycle in July 1998.

The idea of rotating the Presidency supports the learning curve argument, namely that a six-month rotation gives all member states the opportunity to hold the office of the Presidency, and to familiarize themselves with Council and EU policy-making processes. Experiencing the day-to-day management of policy-making alerts any member state to the realities of this. The six-month period is sufficient time to achieve certain policy objectives but not too long to allow abuse of the term of office. Rotation is also significant for the smaller member states as it permits them to have a greater voice in EU affairs than would otherwise be possible. Smaller member states often take full advantage of this; for example, the Luxembourg and Dutch Presidencies of 1991 were highly influential in the drafting and agreement of the TEU.

With particular respect to the European Council and EPC, the Presidency acts as a spokesperson for the EU. Most media attention concerning the EU

| | 1 January–30 June | 1 July–31 December | |
|---|---|---|---|
| 1982 | Belgium | Denmark | |
| 1983 | Germany | Greece | |
| 1984 | France | Ireland | Note: The cycle is arranged |
| 1985 | Italy | Luxembourg | alphabetically according to the |
| 1986 | Netherlands | United Kingdom | name of each member state in |
| 1987 | Belgium | Denmark | its own language, for example |
| 1988 | Germany | Greece | Germany–Deutschland, Greece– |
| 1989 | Spain | France | Ellas. The first and second cycles |
| 1990 | Ireland | Italy | depicted by ······· illustrate the |
| 1991 | Luxembourg | Netherlands | accession of Spain and Portugal |
| 1992 | Portugal | United Kingdom | and the introduction of the |
| 1993 | Denmark | Belgium | alternating rotation. The third |
| 1994 | Greece | Germany | cycle includes the accession of |
| 1995 | France | Spain | Austria, Finland and Sweden in |
| 1996 | Italy | Ireland | 1995, and consequently from |
| 1997 | Netherlands | Luxembourg | July 1998 the balanced |
| 1998 | United Kingdom | Austria | rotation agreement. |
| 1999 | Germany | Finland | |
| 2000 | Portugal | France | |
| 2001 | Sweden | Belgium | |
| 2002 | Spain | Denmark | |
| 2003 | Greece | Italy | |
| 2004 | Ireland | Netherlands | |

**Figure 2.2** Rotation of the Council Presidency.

focuses upon summit meetings, and consequently upon the member state occupying the Presidency. Such attention means that member-state administrations regard their period of Presidential office as extremely important; they try to ensure that the six months runs smoothly and that substantial policy outputs are achieved. Member states do sometimes use the Presidency for domestic purposes. During the first half of 1993, Denmark succeeded in using its Presidency to promote the need to ratify the TEU domestically after the narrow 'No' victory in the first referendum. In contrast, the UK failed in its attempts to quell domestic dissatisfaction with European issues during its 1992 Presidency. However, some member states use the Presidency as a means to promote European issues and heighten public awareness; both the Luxembourg and Dutch Presidencies of 1991 increased public awareness of what was intended by the TEU.

The President in office is often described as a 'broker'. Presidential responsibility for problem solving has increased for a number of reasons. Firstly, the President can be the preferred mediator for member states. As discussed in Chapter 1, the Commission also plays the role of mediator in

Council negotiations. However, the Commission's relationship with the Council, and its success in helping to find agreement is often dependent upon the circumstances at that particular time. Secondly, the increased number of member states means that there are more negotiating styles in the Council, which generates further work for both the Presidency and the Commission in trying to lead member states towards agreement. Finally, the need to find compromises is becoming increasingly urgent as the scope and significance of EU policy-making increases. All these factors have placed a larger burden on the Presidency in its role as broker.

There are numerous ways in which the Presidency can exercise its role as mediator. During a Council session, the President can call for an 'indicative' vote to assess the state of agreement on a proposal. Member-state representatives set out their position – for, against, abstention – but also explain the reasons for such a position (Nicoll, 1984: 38). This enables the Presidency to identify the difficulties, and thus work out how to achieve a solution. Presidential 'confessionals' are another method used to find agreement. The President adjourns the Council and speaks to each member state in turn, asking each delegation to state its position with reasons. If only two or three member states hold differing positions, then the President calls informal bilateral or trilateral negotiations. Through these confidential confessionals, the President is in a better position to establish compromise agreements. The Presidency can also use time pressures to force an agreement. The President sometimes lets the discussion continue late into the evening. One alleged motive for doing so is that ministerial representatives start to worry that they will miss their last flight and consequently agreement is reached.

Member states can, and do, use the Presidency to their own advantage. As shown, distortions in the frequency of sessions are often attributable to Presidential agenda management. The number of 'B' points on the agenda, the number of decisions taken by a Council, as well as the emergence of 'new' Councils are partly due to Presidential management. Partner member states stated that the UK used its 1992 Presidency to block the passage of European employment legislation. Another member state did not schedule a Development Council under its Presidency. There was such an outcry, with accusations that the member state concerned did not care about development issues, that a Development Council was finally scheduled, presumably as a damage-limitation exercise.

The role of the Council Presidency has increased in importance in the last few years. It is no longer just concerned with the day-to-day running of the Council, but with conflict management. However, the significance of the Presidency for steering meetings also has negative aspects, in so far as the Presidency will have its own agenda of what it would like:

> former permanent representative privy to the inside workings of the Council's meetings termed it 'almost impossible' to get the Council to yield decisions which go against the desires of the Presidency. (Troy Johnston, 1994: 25)

One senior Council official stated that all Council sessions are essentially stage-managed by the Presidency, with the assistance of the General Secretariat. However, it is not the case that a member state can only initiate a proposal during its Presidency. The Franco–German initiative for political union during the Irish Presidency of 1990 is a good example. Yet, member states often use the Presidency to serve particular interests.

From this, it is clear that in analysing the Council, it is important to consider the role of the Presidency, as it is a crucial player in Council policy-making. However, there are difficulties in identifying the precise input of the Presidency. For example, details of Presidential confessionals are not recorded. In such cases where there is a lack of information, analysis of the Presidency as a player may only be possible by implication. There is also a question mark hanging over the future of the Presidency, and its abilities in an even larger EU (see Chapter 10).

## Coreper

The Treaty of Rome stated that a committee consisting of permanent representatives of the member states *may* be established, and that the Council could determine the task and power of that committee. The Council quickly seized this opportunity and set up such a committee at an intergovernmental conference of the Foreign Ministers on 7 and 8 January 1958. The Permanent Representatives Committee (more commonly referred to by its French acronym Coreper), quickly established itself as a crucial element in the internal structure of the Council and in the business of Community policy-making, although legal acknowledgement of Coreper did not occur until ratification of the Merger Treaty in 1967.[8] In the ECSC (the European Coal and Steel Community), the Council established a committee known as COCOR (Comité de Coordination de la Communauté du Charbon et de l'Acier) but, in comparison to Coreper, COCOR was a 'loose liaison' (Wallace, H. 1973: 58).

The role of Coreper is that of a bridge between EU and national concerns. Each permanent representative has a dual role, as they must represent the national position whilst keeping the national capital informed of all developments, member state positions, likely outputs, etc. in EU policy-making. Thus Coreper helps to draw up and coordinate national positions on all proposals, and negotiates on these within the Council framework. Although permanent representatives cannot vote, they do indicate voting positions of their national ministers. There is constant and continual consult-ation between Brussels and the national capital. In addition, an absent minister should be replaced by a colleague at a Council session but it is usually a representative of Coreper. As Noël (1967: 229) stresses, it is important to remember that Coreper has no actual policy-making powers so it would be incorrect to consider Coreper representatives as deputies for their respective ministers. Coreper officials simply stand in for their ministers at formal Council meetings, so that at least a representative is privy to the policy discussions even if they have no decision-making powers. Therefore, Busch and Puchala's (1976: 235–54) comment that Coreper can be viewed as a Council in permanent session is misleading, as Coreper representatives do not have the same decision-making powers as their respective ministers. However, the reality is that ministers only take about 10 to 15 per cent of final policy decisions. Most decisions (albeit unofficial) are taken by the working groups and Coreper, approximately 70 per cent and 10 to 15 per cent respectively.

The organization of Coreper is split into two parts. Coreper I consists of Deputy Permanent Representatives; Coreper II consists of Permanent Representatives who have ambassadorial status. In 1962, Coreper was divided into these two elements due to its increased workload as Community activity grew. The number in each member-state permanent representation differs according to geographical factors and national attitudes as shown in Figure 2.3. France has traditionally had a small mission due to the proximity, in relative terms, of Paris to Brussels, whereas Greece has a high number of representatives in its mission. Germany is said in the past to have viewed its mission as a place for civil service training (Wallace, H. 1973: 56–75). When a member state occupies the office of the President of the Council, there is a slight increase in total number of Coreper personnel based in Brussels.

Coreper normally meets at least once a week, and spends on average 119 days per year in meetings. It is noticeable that its workload has remained fairly constant since its formalization.[9] The agenda of a Coreper meeting is similar to that of the Council, but Coreper meetings tend to be less formal. Coreper agendas have roman 'i' and 'ii' points which correspond to Council 'A' and 'B' points. However, there are open points on Coreper agendas,

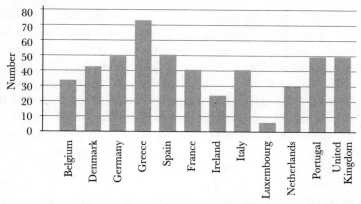

The figures for Portugal and the UK are higher than in 1991 due to their presidential terms of office in 1992

Source: *Guide to the Council of the European Communities 1992.* Brussels 1992.

**Figure 2.3** Number in permanent representations to the Council 1992.

which allow proposals to be modified during the meeting to ensure that agreement will be reached. The President of Coreper I divides the policy proposals between the two components of Coreper. Customarily, Coreper II manages the more general dossiers, in particular those of a more political nature. This includes external affairs, relations with developing countries, energy and nuclear issues, political cooperation, EcoFin affairs, regional policy, trade union questions, and institutional issues. Coreper I, as a rule, considers budgetary affairs, social and environmental issues, transport, fisheries, the freedom of establishment, industrial issues, and replies to questions from MEPs. The preparatory work of Coreper II (and European Council meetings) is carried out by a special body known as the Antici Group, composed of high-level civil servants from each member state together with a Commission official. The Antici Group was set up in 1975, primarily in response to the increasing workload of Coreper II. However, the Antici Group has also established itself as a crucial actor in the work of the European Council.

Other 'specialist' committees within Coreper's organization discuss particular policy areas, with the member state holding the Council Presidency in the chair (refer to Figure 2.1). These include the Political Committee which supports the General Affairs Council on foreign policy matters, the Article 113 Committee dealing with external trade and tariff negotiations, the Special Committee on Agriculture, the Standing Committee on Employment established to coordinate employment policy within the EU framework, and Crest (Committee on Scientific and Technical

Research), which coordinates projects and policies in this area. The Budget Committee prepares briefs, gives opinions upon EU finance measures for non-EU forums and approves budget forecasts for the General Secretariat and the ESC. An Education Committee was set up in June 1974 to draw up and subsequently implement action programmes. The newest committee to emerge is the K4 Committee, dealing with matters falling under the third pillar. However, its members were involved within intergovernmental committees dedicated to justice and home affairs, such as the Trevi Group.[10] In addition, some two hundred working groups assist Coreper in its work. Some are permanent, others temporary so the total varies over time and the General Secretariat has no official list.[11] Committees and working parties meet the most frequently of all the elements of the Council's structure, averaging 1609 days per year.[12] The pace of discussion is usually slow, until the week before the Coreper meeting, when negotiation is speeded-up. Working parties concern themselves with the detail of a proposal and meticulously amend texts until all delegations are satisfied. Some amendments may appear trivial to the casual observer – 'can' instead of 'will', 'could' replacing 'should', 'coordination' rather than 'cooperation', the reordering of paragraphs, etc.[13] However, these changes are crucial to the life of a proposal. The significance of Coreper and its composite committees is that it speeds up EU policy-making processes by partly relieving the Council's workload. This has strengthened the position of the Council as a whole, as it has reduced the risk of overburdening the Council, and as discussed has, to a certain extent, limited the input of the Commission.

Council agendas are divided into 'A' and 'B' points.[14] 'A' points refer to proposals that simply require formal Council approval, Coreper having reached agreement. 'B' points cover all other agenda items that demand further consideration by the appropriate ministers, often the more difficult, politically sensitive policy proposals where ministerial-level negotiations are mandatory. By filtering proposals, Coreper is alleviating the preparatory 'burden' of discussions and identifying areas of consensus (Hayes, 1984: 199). Coreper works in close contact with respective national administrations and alerts them to the pending difficulties of a 'B' point. It makes stringent efforts to reduce the number of 'B' points on a Council agenda, especially as only a fraction of the total number of items requires a 'B' point. However, occasionally the entire Council session discusses a single 'B' point. Nevertheless, the input made by Coreper has undoubtedly increased the speed and efficiency of the process. Moreover, due to the non-permanent composition of the Council, Coreper's role is crucial. Changes in the composition of national government, either through elections or reshuffles, could have implications for the continuity of national positions regarding

EU policy. The permanent nature of Coreper reduces the possible disruption.

Although the structure and organization of member-state administrations is not explicitly dealt with here, some consideration needs to be made of the approach to, and organization of EU affairs by individual member states. Differing national structures affect the operation of Coreper, and the policy-making processes of formal Council meetings. These are due to variations in government organization and administrative style. For example, some member states have separate representatives responsible for economic and financial affairs, while others group these portfolios together. All have a foreign affairs desk, but representation ranges from five in the Luxembourg mission to twenty in the Belgian and Italian missions in 1992. These administrative set-ups show that member states have different EU policy priorities. Consequently, this will affect the information-gathering capabilities of the players and the quality of their input into Coreper on different issues.

## The General Secretariat of the Council

Article 21 of the Council's Rules of Procedure provides for the establishment of the Secretariat.[15] Its role is to assist the Council in its work under the direction of a Secretary-General. The General Secretariat has grown in size, in line with the general increase in Council activity and the formalization and eventual treaty recognition of the European Council. In 1958 there were 238 members of staff in the General Secretariat, rising to 2008 by 1990 (Council, 1991: 26) However, it is still relatively small in comparison with that of the Commission. The General Secretariat is extremely important to the operation of the Council, yet it is not given the academic recognition it deserves for the significant supportive role it plays.

The role of the Council's General Secretariat is that of administrator and adviser to the Council, and to serve the Presidency of the Council. It also performs secretarial duties in the broadest sense of the term, for the working parties, Coreper and the formal Council. The General Secretariat holds a detailed briefing before each Coreper meeting and Council session to help identify and discuss Presidential concerns. The General Secretariat attends all formal Council meetings and some informal sessions, and draws up the minutes of each formal Council session, which must be submitted for approval by the Council within fifteen days of the meeting, as defined by Article 9 of the Council's Rules of Procedure (see Appendix 1). The General Secretariat is also responsible for the translation of all Council documentation into the official EU languages, and for the preparation and distribution of all documentation relating to the work of the Council, both for internal and external view. Moreover, the Secretariat ensures that ministers receive all EP and ESC opinions and recommendations.

The General Secretariat is sub-divided into ten Directorates-General, A to J, with specific policy responsibilities (see Figure 2.4). A major restructuring resulted from TEU implementation and in 1995 the number of Directorates-General rose from seven to ten. Although not as broadly sub-divided as the Directorates-General of the Commission, the policy groupings in the General Secretariat are complementary. The Secretary-General heads the Private Office of the Secretariat, a position held by Jürgen Trumpf until the end of 1999. There is a general consensus that the previous Secretary-General Niels Ersbøll (1980–94), enhanced the status of this position through his proactive approach in preparatory meetings with respective delegations.

The General Secretariat's legal service assists the Council in all issues regarding the preparation of Council acts. This assistance is invaluable, but usually invisible. However, the demanding policy agenda has on occasion focused attention upon the input of the legal service of the General Secretariat. A good example is that of the Edinburgh European Council in December 1992 where Monsieur Piris, Head of the Legal Service, spoke directly to the meeting, which was the first time that a member of the General Secretariat had done so. Moreover, it was Monsieur Piris who found the solution to the Danish problems regarding ratification of the TEU. However, the legal service is rarely invited to attend informal sessions. As several General Secretariat officials pointed out, this is rather short-sighted and potentially hazardous if ministers reach political agreements without considering the legal implications.

The General Secretariat services the entire Council, and is of particular value to the member state holding the Presidency. It provides continuity of information for the Presidency, as it is often the case that a member of the General Secretariat will follow one dossier for several years and is therefore able to offer in-depth knowledge and expertise. When a member state begins its term of Presidential office, it often inherits proposals. The General Secretariat is able to offer detailed information on the state of discussion of such proposals and alert the Presidency to any 'difficult' policy decisions. In addition, the General Secretariat provides the President with a handling brief before every formal Council session. The General Secretariat can also discourage Presidential manipulation of the EU agenda by advising the Presidency of the likely success of negotiations on a particular proposal. Any member state may want to use its period of

**Secretary-General**
financial control

**Private Office**
advisory group,
general information,
documentation, publications,
press information

**Legal Service**

**Directorate-General A**
administration, personnel,
protocol, organisation,
security, infrastructures,
translation and documentation production

**Directorate-General B**
agriculture, fisheries

**Directorate-General C**
internal market, industrial policy, competition

**Directorate-General D**
research, energy, transport

**Directorate-General E**
external relations, CFSP

**Directorate-General F**
EP and ESC relations, institutional affairs
budget and staff regulations

**Directorate-General G**
economic and financial affairs

**Directorate-General H**
justice and home affairs

**Directorate-General I**
environment, consumer protection, health

**Directorate-General J**
economic and social cohesion,
regional, social affairs, education

**Figure 2.4** Organization of the General Secretariat of the Council.

Presidency to promote or demote a specific policy proposal on the Council agenda. The General Secretariat is aware of this and can advise the Presidency of the implications of doing so. In addition, the General Secretariat is a valuable source of knowledge about member-state attitudes towards particular dossiers and provides the Presidency with such information to facilitate agreement within Council sessions. Interestingly, one long-serving General Secretariat official stated that 90 per cent of the time it is the General Secretariat rather than the Presidency that finds a compromise agreement on a specific proposal.

The General Secretariat offers an existing and well-established administrative structure that is beneficial to all member states, but can be of special value to the smaller member states, as it was to the new member states in the past or Austria, Finland and Sweden at present. However, Presidential recognition of the value of the General Secretariat is often belated. The 1992 UK Presidency under-utilized the General Secretariat until the final two months of its term of office. Other member states, namely Italy and The Netherlands have also been guilty of this during their last Presidencies. In speaking with many Council officials, there was a general feeling that some ministerial representatives place little value on the advice and expertise of the General Secretariat, preferring instead to consult their own national experts. Whilst such remarks may be expected from General Secretariat members, this may particularly be the attitude of the larger member states as they feel that they already have adequate administrative structures and expertise, and therefore have no need to use the General Secretariat. However, the General Secretariat is more than a simple secretarial and administrative body, although it also performs these functions very effectively. Many of the staff employed in the General Secretariat have immense and practical knowledge of EU policy-making. Staff may have come from other EU institutions, or from national administrations, which means they can offer different perspectives on the experiences of policy-making. Such advice and diplomacy can prove invaluable in times of protracted negotiation. The total impartiality of the General Secretariat's advice can greatly assist not only the Council's internal operation, but the Council's inter-institutional relations in EU policy-making (Edwards and Wallace, 1977: 25).

The support of the General Secretariat may be invisible at first glance, yet its role in the work of the Council is of fundamental significance and consequence. Whilst Article 151 of the TEU gave formal recognition to the General Secretariat, it failed to outline its role sufficiently. Perhaps this is due to member-state wishes that the Secretariat should maintain its low profile. One hindrance to efficient supranational policy-making is often the lack of coordination between national ministries. Although the General Secretariat cannot solve this problem, it does go part of the way to improving the channels of information available to the ministerial represent-atives of the member states, providing that member states acknowledge and use this. Clearly, the role of the General Secretariat is crucial to the Council's operation, but the analyst may find it extremely difficult to identify its precise input in Council policy-making, due to its invisible and undocumented work. Moreover, as in the case of Coreper, the General Secretariat can be viewed as both a single body and as a part of the Council's structure comprised of individual players. However, due to the invisible nature of the General Secretariat, it may not always be possible to analyse its input and effect.

## Assessing the Council

Analysis of the characteristics of the Council's operation requires consideration of all five of these elements of its structure. They function together to ensure effective operation of the Council. Only ministerial representatives from member states have the final power to take legislative decisions. Yet, as shown, ministers have a strong network of support comprising the Presidency, Coreper and the various working parties, and the General Secretariat in the Council's policy-making process. Along with the ministers, these levels of the Council, whether viewed as individual actors or as structural mechanisms, can affect the way in which the Council conducts its policy-making. The theoretical framework devised in Chapter 4 further conceptualizes how these five tiers can be analysed. What is clear, though, is that the Council, through the development of its internal structures, has consolidated its position and enhanced member-states' grip on EU policy-making. Tangible differences at a structural level do exist however between the various technical councils that constitute the Council. What the case studies will ascertain is whether operational distinctions also emerge.

# CHAPTER THREE

## *Organizational procedures of the Council*

The rules and procedures of the Council crucially affect the way in which it conducts its policy-making. They can be viewed as the action channels of the Council – a term developed in subsequent chapters and employed in the analytical framework. They include the forms that Council meetings take, the mechanics of formal sessions, and the rules that govern Council decisions. An appreciation of these mechanisms adds a further dimesnsion to our understanding of the Council's characteristics, and its preferred modes of operation. Some attention is given to the ways in which Council sessions are, and are not, recorded. Given the informal practices that have evolved in the Council's history though, and the reluctance on the part of member states to advertise all of the inner workings of this still most-secretive of EU institutions, accurate information remains patchy.

### The types of Council session

The Council meets in both formal and informal session, and sometimes in joint session. A formal session can be defined as a meeting of the Council at which a record of the discussion is taken. Formal sessions predominantly take place in the Justus Lipsius building in Brussels, except during the months of April, May and October when meetings are held in Luxembourg. Formal sessions can be 'normal' or 'restricted'. At a normal session, those present include the Presidency, the General Secretariat and the Commission. Ministerial delegations comprise of three representatives at the table, plus numerous assistants, although there is only space for six per delegation.

The Council goes into restricted (or *super-restreint*) session when there are severe difficulties in agreeing on a proposal. It is felt that restricting the number of personnel present in the room may allow more frank and open discussion to take place. Restricted sessions involve only one ministerial representative plus one aide from each member state, together with the Presidency and the Commission. Even the interpreters are often asked to leave the room.

Informal sessions range from the dinner-table diplomacy conducted during the lunchtime break within a formal session, to weekend breaks usually on the initiative of the President-in-office, conclaves, inter-ministerial meetings, and 'ministers meeting *within* a Council session'. Informal sessions pose a problem for any analysis of the operation of the Council as there is no record of the discussion. There may be references to informal meetings in official Council Press Releases or *Agence Europe*, but these are rare. Moreover, no recorded details exist of the working-lunch sessions. In December 1988, an informal political agreement between member-state Foreign Ministers resolved to limit the number of informal sessions held under each Presidency to seven. Yet this agreement had no legal backing as it is informal in itself, and member states still abuse this arrangement by manipulating what constitutes a session. The amended Rules of Procedure for the Council adopted in December 1993 were to include a clause to restrict the number of informal sessions and define the status of such meetings, but this was not approved. Figure 3.1 sets out informal sessions held between 1982 and 1992, based on the available sources of information, and demonstrates that the informal type of meeting is an important organizational fact of the Council.

EcoFin has always held informal sessions, usually before and in preparation for the International Monetary Fund negotiations. Since 1958, Agriculture has tended to have three 'jollies' per year, including one in Berlin to coincide with the January Farm Fair. Most member states hold informal sessions for many policy areas, although Belgian governments have made it clear that they dislike informal meetings. Interestingly, the European Council has also started to convene informally. Some Presidencies primarily call such meetings so that the main summit can deal with more than just one issue, but this can add to the workload of Heads of State or Government, reflected in Lady Thatcher's (1993: 760) comment that such extra informal sessions were 'an unwelcome habit'.

One advantage of informal sessions is the 'socialization' process that occurs. Informal meetings help ministerial representatives to get to know each other in a relaxed setting. As discussed, personal relationships can be crucial to the Council's negotiating process. One respected long-serving EU

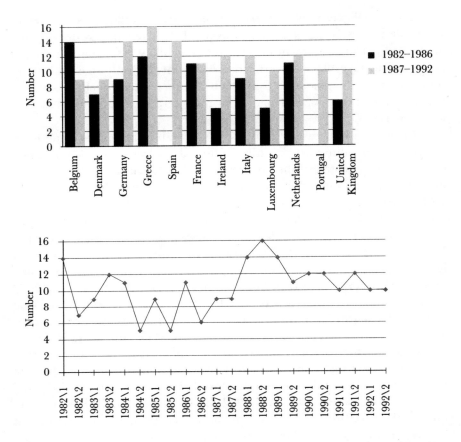

The bar chart shows the number of informal sessions under two Presidencies for each member state (e.g. Belgium 1982 and 1987, with the exception of Spain and Portugal who only acceded in 1986). Refer to Figure 2.2 for the differing cycles of the Presidency. The graph shows the overall number of informal sessions since 1982, where /1 refers to the first semester of the year, /2 to the second. Data taken from *Agence Europe*.

**Figure 3.1** Informal sessions of the Council 1982–92.

official feels that informal sessions are being relied upon so heavily that they are now beginning to resemble the formal variety. This may have undermined the socialization process, but it is not possible to investigate this due to the lack of information about informal sessions; the analyst has to rely purely on comments from 'insiders'.

The most common informal session is the accepted and acknowledged practice of a working lunch within a Council session, at which political bargaining is 'dinner-table conversation'. The lunchtime session is especially significant, as it is usually the first opportunity for ministers to have an informal chat in a more relaxed, sometimes light-hearted atmosphere. In addition, it is often the case that the working lunch addresses the more difficult issues on the Council agenda. Referring to EcoFin, Nigel Lawson (1992: 912) states:

> It was the custom to conduct the formal business at EcoFin Council meetings during the morning and afternoon sessions, leaving the trickier, more important, and more interesting matters for informal discussion over lunch, when no minutes were taken and to which no reference would normally be made afterwards, not least to the press.

Only the ministers, the Chairmen of Coreper I and II, and the Secretary-General or Director-General of the Council are present at the working lunch. It is felt that ministers may be more flexible without their advisers present. As one Council official put it, the *salle à manger* has come to resemble a Council meeting room:

> Once upon a time, this [the lunchtime session] was improvised, with whispered interpretation. But now, at the insistence of the Danes in 1987, the luncheon room is wired and the interpreters sit in a booth, but with a curtain drawn so that they do not have to watch the spectacle of food being eaten.

The Council specifically requested an additional dining room for the new Justus Lipsius building due to the accession of Austria, Finland and Sweden. Yet, this request also emphasizes the importance that the Council places upon dinner-table conversation. There is usually no fixed agenda, although some Presidents make it clear what they want to talk about.

Other types of informal session include the weekend 'get-together' organized by the member state holding the Presidency. Officials of the General Secretariat of the Council are not normally present at such occasions. The terms 'conclave' and 'inter-ministerial meeting' are employed when ministers of the Council meet to officially discuss issues outside the competences of the Treaties. Whether these gatherings also consider EU issues is questionable but highly likely, although no-one would ever admit as much. The same can be said for those meetings entitled 'Ministers of *x* (for example Health) and Representatives of the Governments of the Member States meeting within the Council'.[1] These meetings deal with extra-Treaty issues but the distinction between such issues and Community issues can be blurred.

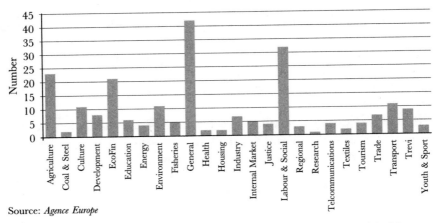

Source: *Agence Europe*

**Figure 3.2** Informal sessions of the Council by policy area 1982–92.

Figure 3.2 indicates that those Councils that deal with the most highly significant policy areas meet more frequently in informal sessions, namely General Affairs, EcoFin, and Agriculture. A similar pattern was found in the previous section of this chapter for the frequency of formal meetings in these policy areas. The figure for informal General Affairs Councils may be distorted by the need to convene such meetings to discuss issues outside EU competences but which nevertheless have an impact upon European affairs. The high number of informal Labour & Social Affairs meetings is a result of the new competences given to this Council by the SEA. Figures are also relatively significant for other new or developing policy areas, namely Culture, Environment, Transport and Trevi (prior to TEU introduction of Justice and Home Affairs).

Most informal Council meetings seem to take place towards the end of each Presidency (see Appendix 3) and there is little difference between the number of meetings held in each Presidential cycle. Figures show that the most popular months for informal sessions are April and May during the first semester and September and October during the second semester. Overall, informal meetings are mainly held in September, but this is probably because there is little activity during late July and all of August. Relatively few meetings are convened in January, June or December, perhaps because preparations for the European Council meetings tend to dominate Presidential activity during June and December.

The main advantage of informal sessions is that a relaxed setting is often more conducive to reaching agreement. Although there is no concrete evidence that this form of discussion helps, the general impression given is that informal sessions are enjoyable and often productive. One former minister felt that the informal conversations were often useful, sometimes absolutely crucial, but stressed that informal meetings were not *more* important than formal deliberations. No agreements, conclusions, etc., reached in informal sessions have legal status; they still require formal approval in the framework of a formal Council session. However, this legal distinction has not deterred some member states from using the outcomes of informal meetings to their advantage. For example, a set of conclusions adopted at an informal session of the Transport Council during the 1989 French Presidency had no legality in itself but was persistently quoted by French representatives in subsequent meetings. The absence of the General Secretariat at informal sessions can have a detrimental effect upon any consensus achieved as often the political agreements are reached without consideration of the legal implications. Another former minister stressed the importance of informal sessions for non-decisions, in other words for enabling member states to identify each other's positions through general discussion, but where no formal agreement is sought, discussed more fully later in this chapter.

Joint sessions, sometimes referred to as jumbo Councils, occur where there is a clear policy overlap such as that between internal market and consumer protection issues or finance and agriculture. Joint Energy and Environment sessions began to occur due to the need for better coordination between these policy areas. However, this type of session is not considered very productive or effective, hence the reference by some to 'jumble' rather

| Year | Joint session | Total |
|------|---------------|-------|
| 1982 | EcoFin & Labour & Social Affairs | 1 |
| 1983 | Labour & Social Affairs & Education | 1 |
| 1984 | None | 0 |
| 1985 | None | 0 |
| 1986 | Internal Market & Consumer | 1 |
| 1987 | EcoFin & Agriculture | 1 |
| 1988 | Internal Market & Consumer | 1 |
| 1989 | None | 0 |
| 1990 | Environment & Energy | 1 |
| 1991 | Environment & Energy | 1 |
|      | Youth & Labour & Social Affairs | 1 |
| 1992 | Environment & Development | 1 |

Source: *Annual Reviews of the Council's Work.*

**Table 3.1** Formal joint sessions of the Council 1982–92.

than 'jumbo' Councils.[2] Table 3.1 shows that joint sessions are only held on average once a year at most, suggesting that this type of session is only convened when there is a distinct overlap of issues. Figures for informal joint sessions, for which documentation is sparse, show that there were only two informal joint sessions between 1982 and 1992, (Education and Youth, General Affairs and EcoFin), both under the UK presidency of 1992.

The reasons for these low figures for both formal and informal joint sessions are three-fold. First, there is the issue of ministerial representation, which links back to previous comments on ministerial status. For example, Environment Ministers tend to dominate joint sessions with Energy Ministers despite their more junior position in national administrations. This is partly because the Environment Council convenes more frequently than the Energy Council and therefore Environment Ministers are better acquainted. Consequently, such joint councils are not always regarded as productive events due to the dominant position of Environment Ministers over their colleagues in Energy. Second, there is the problem of ministerial coordination. Member states are often settling their own internal rows in joint Councils. One senior General Secretariat official indicated his frustration with member states who do not coordinate their policy positions more effectively, as it can make a real difference to the actual negotiations, giving the example of the UK as being good at this in contrast to Italy. Finally, there is often difficulty in defining the agenda and substance of the meeting. Although there may be logical policy overlaps to discuss, the problem arises in deciding exactly what to examine without upsetting any of the member states concerned. For example, the German Presidency, during the first half of 1983, convened a joint Social Affairs and Education Council. There was a lack of detail in the debate, it was considered a waste of time as no matters of substance were discussed, and it was felt that the meeting was convened only for show. However, joint sessions involving the Internal Market and Consumer Councils have proved successful. This perhaps illustrates the importance of there being a distinct policy overlap, where common objectives and priorities exist.

From the above, the Council clearly uses a variety of action channels. These different types of Council session can affect the 'pulling and hauling' process of negotiation. In particular, it appears that the Council uses informal meetings when agreement is proving difficult. These may be crucial to the outcome of Council policy-making at any given moment. However, precisely because these meetings are informal, they are undocumented. It is also important to note that the action channels used by the Council may vary during the discussion of a particular proposal, which may affect the negotiating process and consequently the final output of the Council's policy-making process.

## A typical formal Council session

To arrive at a better understanding of how the Council works, it is worth considering the mechanics of a formal session. A Council agenda will include, in order:

- Formal approval of the agenda.
- Formal approval of 'A' points:
  (i) formal approval of Council minutes.
  (ii) approval of answers to EP written questions.
  (iii) miscellaneous adoptions already agreed by Coreper.
- Main items – 'B' points.
- Any other business.

Coreper discusses the draft agenda three weeks before a Council meeting, and then a provisional agenda is circulated at least fourteen days in advance of the actual Council session. As discussed, 'A' points refer to those matters which only require Council approval; the ministers do not have to debate such items as Coreper will already have finalized agreement on them.[3] 'A' points are normally dealt with in the next scheduled session of the Council (that is any of the Councils, not necessarily the Council covering the particular policy area). Ministers can exercise the right to express an opinion on such agenda items, but if a member-state's position requires further discussion, a decision is usually postponed unless the Council decides that this is not appropriate. As a rule, about two-thirds of Council decisions are dealt with as 'A' points (Council, 1991:22).

'B' points require ministerial discussion, as Coreper has not been able to agree a position on them. There are also false 'B' points, such as agreements with third countries, which are not contentious, but where it would be politically incorrect not to discuss them at ministerial level. Discussion of the 'B' items establishes the Council's position or decision. The Presidency normally calls for a *tour de table* where each minister comments for five minutes on a 'B' point. After this, the Council examines the proposal in greater detail. It may only concentrate upon certain aspects, or become bogged-down in one section. Therefore, the length of discussion on any one 'B' point varies considerably.

The Presidency asks numerous questions after the discussion of a proposal has ended. From the responses given, the Presidency deduces the likely outcome of a vote. The President knows that member states are likely to adopt a maximalist position at the outset, and that because of this the Presidency has a certain amount of room for manoeuvre. However, if there is a large divergence of opinions and positions between the member states,

61

the Presidency may use the 'confessional' tactic. Although voting usually occurs on the initiative of the President, a clause added to the 1993 Rules of Procedure allows any member state or the Commission to open a voting procedure, providing that a majority of the Council members agree.[4] An asterisk by an agenda item indicates that a vote may be requested. When it comes to voting in a Council session, on most occasions, member-state representatives just nod or remain silent. They tend only to raise their hands in cases of qualified majority voting, while the Presidency frantically calculates the majority threshold.

Areas in which there may be difficulty in reaching a decision are sometimes put on the agenda as 'any other business'. This usually refers to fundamental political objections by a member state or the EP. These items are not classed as 'B' points, because it is unlikely that any sort of resolution will be possible, and the main items on a Council agenda normally require some form of action or decision.

The atmosphere of a Council session is also important in understanding how the Council works. The following comments are based on the author's attendance of a number of Council sessions during 1993 and 1994. Obviously, the content of these meetings cannot be disclosed but the remarks give a flavour of what a Council meeting is like. First, there is the bustle of the meeting. The ministers sit at the table, and behind them representatives and advisers come and go from the room, which can often be distracting. Such noise and bustle is more common in those Council meetings with 'high' political agendas (for example the General Affairs Council in its discussions over the Yugoslavian crisis or the EcoFin Council when debating EMU.) From the agreement reached at the Edinburgh Council in December 1992, it is possible to get a better flavour of Council sessions, as the public can view the so-called open sessions on television screens in the press rooms in the Justus Lipsius building. Second, there can be a language problem in trying to communicate quickly in a Council session. Most delegations tend to listen to their colleagues in French as, although the interpreters are of a high calibre, translation often loses the tone and implicit meaning of a statement. Third, Council etiquette is very noticeable. Member-state representatives observe the practice of thanking the President for inviting them to speak, and the previous speaker for their comments, even when tensions are high.

It is possible to analyse formal Council sessions as these types of meeting are, to a certain extent, documented. The nature of a particular formal meeting – the agenda, the input of Coreper, the duration of the meeting, the tactics employed by member states and the role of the Presidency – provide insights into the negotiations and give some indication of the final decision output.

## The methods of decision in the Council

Voting procedures in the Council vary according to the policy area under discussion. There are three categories: simple majority voting, qualified majority voting and unanimity. The use of simple majority voting (currently eight out of fifteen votes) is mainly for procedural decisions such as the adoption of the Council's Rules of Procedure. The Treaty of Rome provided for the use of qualified majority voting but expected unanimity to be the 'norm' in voting procedures for the period of transition 1958 to 1970. Qualified majority voting would gradually come into force. The current breakdown of votes per member state under qualified majority is shown in Figure 3.3. However, the Luxembourg Compromise of 1966 restricted the use of qualified majority voting, and between 1966 and the early 1980s, qualified majority voting was only used for budgetary and administrative decisions (Lequesne, 1991: 20).

The Luxembourg Compromise solved the six-month empty chair crisis in the EC during July to December 1965. The French government walked out of the Council in response to the other member states linking a decision on the CAP (Common Agricultural Policy) to EC financing in general and the EP's budgetary powers.[5] The solution was really an agreement to disagree, espoused in the Luxembourg Accords, 28 and 29 January 1966. Clause I states that

> where, in the case of decisions which may be taken by majority vote on a proposal from the Commission, very important interests of one or more partners are at stake, the Members of the Council will endeavour, within a reasonable time, to reach solutions which can be adopted by all the Members of the Council while respecting their mutual interests and those of the Community, in accordance with Article 2 of the Treaty.

Consequently, any member state perceiving a threat to its national interest could invoke this accord. The power of the veto was rather fragile until the 1973 enlargement. With the addition of more sceptical members like Denmark and the UK, there was concern that the Luxembourg Compromise would increasingly be used. However, there is an unwritten understanding that the Council seeks agreement and the word 'veto' is never officially used in meetings. Moreover, the President of the Council will not usually call a vote if the threat of a veto exists.

The belief at the time was that the Luxembourg Compromise would slow down Community policy-making as it would take far longer to reach agreement. However, even before SEA ratification, the time taken to adopt

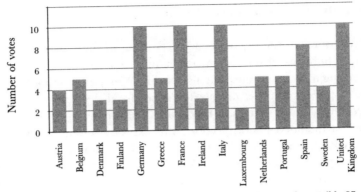

Decisions taken by qualified majority voting require a total of 62 out of a possible 87 votes where the Council is debating a Commission proposal. In other cases, those 62 votes must include votes in favour by at least 10 member states.

**Figure 3.3** Qualified majority voting in the Council 1999.

a proposal significantly decreased. Between 1975 and 1986, the average number of days to adopt a proposal declined by 30 per cent (Sloot and Verschuren, 1990). Nicoll (1984: 36) argues that it is debatable whether qualified majority voting would have become normal procedure even without the 1965 crisis. By using qualified majority voting, the Council puts a member-state representative in the difficult position of returning to their country and explaining that although not in agreement with $x$, the other member states support $x$, and there is no choice but to accept. Any member state is likely to find itself in that position at some time or other. The Report of the Three Wise Men described the Luxembourg Compromise as a fact of Community life.[6] For the Council as a whole, it is often easier to reach unanimity. What matters is the knowledge that a vote *could* be taken even if it is not. Amendments to the Council's Rules of Procedure in 1987 required that provisional agendas indicate those items that could be subject to a vote. However, evidence suggests that although the possibility exists, it is not at the front of ministers' minds when conducting Council negotiations. One official from the Council's Secretariat described qualified majority voting under the SEA as 'irrelevant'; that the consensus approach dominates. Another stated that despite qualified majority provisions, proceedings on most matters start from the premise that it would be desirable to achieve a consensus and a lot of effort goes into finding this. Significantly, the Internal Market Council has only used qualified majority voting for one-third to one-half of proposals, even though the SEA called for qualified majority voting for nearly all proposals relating to the completion of the internal market. It should be noted that data on the use of qualified majority voting is rather unreliable. Records of its use remained secret until 1994. Council press releases now state when proposals have been adopted by qualified majority voting, yet it is probable that a majority decision was reached without an actual vote.

The seeming reluctance to avoid using qualified majority voting stems from the fact that if a proposal is blocked under the qualified majority procedure it will be lost, and generally member states want to promote rather than hamper decisions. To abstain in qualified majority voting procedures is equivalent to a negative vote, which is not the case with unanimity – discussion will continue until all agree. Even the Official Handbook of the Council (1991: 41) points this out:

> This sometimes results in the paradoxical situation where a decision for which a qualified majority cannot be reached, because the 54 [in 1991] votes needed have not been attained, is taken more easily unanimously as a result of abstention by certain members of the Council who do not wish to vote in favour but do not want to prevent the Act concerned from going through.

The Luxembourg Compromise is still alive, but seldom used. At the Paris European Council of 1974, the member states agreed that 'an end should be put to the Council's practice of making agreement even on the less important questions conditional upon the unanimous consent of the Ministers'.[7] However, this declaration came to nothing: the threat of the veto remained. Interestingly, though, since the 1980s member states have only tried to use the veto three times, and each time were unsuccessful. In 1982, the UK tried to veto the agricultural prices settlement but failed, due to a lack of backers. In 1985, there was a German veto on cuts to cereal prices, but the Commission used its management powers to overrule this (Vasey, 1988; Swinbank, 1989). Greece invoked the veto in 1988 as it objected to the proposed devaluation of the green drachma in the agricultural prices settlement, but the Greek government found itself isolated. In 1993, France said that it had invoked or could cite the Luxembourg Compromise in relation to the GATT agreement. However, this decree was purely for domestic purposes, as it was never mentioned in the Council session. What is most striking is that on all these occasions it was agricultural prices that caused member states to try to use their veto. Teasdale (1993) states that the SEA killed the Luxembourg Compromise. However, this is not the case. Greece tried in 1988, and there may be cases that went unreported. It is more precise to state that the veto still exists, but that member states prefer to seek other solutions to their difficulties. The issue of enlargement has raised questions about future methods of decision in the Council. Some argue that in an enlarged Council reaching unanimity will become more difficult, and therefore there is a call to increase the use of qualified majority voting. Others, however, prefer to maintain the status quo (discussed further in Chapter 10).

Member states seem to avoid using formal voting methods in the Council. Consequently, it may also be useful to consider the informal rules of decision. The competence of the Presidency is of particular significance to the operational style of the Council. Every decision in the Council is subject to the formal methods of decision. In reality, the Council often prefers a consensus approach, without resorting to a vote. Frequently this is reliant upon the skilful manoeuvring of the Presidency in office. The Council's decision rules, both formal and informal, may crucially affect the way in which the bargaining activity occurs. Therefore, analysis of decision rules appears to provide important insights into how the Council works.

## Council decision outputs

In assessing the outputs of Council policy-making, it is possible to detect the extent of agreement from the terms employed. The Council may adopt one of the various types of legislation, as detailed in Chapter 1. It may also adopt a proposal or report, which means that further consideration and discussion will follow. All of these decision outputs can often have 'formal' inserted in front of the term 'adoption'. In the case of the types of legislation, this means that the Directive, Regulation, etc., will now enter into force on the date stipulated. The formal approval of a proposal or report normally implies that action will be taken at the next appropriate Council session. In addition, the Council often requests further reports from the Commission, Coreper or the relevant committee/working group.

The Council also uses 'code-words'. For example, 'instructed Coreper' means that there was little agreement in the Council; the Council requires more detailed information so that the difficulties can be re-addressed. There is also a certain amount of etiquette employed by the Council as it will always 'ask', 'invite', or 'request' its institutional partners to discuss the matter further, prepare a report etc. In addition, the Commission will submit to the Council a 'communication' rather than a proposal when it wants to test the water. Presumably, if a proposal had previously been submitted as a 'communication', it is probable that significant amendments have been made and the chance of adoption is relatively good.

Other 'speech acts' can be unclear. Examples of those that appear consistently are 'discussion', 'exchange of views', 'common position', 'substantive agreement', 'proposal examined'. They all show that the issue concerned requires deeper consideration; they are interim actions. However, the extent of the agreement so far is unclear. Hence, these non-decisions need to be considered. Bachrach and Baratz (1963) define non-decisions as deciding not to act or not to decide. This is different from their concept of 'non decision-making' which concerns the prevention of issues from needing a decision. For Bachrach and Baratz (1963: 632), non decision-making is 'the practice of limiting the scope of actual decision-making to "safe" issues by manipulating the dominant community values, myths, and political institutions and procedures'. Their argument, developed from an earlier article, is that a model is needed that will assess both decision-making and non decision-making. They provide a starting point for this but do not offer such a model. This analysis of the Council is concerned with those issues that have already entered the decision-making process, but on which agreement cannot be reached immediately: in other words, it is concerned with non-decisions as opposed to non decision-making.

In EU policy processes the Council often decides not to act or not to decide at a particular time on a given proposal. In such circumstances, the Council may choose to delay consideration of the proposal until its next meeting, or it may be sent back to Coreper for further consideration, or even back to the Commission. Parry and Morris (1982: 19-35) argue that so-called non-decisions really fit into the category of decisions, basing their argument on the assumption that non-decisions are decisions but not necessarily 'key' decisions. In other words, they may be conscious or unconscious decisions (Bachrach and Baratz, 1962). This point of view has particular relevance to the Council. A decision on one particular proposal may force a decision on another proposal, due to package deals or tactical manoeuvring by a member state or the Presidency. Parry and Morris (1982: 19-35) propose that there are decisions not to decide as yet, or incremental decisions that consequently commit the policy-maker to a 'key' decision later. Therefore, non-decisions in the Council are of significance to the evaluation of the Council's policy-making approach. They are not necessarily negative, except in cases where an issue under discussion is finally dropped from the agenda.

The Council may decide not to act at a particular moment, or to postpone a decision to a later meeting. In this sense, member states may be taking an incrementalist approach as it may not be the objective that is disputed, but the means to achieve that particular goal from the menu of alternatives available. Frequently, the Council adopts such practices to ensure that a proposal will not be lost. Council representatives are often familiar with each other's policy positions and recognize that if a decision is forced, then it may be negative. To postpone a decision gives Coreper or the particular working group time to resolve outstanding contentious issues, or allow national ministers to return to their capitals and discuss the possibility of altering a position, linking agreement through a package deal, etc. Therefore, non-decisions may be valuable indicators of the policy approach adopted by the Council.

One final factor that might be worth considering is the time taken to adopt a proposal. Although analysis can only focus on the time taken once the proposal has entered the formal policy-making process (in other words from when the Commission submits the proposal to the Council), it may provide some indication of the efficiency of the Council, providing the subject area and complexity of the proposal is taken into account. Only four councils have been selected for special consideration here, so it would be dangerous to apply any findings to the Council as a whole. Nevertheless, the time taken to adopt a proposal may provide additional insight into the Council's operation.

## Documenting a Council session

For all formal Council meetings, the General Secretariat draws up the minutes, which tend to be based on the press releases issued by the Secretariat one day after the Council session. Any Council can adopt the minutes, but in practice it is usually the next available meeting. Council minutes were subject to a thirty-year law of restriction until the transparency decisions in 1992. Council minutes from the 1960s are very different from the minutes that the Council produces today, both in their structure and content. They were much longer and more detailed. They did not give verbatim accounts of Council discussions, but did set out the positions of the member states, Presidency and the Commission. Moreover, the minutes of the 1960s, unlike today, actually specified the documents that the delegations wanted Coreper or the Commission to examine.[8] Council minutes are now much shorter and Article 9 of the Council's Rules of Procedure stipulates this slimmer structure (see Appendix 1). Since 1973, Council minutes have been drastically reduced in length and detail due to the increased workload of the Council. Consequently, Council Press Releases are fairly similar to the official minutes, and tend to only omit statements by member states or the Commission. As a result of the Edinburgh Council conclusions, the public is now entitled to obtain Council minutes. However, as demonstrated in Chapter 10, access involves a lengthy process of justification by the applicant, which is not always granted.

Minutes of working parties comprise a summary of the key points, whereas Coreper minutes are more detailed. The General Secretariat is also responsible for the drafting of these, but they often take one week to reach member-state delegations. However, both Coreper and working party minutes are not available to the public, which adds to the information deficit when analysing the Council.

Although Council meetings are documented, the precise details of the negotiations are kept secret. The capital offence in the Council General Secretariat is to reveal member-state positions during the negotiating process. The 'obligation of professional secrecy', as set out in the Rules of Procedure, governs Council minutes. However, leaks do occur. There has been one accidental publication of Council minutes in the Official Journal of the EC (Nicoll, 1993).[9] Normally, member-state delegations will target the Press if they want to make a statement about the outcome of a Council meeting, or make their position clear about a decision taken. Therefore, press reports of Council policy-making activity can help the analyst, providing such sources are used carefully.

## Council action channels

Analysis of the organizational procedures of the Council provide important indications of the dynamics of bargaining in the Council. The Council's action channels include the types of session, the role of Coreper, and the decision rules. It is important to analyse the nature of formal sessions, whether informal or joint sessions were used, and the outcome of each meeting. All of these variables affect the way in which the Council conducts negotiations. Moreover, these action channels may alter as policy negotiations proceed, and the still-relative secrecy of meetings makes obtaining factual details of the Council's work difficult, especially in the case of informal meetings. Analysis of the formal decision rules, as prescribed by the Treaties, not only provides important insights into the preferred decision methods of the Council, but contributes to the debate on the actual use of qualified majority voting.

# CHAPTER FOUR

# *A framework for analysing the Council*

The role and position of the Council within the EU has not evolved entirely according to the theoretical predictions made since the establishment of the ECSC. The various theories of integration all have their own assumptions and consequently their own conclusions, as Puchala's (1972) analogy of several blind men trying to understand the appearance of an elephant demonstrates. The problem is that integration theory does not provide the analytical tools required to analyse the character of the Council. Integration theories help the analyst to place the Council in its institutional context, and assess the process of European integration in general terms. However, they are not, nor do they pretend to be, appropriate tools for examining the nature of the Council's operation. What are required are methodological tools that take into account that while the Council legislates, it also negotiates. During its legislative proceedings, the component elements of the Council, the member states, engage in negotiation. Therefore, it is appropriate to base the proposed framework on both policy analysis and negotiation theory. The justification for using elements of a number of theoretical approaches lies in the fact that the Council is *sui generis*. Designing a framework that draws upon both these areas of theoretical concern should enable a better understanding of how the Council works.

At the outset, it is essential to qualify two points. First, the terminology employed in such analytical endeavours can all too often obscure aims and purposes. 'Theory' and 'model' are frequently used interchangeably, even though their meanings are quite different:

Whereas a theory claims to be correct and hence excludes the validity of rival theories, a model is merely a convenient way of looking at things from a specific angle; the former can be considered as 'true' provided it cannot be falsified, the latter can be merely regarded as convenient or useful. (Frankel, 1973: 16)

The term 'analytical framework' rather than 'model' is employed here to re-emphasize that the aim is to establish a framework that can be useful in analysing the policy characteristics of the Council without setting out to construct any specific theory.

Criticism could be levelled at the fact that there are some omissions in the theoretical literature considered here. However, it is not possible to provide a comprehensive consideration of all the approaches that could be used. Such an exercise is beyond the practicalities of the scope of this book. It excludes other theoretical approaches, such as the numerous variants of the rational model (although the rational model is discussed as it forms the basis of other policy-making theories), and cybernetic theory, as they are not appropriate to the purposes here. That is not to say that the proposed analytical framework is the *only* approach that could be taken, but as will be shown, it does appear to be the most appropriate one according to the author's criteria.

## Devising a framework

The aim, then, is to construct a framework flexible enough to tackle the complexities of Council policy-making. Analysis of two main bodies of theoretical literature – policy analysis and concepts of negotiation – concentrates upon their heuristic value; they are being considered to see how helpful they are in explaining the operation of the Council.

### *Policy analysis*
From an initial examination of policy-making literature, certain approaches to policy analysis can be 'transported' and adapted to the particular case of the Council. Policy analysis considers the entire process, from the forming of a proposal to its implementation, yet this analysis of the Council excludes policy implementation. Consequently, only those approaches which appeared flexible enough to be adapted to the particular case of the Council are included here.

The rational policy-making model approaches the world of policy-making as it 'ought to be', as opposed to what it is in practice, and has underpinned the development of policy analysis. The basic premise is that policy-makers select alternatives in a rational manner to achieve the desired goals, and that actors aim at optimal choice. The most prominent writer on rational policy-making is Herbert Simon, who offers a three-stage framework for achieving a policy decision (Simon, 1957). It is only possible to use the traditional rational model in choices involving the unitary actor rather than collective decisions. In the Council, a particular policy choice may not be the one that maximizes the objectives of all the member states. A delegation may compromise on one decision to achieve its objectives in another, because the second decision is more valuable than the first decision to that particular delegation (otherwise known as log-rolling or package deals). The other main criticism of the rational model is the condition of perfect information. One must surely question how the rational policy-maker can assess all the options available and all the consequences of those options in the manner suggested by Simon. In the context of EU policy-making, all players will try to obtain as much knowledge (or maximum knowledge) about a given proposal before taking a decision. Although each player would hope to have as much information as possible, it is hard to imagine anyone involved in EU policy-making stating that they knew everything about a particular proposal and its likely consequences if implemented. The criteria that a player uses to sift through the information may also affect the knowledge that they acquire about a particular proposal; in other words, how objective is the player in filtering the information? Furthermore, the information available to a particular actor may be different to that of their policy-making partners. The process of information gathering varies between member states due in part to the differences in their policy agendas, and variations in their administrative structures.

The incrementalist model of policy-making places greater emphasis on the need to define the objectives of a policy, and is often the approach identified with Lindblom (1959; 1968; 1979). His work was a response to the vast amount of literature on rational policy-making which appeared at that time. He criticizes it because it 'assumes intellectual capacities and sources of information that men simply do not possess' (Lindblom, 1959: 80). The starting point of the incrementalist model is not an ideal goal but an objective that takes into account those policies already in operation. This is considered to be more politically feasible, defined as the method of 'successive limited comparisons'. This means that consideration of policy options only involves those that are relevant and specific to the desired outcome, and consequently, small, incremental changes characterize policy-making. Lindblom acknowledges that in his method there is no built-in safeguard that all relevant values will be considered, and that some alternatives may thus be overlooked because they do not emerge from the existing situation. The capabilities of the players, and the information and resources available, affect consideration of the means to achieve the desired result. However, he sees this approach as realistic, because this process of 'muddling through' is often how policy is made (Lindblom, 1959: 88).

In a later contribution to the literature, Braybrooke and Lindblom (1963) develop the incrementalist method further, terming it 'disjointed incrementalism'. Their strategy develops from a belief that it is necessary to distinguish the difference between decisions effecting a large or a small change, and suggest that an incremental change is one that occurs within a short time and offer five years as a measure. They use the term 'disjointed' due to the fragmentary nature of the process. In essence, policy-makers separate problems into small segments so that marginal, as opposed to large choices, can be made. Analysis only considers the relevant, the concrete, and the familiar. The motive behind this approach is much the same as that of the 'successive limited comparisons' model – namely that it accounts for the intellectual and information limitations of the real world. However, there is a much sharper focus than Lindblom provides in his earlier contribution.

A major criticism of the incrementalist model of policy-making is that it does not include a longer-term view of policy alternatives. Incrementalism is the continuation of previous policies with the least possible change. In other words, there are no major upheavals in the policy-making process. Therefore, it is only useful as an approach to policy analysis if the nature of the problem is relatively stable. Incrementalism does not deal with larger decisions, in other words those decisions which result in a more fundamental change. The difficulty in applying this approach to the EU, and thus the Council, is that although the EU has not altered its underlying principles and goals, it has been forced to make large changes to its policy intentions as a result of the conflict that arises between member states, and enlargement. The constantly changing environment may from time to time demand upheavals in policy-making, either in specific sectoral areas or in the general approach, to achieve the overarching principles of European integration. EU action programmes exemplify this problem of distinguishing between large and small decisions. Action programmes involve a number of smaller policy decisions in order to achieve the larger decision of adopting and implementing an action programme. Within the Council 'the result is a bargaining process which is certainly disjointed and where even modest incremental change has to be viewed as a major achievement' (Wallace, H. 1983b: 65). The strength of the incremental policy-making approach is that it acknowledges the means available to achieve the desired outcome. In this sense, it is more realistic than the traditional rational model because it shows how policy-making is constrained by the available resources and information available. It bases choice on experience. Therefore there may be a better

73

understanding of the limitations in achieving the desired outcome. It could be argued that the Council is now an established policy-maker. Basing decisions on experience may be applicable to the Council, as member states often know where the fault-lines in the negotiating process occur. By considering the goals of a particular policy and the means to achieve such goals at the same time, incrementalism takes into account possible constraints in the policy-making process. Therefore, it would seem that the incrementalist approach to policy-making might well constitute a useful part of the analytical framework being devised here.

Etzioni (1967) offers an alternative model of policy-making which tends to fit between the models of Simon and Lindblom. He devises this third approach to policy-making because he feels the rational model is rather utopian, and like Dror *et al.* (1964), believes that the incrementalist model is too conservative for analysing policy-making (Etzioni, 1967: 385). The mixed-scanning approach identifies two processes for policy-making. The first is detailed (rational) scanning of some sectors, whilst the second is a slimmed-down review of other sectors. What is stressed is that within each of these processes there can be several levels of varying degrees of detail. Etzioni argues that the amount of consideration or scanning of the alternatives differs according to the level required in a particular case. For example, if the policy-making environment has altered, then there will need to be more detailed scanning to account for these changes. Consideration of the alternatives will also need extending in cases where an incremental change has not proved sufficient for the desired outcome. He adopts this two-phased multi-level scanning approach to limit, where necessary, the details in fundamental decisions, and to ensure that incrementalism is not so short-term in its consideration of the alternatives.

The advantage of this approach is that it can respond to changes in the policy environment more adequately than the incrementalist approach to policy-making. However, there is a major drawback in the mixed-scanning approach; namely the difficulty that could arise in distinguishing between fundamental and incremental decisions. The 'disjointed incrementalist' approach of Braybrooke and Lindblom was also subject to such criticism. According to Etzioni (1967: 389–90), fundamental decisions ignore the specific details; they are based purely on the overall goals of the policy-maker. Incremental decisions provide the details, but within the strict context of the fundamental decisions. It is highly probable that the policy-makers who use this approach will have different ideas and criteria regarding what constitutes a fundamental as opposed to an incremental decision. In the context of the Council's policy-making process, member states may not agree on the nature of a particular decision. Treaty revisions, such as the

SEA and the TEU would clearly be regarded as fundamental decisions by all Council members. However, action programmes or framework directives could also be regarded as fundamental decisions by some players, even though they involve a number of smaller decisions. The mixed-scanning approach is an attempt to deal with the difficulties associated with both the rationalist and incrementalist models of policy-making. However, in doing so it heightens the problem of differentiation between the type of decisions. The Council often faces such a problem. Each member state has different policy priorities, and at a given moment, one member state may consider a particular proposal to be of a more fundamental nature than another member state. Thus, to be able to agree on which are the fundamental and which are the incremental decisions could prove difficult. However, it may be possible to resolve conflict over the status of a proposal through the bargaining processes between member states. The importance of bargaining will be dealt with in subsequent sections. Hence, bearing in mind the potential that it offers for overcoming some of the limitations in the incrementalist approach, mixed-scanning may warrant possible inclusion in the framework for analysing the Council.

Allison (1971) develops two models to counter what he deems as being the limitations of rational policy models. He posits the rational model as adequate for explaining the behaviour of an individual, but believes that analysis of organizations or governments requires a deeper foundation. Consequently, he introduces the 'organisational processes paradigm' and the 'governmental (or bureaucratic) politics paradigm'. He terms them conceptual models, using the analogy of a lens. Essentially, Allison's argument is that each conceptual lens will view the making of a particular decision differently, and illustrates this when he uses the Cuban Missile Crisis to test each paradigm. Allison's organizational processes paradigm views governmental action as organizational output; such output is partly coordinated by a unified group of leaders. The governmental politics paradigm focuses attention upon these leaders. Consequently, a distinct overlap emerges between these two paradigms. The governmental politics paradigm simply adds greater focus to the context of the organizational processes paradigm by considering the players. This is presumably the motive for a formal merger by Allison and Halperin, who combine these two models to form the bureaucratic politics paradigm (Allison and Halperin, 1972). Prefiguratively, Allison states that both models could be used in conjunction, if one considers organizations as players (although he makes it clear that even in so doing, elements are still missing).[1] This section deals with this revised version by Allison and Halperin. The bureaucratic politics paradigm focuses on the importance of interests in affecting government action. In other words, the players and their interests are crucial in shaping policy-making and implementation. Allison and Halperin identify the determinants of governmental action as the individuals within a government, and the interactions between them. Action, in this sense of governmental action, is achieved through bargaining. Organizational processes and shared values affect this bargaining process ('pulling and hauling'), and Allison and Halperin consider these factors as constraints of the model. Before dealing with these constraints, it is useful to sketch out the essential elements of this 'new' paradigm. It will then be possible to examine the extent to which the paradigm could be included within a framework to analyse how the Council conducts its policy-making.

Actions are 'the various acts of officials of a government in exercises of governmental authority that can be perceived outside the government' (Allison and Halperin, 1972: 45). To comprehend a particular governmental action, the analyst must recognize and understand how bargaining within the relevant policy-making process occurred, and how it affected the final output. To do this, Allison and Halperin stipulate that it is necessary to identify the 'action channels', the 'regularised sets of procedures for producing particular classes of actions'. It is these procedures that condition the structure of the game, by determining the players and the context.

> The decision that triggers the game and the rules of the game assign the action to a player and pick the action channel. However, there are likely to be several sub-channels. Players will manoeuvre to get the issue into the channel they believe offers the best prospects for getting the desired result. (Allison and Halperin, 1972: 52)

The analyst needs to identify the players and their interests to understand how a government decides or acts. Allison and Halperin highlight senior players as the most dominant actors in the game, but point out that junior players (lower level officials, interest groups, the public and the press) do have a role. They also argue that organizations can be treated as players if acting as a single unit. This fully acknowledges that there are many players in the game and moves away from the problems associated with policy approaches designed for understanding the unitary actor, but used inappropriately in the analysis of collective policy-making. In his earlier 'governmental politics' paradigm, Allison states that although the 'Chiefs' take the formal decisions, it is important to identify the role and input of the 'Indians'. However, Allison fails to mention sufficiently the part junior officials play in the preparation and taking of decisions. In the bureaucratic politics paradigm, this is developed through the distinction made between decision games and action games. Decision games are defined as 'the activity of players leading to decisions by senior players', whereas action games are 'activities that follow from, or proceed in the absence of' decision games (Allison and Halperin, 1972: 46). 'Chiefs' dominate the decision games but 'Indians' can, and often do participate in action games. This is highly important, because to understand the nature of the policy-making process it is essential to recognize that many issues and choices are interlinked.

A decision game proceeds according to the action channel with some players planning their moves, others opting not to do so. In either case, the result of a decision game will be a policy, a decision, or the avoidance of a decision. Action games try to explain how the actions of players within a government affect the overall outcome of policy-making. Allison and Halperin propose a number of factors that can affect action games: policies about the outcome, decision games about the outcome, decision games about other outcomes, actions without higher level decisions, manoeuvres in decision games and finally the routine behaviour of organizations. The essence of action games is that the final outcome is more than just the policy desires of the governmental leaders. Krasner (1972) argues that this distinction obscures the power of the President (or governmental leader) in policy-making. However, it is often the case that there may be different actions taken by players from many parts of the organization that combine to affect the final outcome.

One needs to consider not only the hierarchical position of a player, but also their goals and interests, which can be national, organizational, domestic and personal in nature.[2] Choices made by players in both types of game evolve from their perceptions of the interests at stake. Consequently, analysis must also take into account these interests and their determinants. Within these interests, it is essential to recognize that party and ideological interests also play a part, although Allison and Halperin are less explicit about this. Recognizing that players (either nations or units within a governmental organisation) view issues differently is essential. As Allison and Halperin put it, different players will see different 'faces of the issue'. Players' interests compete within the framework of the decision or action game: success is dependent upon their individual bargaining ability or power, the organizational routines and 'shared values'. These are the essential aspects of the paradigm – the 'pulling and hauling' involved in the making of governmental action. Allison and Halperin deal with these factors separately, according to the 'type' of game. However, it may be more useful to consider these factors collectively, because there are not only repetitions, but overlaps. Furthermore, it is usually a combination of such factors that affects success.

The bureaucratic politics paradigm argues that the degree of a player's success is affected by (a) their bargaining advantage, (b) the skill and will in using this advantage and (c) other players' perceptions of (a) and (b). These combined three factors denote the 'pulling and hauling' process of the game. Allison and Halperin do not go into much detail here, although this bargaining advantage is crucial to the outcome. The ability of a player to bargain is affected by a number of factors. These include the player's:

- formal authority and responsibility (stemming from the player's hierarchical position);
- actual control over resources;
- expertise (specialist and technical);
- control over information;
- ability to affect other players' objectives;
- personal persuasiveness.

The skill and will of players in using this bargaining advantage are obviously crucial. Players need to take into account the bargaining advantage of other players to use their own bargaining advantage to best effect. As Allison and Halperin note, this skill can vary between players, and those less skilful may have to rely on simple argument. The will to use the bargaining advantage can depend upon the importance of the issue to the particular player, or whether the issue under discussion is linked to other policy discussions (package-deals). In addition, a player may decide not to use their bargaining advantage if it is clear that this will not have the desired effect at that particular moment in the policy-making process. A player's success can also be affected by other players' perceptions of their bargaining advantage and skill and will to use this advantage. A player may be more successful at 'pulling and hauling' if the other players regard them as having a greater advantage than is actually the case. Clearly, players often attempt to convince others of this, but it may be the case that a player regards themself to be in a weaker bargaining position.

Organizational routines also affect this 'pulling and hauling' process. In identifying the effect of these, Allison and Halperin acknowledge that much of their analysis derives from Allison's former organizational processes paradigm, yet they only refer to a number of elements of the latter. It is rather unclear whether one should consider all aspects of the paradigm or only those parts cited in the bureaucratic politics paradigm. However, implicitly contained in Allison and Halperin's work is a desire to simplify, and thus achieve better understanding of governmental action. Therefore, this consideration will only focus upon those aspects cited by Allison and Halperin.

Organizations supply the information and the options available to individual players to enable them to make decisions. According to the paradigm, information – both quantitative and qualitative – may vary between players, as organizational procedures perform the task of supplying information differently. In particular, standard operating procedures (rules, procedures, conventions) limit the flexibility and long-term nature of action. Allison and Halperin argue that the 'menu of alternatives' available is far more limited in a bureaucracy than if drawn up by independent experts. An organization has to work within the confines of its existing goals and resources, whereas an independent expert will be able to widen his/her consideration. Consequently, organizations have established certain routines and procedures which structure the capabilities of the players in making a decision. Moreover, these routines are normally 'standard' which often results in incrementalism. When a one-off situation occurs, Allison and Halperin state that there is a tendency to try to adapt existing procedures, rather than attempting to construct new procedures. The bureaucracy would regard this as being outside its capabilities and somewhat radical in approach. 'A program, that is a complex cluster of standard operating procedures, is rarely tailored to the specific situation in which it is executed' (Allison and Halperin, 1972: 56).

The concept of shared values is 'new' to the bureaucratic politics paradigm, in the sense that it is under-developed in Allison's previous work. It concerns the significance of shared values within the society as a whole, and within the bureaucracy. Allison and Halperin, as shown, mention perceptions of an issue when they consider the determinants of a player's position on an option. The notion of shared values is the idea that these perceptions arose partly from societal attitudes to, and images of, a given issue, and it is these attitudes and images that form the national interest. Furthermore, even if a member of the bureaucracy does not accept the values behind the shared attitudes and images, it is unlikely that they would argue otherwise for the simple reason that this might threaten their position. The paradigm is re-emphasizing the importance of the national interest, and how it exists within the society and within the organization. This constrains the pulling and hauling process, which subsequently affects the choices and outcomes of governmental action.

Having considered the essence of the bureaucratic politics paradigm, the task now is briefly to assess its usefulness and then to decide whether it can be extended beyond the state to cover the Council. First, it is true that Allison and Halperin's paradigm is culture-bound. They seem to ignore the fact that they base their model on the United States experience of policy-making and therefore that it may not be as applicable to other, less open, systems. They also offer no evidence to prove their model's value in empirical analysis, but merely articulate recommendations to American policy-makers. Putnam (1988: 431) feels that 'the theoretical contribution of this literature did not evolve much beyond the principle that bureaucratic interests matter in foreign policy-making'. Allison argues that the main dilemma facing an empirical test of the governmental politics paradigm is that accurate accounts of the bargaining process are hard to find. This difficulty also arises in the testing of Allison and Halperin's later paradigm. The piecing together of documents, newspapers, interviews, etc., is 'an art', and it is only possible to 'test' the paradigm if such sources are used carefully (cross-referenced and corroborated). This is a constant reminder that Allison and Halperin do not consider this to be a model or a theory, only a 'rough-cut framework', best formulated as a paradigm (1972: 43). The bureaucratic politics paradigm may be *a* method, but not *the* method of analysing governmental action due to these limitations; indeed Rosati (1981) argues along similar lines. What balances this to some extent, and accounts for the paradigm's attractiveness in the context of analysing the Council, is the way in which it emphasizes and draws upon the complex internal dynamics of policy-making within large, sophisticated organizations. Although Krasner would disagree, the bureaucratic politics paradigm is a useful alternative method of analysing the determinants of governmental action. Krasner (1972) feels that too little emphasis is placed upon the clarification of objectives, arguing that it is all too easy to blame the bureaucracy for inaction or failure; what should be considered first are the objectives that are being sought. Wessels (1990) believes that the patterns of administrative interaction within the EU (and implicitly the Council) warrant further research due to 'fusion' and 'diffusion' that has emerged in policy-making. The bureaucratic politics paradigm seems to provide the analyst with certain tools that enable them to examine the policy-making process within a complex organization such as the EU, or a particular part of its structure, namely the Council.

The Council is the final decision-maker in the EU and is not legally charged with the formulation or implementation of policy; that is the role of the Commission. The Council can be viewed as a government consisting of a number of players, where the member states and the interactions between them determine the actions of the EU.[3] Action by the Council is the result of bargaining activity, pulling and hauling. Moreover, the Council is also an organization that acts as a single actor within the EU policy network and has its own internal processes.[4] Accepting these points, there may be some value in using the bureaucratic politics paradigm to analyse the operation of the Council, given that there appears to be a strong degree of 'fit' between the two.

It is essential, then, to identify which aspects of the paradigm might be useful in furthering this analysis of the Council. As demonstrated in the preceding two chapters, the first aspect to consider is who the Council *players* are and what are their *interests*. In looking at the players, the status of ministers must be identified. Senior players dominate the Council forum, which may affect the manner in which decisions are likely to be achieved. Therefore, it is essential to identify who these people are. In assessing policy-making in the Council, the ministerial relationships must be considered, and how these affect the nature of the particular Council. This includes the personal relationships between ministers. For example, ministers of Councils that meet on a frequent basis are better acquainted. This may affect policy discussions, as ministers may be more aware of each other's tactics and approaches. Stemming from this, another consideration is the length of time a minister has held office. This not only affects the personal relationship between ministers, but also the stability of the particular Council. Long-serving ministers will be better acquainted with the rudiments of EU policy-making, both in terms of the objectives, and the policy-making processes. The extent of Coreper involvement in a decision may also be important, as often it is Coreper that arrives at agreement. In analysing the interests of the players, it is necessary to focus upon the interests of the individual *combined with* the perceived interests of the member state represented by the individual.

It is also imperative to analyse the extent to which there are shared values at the Council level. This links with the players' interests, as one needs to distinguish between the amount of common belief in a particular policy and the national interest of achieving the particular decision. One can assume that there is a shared belief between member states about the overall goals of the EU, otherwise members would secede. However, it is not always the case that there are shared values over a specific policy. Lines of conflict emerge between member states in many forms, such as the economic philosophy or political ideology of a member state, and the costs and benefits of policies. Therefore, it may be helpful to look at the subject area of the proposal (and of the technical council) as this often characterizes the policy-making approach, and the extent to which member states share the same values on a particular subject area.

Chapter 3 examined the Council's rules and procedures, in other words its *action channels*. It must be clear what constitutes a Council session. All decisions must be taken within a formal Council meeting, usually in the Justus Lipsius building. However, Council policy discussions also operate on an informal basis. Informal sessions permit 'off-the-record' discussions, allow for difficult issues to be flagged at an early stage, and enable solutions and compromises to be reached. The method of decision or the rules of decision may also be potent variables in characterizing the Council. Such rules can not only affect the way in which the Council conducts its deliberations, but may affect the policy output. Formal rules relate to the voting method employed: simple majority, qualified majority or unanimity. Informal rules relate to the consensus-seeking approach of the Council, achieved through presidential manoeuvring. The competence of the Presidency may affect the operational style of the Council. Every decision in the Council is subject to the formal methods of decision. In reality, the Council often prefers a consensus approach without resorting to a vote. Frequently this is dependent upon the skilful manoeuvring of the Council Presidency. In addition, analysis of the Council's approach to policy-making must account for non-decisions as discussed in Chapter 3.

The final area that could usefully be assessed is the bargaining activity of the Council. The *bargaining advantage* which an individual member state may have must be identified, together with the *skill and will* of the particular delegation to use this advantage. The constituent elements of bargaining advantage (see previous list) are crucial. Therefore, it is necessary to look at the player's status, as this will affect their authority and responsibility to take decisions. The ability of a player to persuade is an important factor and is often due to the diplomatic, ministerial experience of a representative. Furthermore, member-state contributions to the EU budget vary. As a result, it is often the case that the larger contributors will want the greatest control in deciding an 'expensive' policy decision. It is also important to identify when the bargaining activity between players occurs (the 'pulling and hauling'), and the location of such activity (the action channel). This provides the analyst with some indication of the dynamics of bargaining. In examining the Council, it may be the case that one particular outcome of the 'pulling and hauling' may not be the final legislative output of the Council. There may be some difficulties in characterizing the precise nature of the Council's 'pulling and hauling' process due to the lack of detail in Council documentation, yet this is an essential factor to consider when analysing the operation of the Council, and needs to be included in the framework.

Another approach that may be useful to include in this analytical framework is policy-style analysis, through Richardson *et al.*'s (1982) three categories of 'problem solving', 'bargaining' and 'confrontation'. Although policy style refers to both the approach to policy-making, and to the implementation of policy, it may offer some insight into identifying the character of the Council. Scharpf (1988) adopts Richardson *et al.*'s above-mentioned three-fold classification of 'problem-solving', 'bargaining' and 'confrontation' in an article that specifically discusses policy-making in the EU. He justifies this by arguing that whilst other scholars offer categories (March and Simon's 'problem-solving', 'persuasion', 'bargaining' and 'politics', and Olsen's four labels of 'problem-solving', 'bargaining', 'mobilisation', and 'confrontation'), 'substantive agreement on the distinctions actually subsumed under these different labels seems to be remarkably high' (Scharpf, 1988: 258). Both Richardson *et al.* and Scharpf provide a convincing case for restricting the number of labels of policy style to three due to the need for simplicity and clarity of definition, hence only these are examined here.

Scharpf states that policy styles combine with decision rules to characterize a particular system, which may be of particular use to this analysis of the Council. 'Problem-solving' is the label given to the policy style in which the actors in the policy process have the same values. There is a pursuit of common goals and consequently a high degree of cooperation in trying to find solutions. Richardson *et al.* point out that an overarching consensus on the main objectives often compensates for the differences over specific, lower-order goals. 'Bargaining' is employed if self-interest is the main concern of the policy-makers. Consequently, compromise is the norm. The style is one of slow, protracted negotiation and coalition-building. In an article looking at theoretical approaches to policy research, Scharpf (1989) operationalizes this as 'own gain maximisation' arguing that 'bargaining is conducive to the common search for compromises through which both parties are able to improve their position compared to the status quo'. 'Confrontation' relates to the policy style in which winning is the key, where nothing matters except victory. There is naturally a high level of conflict which is not reduced through negotiation or bargaining.

'Confrontation' appears the least applicable to the Council but should not be dismissed, given that there have been occasions where this strategy has to an extent been employed by member states. Policy-making in the Council is not usually viewed as a zero-sum process. Within the Council, member states often agree upon the main goals or objectives. In 'confrontation' there is no such agreement. However, de Gaulle in the 1960s and Mrs Thatcher in the 1980s achieved policy changes through their confrontational approaches, allowed for by the unanimity rule. Clearly, the Council's approach since SEA implementation (and the extension of qualified majority voting) needs to be considered.

To employ the 'problem-solving' label to characterize the Council requires that Council actors have the same values. Member states and thus their ministerial representatives in the Council do adhere to the principles and overarching goals of the EU. However, disagreement often exists upon the appropriate methods to achieve these goals. Consequently, issue-linkage is frequently used. Issue-linkage can be described as a negotiating tool in Council policy-making processes in which issues are linked to negotiate policy decision trade-offs.[5] Even if there are sacrifices, it is not necessarily the case that a member state will be immediately compensated through a package deal. It would be wrong to conclude, however, that the Council does not adopt a problem-solving approach. It may be the case that member states view issue-linkage as a form of 'problem-solving' for particular policy areas.

However, 'bargaining' appears to be the most appropriate label for the Council as a whole. Disagreement is acceptable in 'bargaining' whereas it is not in 'problem-solving.' When the Council operates under unanimity it is often the case that member states cooperate more in their bargaining to find a solution so as to avoid the possibility of a veto and the potential loss of the proposal. The increased use of qualified majority voting may weaken this approach of policy-making in the Council. These three policy labels offer possibilities for more detailed and sophisticated characterization of the Council. These styles also complement the bureaucratic politics paradigm as, among other aspects, the notion of shared interests and the importance of rules and procedures is again evident in 'problem-solving', 'bargaining' and confrontation.'

### The nature of negotiation

This chapter has already identified the importance of Allison and Halperin's notion of 'pulling and hauling' in policy-making, and the possible characterization of the Council's style as one of 'bargaining'. It may therefore be helpful in constructing a framework for analysing the Council to consider further aspects of negotiation. Although most of the existing theoretical approaches to negotiation derive from international relations literature, there may be a case for adapting and applying certain elements of negotiation analysis when examining the Council. The Council deals with far more than foreign policy affairs, but in all of its policy-making areas it negotiates. This negotiating process is crucial and requires explanation. As with the previous consideration of policy analysis, it is important to stress that this section is not attempting to deal with all elements of negotiation theory. For example, this analysis does not enter the world of game theory which tends to regard players as unitary actors who are equally rational and assumes that there will be perfect information. This section only considers parts of negotiation theory that appear relevant to this search for an analytical framework, and that build upon concepts raised in previous sections of this chapter.

Definitions of negotiation tend to conform to the idea that it is a process in which proposals are put forward and discussed with the aim of reaching agreement.[6] Bargaining processes can be tacit or explicit, formal or informal, distributive or integrative. Distributive bargaining is a fixed-sum process in which there are winners and losers, as opposed to integrative bargaining (or variable-sum) in which there is a maximization of benefits for all. Bulmer (1985) argues that the European Council conforms to both distributive and integrative bargaining. His conclusions contributed to a better understanding of the characteristics of the European Council. For the purposes here, it may also be helpful to assess the bargaining nature of the Council as precisely as possible. For negotiation to take place, there need to be common interests and at the same time issues of conflict surrounding such common interests. 'Without common interest there is nothing to negotiate for, without conflict nothing to negotiate about' (Iklé, 1964: 2). As Allison and Halperin pointed out, the idea of shared values or beliefs can affect the 'pulling and hauling' process. Member states of the EU sometimes share common interests but conflict over the means to achieve these goals. At other times, there is disagreement over the goals of a particular policy. Consequently, member states negotiate within the Council and the strengthening of the Council's position within the EU's institutional structure was inevitable due to member-state desires to control the negotiation of policies (Wallace, H. 1983b: 62).

Iklé proposes five objectives of negotiation, but stresses that negotiating parties will always pursue a mixture of these. Iklé, unlike Schelling (1960), avoids the use of game theory language and thus makes his work far more accessible to the non-specialist. Frankel (1973) praises Iklé's work for its flexibility and realism. Iklé's five objectives are extension agreements, where negotiation is simply routine (such as renewing a trade agreement); normalization agreements (to end conflict); redistributive agreements (to alter existing arrangements); innovation agreements (to establish new arrangements); and, finally, wishing to achieve some aim but not necessarily hoping to reach agreement. This latter objective refers to the 'side-effects' of negotiation, where players use the bargaining process for maintaining contact, intelligence gathering, and propagandist motives.

Barston (1983), however, feels that Iklé's five classifications are useful for antagonistic relationships but are difficult to employ for less conflictual negotiations. Barston's criticism is partly warranted – his example of negotiations for timing a ministerial visit makes it clear that there are additional levels of negotiation to those classified by Iklé. However, the importance of Iklé's classifications for this analysis is that they illustrate how the type of agreement that is sought can affect the actual bargaining process.

For example, it is likely that little conflict will occur in pursuing an extension agreement because the agreement is merely maintaining the status quo. This contrasts with redistributive agreements which propose alterations to the existing arrangements. Consequently, there may be a high level of conflict between the actors in policy-making, and agreement will require concessions. Innovation agreements may also result in conflict because they are 'new' in terms of the desired outcome. Moreover, disagreement may also occur between the policy-making actors because there are differences over how innovative the agreement is. This links back to an earlier point made in the discussion of the incrementalist and mixed-scanning approaches, namely the difficulty in distinguishing between fundamental and incremental decisions. Thus, identifying the nature of the agreement that is being sought may indicate the type of bargaining process that is anticipated, and therefore could be useful when looking at the Council.

The language employed in the negotiating process is an important indication of the degree of bargaining success. The Council, and the EU, are often criticized for abstruse use of language. Conclusions of the European Council held at Birmingham (October) and Edinburgh (December) during the 1992 UK Presidency called for greater transparency, which included a policy of greater clarity regarding language used. A number of decisions have been implemented as a result (see Chapter 10). Language or 'speech acts' indicate the level of commitment amongst the negotiating partners.[7] Usually, the more specific the language, the greater the level of agreement. Examples of specific language used in the Council are 'agreement in principle' where Coreper and the Commission just need to finalize the text, and 'to be discussed at next session' where there is partial agreement but the proposal requires further discussion. Disagreement can be implicit in the ambiguous language used, for example 'exchange of views' where the level of agreement is unclear. The terminology used, explicitly or implicitly, allows the analyst to deduce the level of agreement reached. Consideration of 'speech acts' of the Council may help to evaluate the success of the Council and thus aid analysis. Obviously, the term 'speech acts' is used in its widest sense; it does not involve traditional discourse analysis, as only written reports of Council sessions are available. It is only possible to suggest rather than state how successful the bargaining process has been, as official minutes are secret, and therefore analysis relies on secondary sources, yet analysis of 'speech acts' may be worthwhile.

Although Barston offers no alternative to Iklé's five-fold classification of the objectives of negotiation, he does propose three sets of variables which shape negotiation processes. These are extremely helpful in establishing the factors that affect bargaining, and can be identified in the Council negotiations. The first variable to consider is the negotiating setting. This refers to whether the process is bi- or multilateral, whether the parties are in regular or friendly contact, the degree of international tension (be it related or unrelated to the actual negotiating issue), the level of domestic support, and whether the negotiation is being conducted within an established institutional framework. In relation to the Council, relevant factors might include the type of session, the timing of the proposal, the domestic and international context that member states are operating under at that particular time, and the relationships between the players. The latter was also shown to be an important variable in the bureaucratic politics paradigm, as personal relationships can often affect the bargaining advantage of a player. Contact between actors not only refers to ministerial contact, but also to dialogue between the Council and its institutional partners (Commission and EP), be it formal or informal. Presidential 'confessions' could also be included, where the Presidency of the Council holds informal confidential consultation with member-state ministers. All of these personal contacts are crucial as they enable each player to know their negotiating partners' positions, and thus allow for the building of coalitions.

The second set of variables proposed by Barston is the available assets or capabilities of the negotiating parties. Included in this category are the number and skills of the personnel involved, and the level of specialist expertise. In the Council, it is often possible to distinguish the bargaining skill through the nature and status of the ministerial representation of each member state and the number, experience, and official position of personnel in the permanent representations. These points also overlap with the bureaucratic politics paradigm, where Allison and Halperin highlight the importance of the skill and will of players in the bargaining process. Expertise and skill contribute to the bargaining reputation of a player, which is an essential part of a player's negotiating strength.

The final category is the contingent variables, in other words the internal politics of the various negotiating positions. The interplay of domestic and European interests in Council negotiations cannot be ignored. Fisher's work identifies the principles of conflict strategy, emphasizing the importance of the internal, domestic situation of negotiating partners (Fisher, 1969). On the one hand, there may be an internal battle between governmental departments to establish a national position. For example, the Treasury and the Ministry for Agriculture, Fisheries and Foods engage in extensive negotiations over priorities to arrive at a UK governmental position on the Common Agricultural Policy. On the other hand, internal politics may also play a part in the actual Council negotiations as players can use their own domestic constraints, or exploit those of their negotiating partners to achieve a concession or agreement. The national context may also be relevant in joint councils where the individual national representatives arrive inadequately prepared, and find themselves in conflict with a member of their own delegation.

As shown, the objectives of any particular negotiation will affect its conduct. The language employed may indicate the degree of success achieved in the negotiating process, whilst the internal politics of the negotiating positions can be used in the final negotiating process. The three sets of variables, namely the negotiating setting, the capabilities of the players and the internal politics of the players' positions, are helpful in clarifying the negotiating process of the Council, and emphasize the importance of bargaining. The points made about the nature of negotiation need therefore to be integrated into the framework that is being devised for analysing the Council.

## Constructing an analytical framework

From the consideration of the Council's structure and procedures, and in light of the assessment made of various models, a number of variables can be proposed which enable us to more adequately analyse the character of the Council.

### The proposal

By looking at the aims and substance of the proposal, the analyst can assess the probable positions of member states and therefore deduce the likely form of the negotiating process. Although not explicit, it is possible to analyse member-state positions from their attitudes over time, or their specific policy concerns and domestic pressures at a particular moment. It may be useful to distinguish between the levels of common agreement and commitment compared with individual national concerns. As already discussed, although it is implicit that the member states of the EU do share many beliefs about the aims and purposes of EU policy-making, differences sometimes exist in the degree of common interest and the means to achieve such goals. In addition, the objectives of a particular policy proposal (extension, redistributive or innovation) and the type of proposal (Directive, Regulation, Decision, Opinion or Recommendation, and the procedure required) may indicate the ease with which a decision will be reached, together with the players and their interests. Therefore, in identifying the proposal, it may be useful to consider the subject area of the proposal, the objectives of the proposal, and the extent of conflict between the players' beliefs about the aims of the EU policy area and their own perceived national interests.

## *Council actors*

When analysing any decision of the Council, it is essential to consider the players or actors involved in the policy-making process. It is necessary to identify whether Council actors are senior or junior ministers, or officials. The hierarchical position of the players is important as the status of a player affects their bargaining advantage (which will be discussed shortly). Although Council players are usually senior in rank, some players may be more dominant in the Council's policy-making process. It is important to identify the Presidency. Clearly, the member state presiding over Council meetings may give an indication as to the likely character of the Council at that particular time. As discussed, member states are able to influence and manage the agenda when in office so it is important to take this into account. In addition, the skill and ability of the Presidency may be crucial to the policy-making process. Personal relationships between players are also significant. Ministers of councils that meet frequently are better acquainted and therefore are likely to be more aware of each other's probable positions and negotiating tactics before the session has started. It may be that Council decisions are really made outside the formal processes and are based upon the strong personal links between players. Therefore, in identifying the Council players, it may be useful to consider the ministerial status of players, the skill and abilities of the Presidency, and the personal relationships that exist between players. It may also be necessary to consider the work of the European Council if an issue was 'pushed up' to this level. The interests of players can be individual, national, or organizational, but usually a combination of these. As discussed, individual and national interests may be motivated by party or ideological interests. Member states use the Council's structure to pursue their aims and negotiate accordingly. At the individual level, players may desire a particular decision to enhance their own positions at domestic or international level. At the national level, players may pursue a policy line that conforms to their own governmental policy, or use domestic constraints to achieve a compromise. It may be the case that member states use the various tiers of the Council to promote their aims. In addition, member-state representatives may use different types of session as a means of pursuing their individual or national aims. Therefore, in identifying the players' interests, it may be useful to consider the individual interests of players, their national interests, and the extent to which these are combined by players in the formulation of their policy positions. Consideration of individual interests (such as career ambitions proposed by Allison and Halperin) may prove difficult, though, as there is insufficient information available.

## *Bargaining advantage of Council actors*

As shown in Chapter 2, the player's status affects their bargaining advantage. Some ministers are more junior in their own national administrations than those of other member states but work together within the Council forum. Their internal political weight can thus affect their bargaining ability, as can their particular policy responsibilities. For example, Belgium sends its Minister of Finance to the EcoFin Council, whereas Greece sends its Minister for Economic Affairs. The responsibilities and power that these two ministers have may vary, which could affect their bargaining advantage. In analysing the bargaining advantage of players, it may be useful to identify the status, the capabilities, the expertise, and the EU budget contribution of players. However, the bargaining advantage may change at any given moment in the policy-making process. This may be due to the choice of action channel, the decision reached at a particular moment as a result of 'pulling and hauling', alterations in the political climate for each member state, or changes in the players involved. Therefore, it is necessary to consider the bargaining advantage of players prior to any Council decision, and the bargaining advantage within the action channel being used at a given moment. This two-fold examination of the bargaining advantage of the players allows the analyst to account for the changes that might occur during the policy-making process as a result of 'pulling and hauling'.

## *Council action channels*

Chapter 3 demonstrated how the rules and procedures of the Council can affect the decision output of a proposal. Whether the discussion was held (and agreement reached) in formal or informal session may indicate the level of difficulty that existed in reaching a final decision. Although decisions are not officially reached in informal meetings, this type of session is often more fruitful in achieving decisions. The voting rules affect the conduct and output of decisions made by the Council. The Council has traditionally employed a consensus approach. It is important to ascertain whether this is altering due to the SEA extension of the use of qualified majority voting. Moreover, the legal base for a decision (the treaty article that is used to formulate the proposal and which stipulates the method of decision) affects discussion. Occasionally, member states will try and alter the legal base of a proposal to obtain the desired voting method. National procedures and structures will have an impact upon the Council's own operation. Although this is beyond the scope of analysis here, it is worth remembering when trying to characterize the Council. As discussed, Coreper and the General Secretariat are comprised of individual players, but it may prove extremely difficult to analyse them as Council actors. However, they are also Council action channels. Coreper is not only used as a means of filtering proposals and alleviating the Council's workload, but is also a means of facilitating agreement. The Council often refers discussion of a particular proposal back to Coreper if agreement is proving difficult. The extent of Coreper involvement in reaching agreement on a particular proposal provides an important indicator of the action channel used. The choice of Coreper as the preferred action channel at a particular moment may give some indication as to the nature of the proposal and the decision output. Coreper agreement, appearing as an 'A' point on the Council agenda, usually implies that the agreement was not problematic and that a high degree of consensus existed. Although the Presidency is an important player in the work of the Council, there may be occasions where the precise input of the Presidency cannot be identified. However, using the Presidency's skills to facilitate agreement is employing a particular action channel of the Council. The General Secretariat is not only concerned with preparatory work, but may on occasion be involved in informal policy discussions, and help in reaching agreement on a particular proposal. Therefore, in considering the action channels, it may also be useful to identify when and why Coreper dealt with a proposal, if the Presidency was used as a broker in the negotiations, and if the General Secretariat was involved. The lack of documentation hinders such analysis, but examination of 'speech acts' may help. In identifying the action channels, it may be useful to consider the type of session, the rules of decision, the role of Coreper, the Presidency, and the General Secretariat, and if possible the different national organizational procedures. It is also important that the design of the analytical framework acknowledges that action channels may alter during the negotiations on a particular proposal. This may affect the bargaining advantage of the players, the decision reached at that time, and consequently the final output.

### Council outputs

In characterizing the Council, it may also be useful to consider the type of decision. This involves analysis of the decisions reached during the negotiating process as well as the final output. The interim decision outputs may affect not only the bargaining advantage of the players, but the subsequent choice of action channel, which again may affect who plays, and their bargaining advantage. Non-decisions of the Council are also of significance. They are not necessarily negative, except in cases where an issue under discussion is finally dropped from the agenda. They may be useful to consider because often the Council decides not to act, or not to decide at a given time. Such non-decisions are important, as not only do they indicate how the Council may prefer to work (and this may be linked to the policy area), but they can help shape other policy options, and also account for delays in the policy process which are sometimes used to criticize the Council's operation. In this respect, it could be useful also to look at the language ('speech acts') used as an indication of the nature of decisions arrived at in the Council, and the time taken to adopt the proposal. It may be possible to analyse whether the interim decisions and the final output of Council policy-making are incremental or fundamental in nature. This may provide important insights into the preferred approach of the Council in its negotiations. Such analysis may also help the analyst to characterize the Council through the three labels of policy style – 'problem-solving', 'confrontation', and 'bargaining'. Therefore, in identifying the nature of Council decisions, it may be useful to consider both the decision outputs throughout the negotiating process, as well as the final output. Analysis of 'speech acts', the time taken, and the nature of the decision may be helpful in this respect. The use of the policy style labels may provide an indication of the character of Council policy-making.

## The design of the framework

The simplest way of designing an analytical framework is to devise a 'check-list' which can be used to consider a particular decision process in the Council. Although this is a somewhat crude method, it depicts the dynamics of Council policy-making, and is flexible enough to work even when some considerations are not relevant at a given time. The analytical framework is represented in Figure 4.1. The design of this analytical framework is based upon simplicity and flexibility. There are many variables that may need to be considered when analysing the Council. This framework includes only those which have been shown to be the most relevant to this analysis. However, this does not mean that all these variables will aid analysis in every case. It may be that only some are useful for particular councils, or that only certain variables are applicable at a certain time. In addition, the analyst can only consider those variables for which there is sufficient information. Yet, including all the variables in this framework provides the analyst with the flexibility needed in this type of analytical endeavour.

It is not possible to give an exhaustive account of the Council's entire policy-making process for a particular proposal, due to the quality of information available. However, the design of the framework allows the analyst to assess those variables for which there is sufficient information. This does not undermine the usefulness of the framework, as it is still possible to carry out a structured analysis of the Council's operation even if only

To analyse the Council's operation, consider:

**The Proposal**
its subject area, its objectives,
its 'type', its origin, member-state positions

**The Actors**
who plays, their status,
their relationship, their interests

**The Bargaining Advantage**
**[prior to the selection of action channel(s)]**
authority, expertise,
budget contribution

**The Action Channel(s)**
its type, decision rule

**The Bargaining Advantage**
**[within the action channel(s)]**
authority, expertise,
budget contribution

**The Decision**
**[within the action channel(s)]**
nature of decision, 'speech acts',
policy style

**The Final Output**
nature of decision, 'speech acts',
time taken, policy style

Note: Changes may occur in all of these variables at any given moment within Council policy-making.

The part of the process within the small box is likely to be repeated.

**Figure 4.1** The Council: an analytical framework.

some of the variables can be analysed. As discussed in previous chapters, there is little academic analysis of the operation of the Council as a complete structure. Therefore, consideration of only some of the variables in Figure 4.1 is more likely to provide insights into the character of the Council than existing analytical methods. The framework suggests that each variable should be considered, but is designed in such a way that if a variable appears inappropriate or cannot be analysed due to insufficient information, it can be put aside and should not hinder analysis of the Council. Nevertheless, the potential relevance of each variable should be evaluated in so far as available information allows it.

The section within the small box in Figure 4.1 may be repeated once or more. The decision within the action channel may not be the final decision, a different action channel may subsequently be chosen, which may alter the bargaining advantage of the players. It is also important to note that the variables given in Figure 4.1 are subject to change at any given moment. This should be remembered when analysing any case of the Council's operation. For example, the original proposal may alter as a consequence of the bargaining advantage and the decision output. The actors may change as a result of the selected action channel, the bargaining advantage, or the decision output. The bargaining advantage may alter after the action channel has been selected, during the pulling and hauling, or after the decision output. The action channel is also subject to change if the proposal, actors, or the bargaining advantage alters. If only one particular case of Council policy-making was analysed, and there was sufficient information, then each stage of Council policy-making could be considered in turn. However, it is not possible to provide a full and detailed secondary account of the Council's policy process for the cases that follow, due to the information deficit.

## Using the framework

This final section shows how to operationalize the analytical framework in abstract terms. First, the proposal should be examined. Its subject area may indicate whether the Council is involved in an easy or difficult decision-making process. An assessment should be made as to whether the proposal is a single issue, part of an EU action programme, or linked to other EU policy areas. This may affect who plays, which could influence the bargaining advantage. In addition, the nature of the proposal (its objectives and 'type') could affect the choice of action channel which may determine the bargaining advantage of the actors involved. The proposal itself may also provide indications as to the output. Member-state attitudes towards the proposal should also be analysed. This will involve consideration of each member state's general attitude to that particular policy area, as well as an examination of the domestic and international context at that time. It may only be possible to suggest the likely attitude of member states through implication analysis, as precise information on their views on a particular proposal may not be available.

The actors should then be identified. Who is involved in the decision-making process should be established, as this may affect the proposal in terms of attitudes to it, and subsequent possible modifications. Who plays, their interests, status, and inter-relationships may significantly affect where the bargaining advantage lies in the Council at that particular moment. Actors may also be able to dictate where negotiation takes place and under what rules, in other words they may be able to influence the choice of action channels. Any changes to the actors involved, either as a result of the choice of action channel, or the interim decision output, should also be considered. Finally, identifying the actors may give some insight into the likely final output of the policy-making process of the Council.

The bargaining advantage prior to the selection of an action channel(s) should also be considered. An examination should be made of who has the policy-making authority and expertise. It may also be useful to consider the EU budgetary contribution of member states, as it may be the case that the financial costs of a proposal affect the bargaining advantage of the ministers involved. These factors may influence the way in which the Council works, not only in terms of who is involved in the process, but also the decision methods that will be used. Bargaining advantage may also influence the nature of the proposal during discussion as negotiating power may alter its form and content. Finally, examining the bargaining advantage of the actors may also allow analysts to predict the output of the policy-making process in the Council.

The action channel(s) involved should then be identified. This may give an indication of the actors involved, as some actors may prefer informal to formal sessions, or may prefer a consensus approach to decision-making rather than a vote. Action channels may also influence the bargaining advantage of players. The forum (Coreper, or session type) and method of decision might have an effect on the negotiating strengths of the actors. In addition, the proposal itself could be affected by the action channel that is being used. It may be the case that the action channel influences member-state positions and consequent responses to the proposal. The decision outputs of the policy-making process may be guided by the action channel used.

The bargaining advantage within the action channel should then be assessed. A re-examination is essential, as the action channel may have altered the bargaining advantage of the players. As in the previous examination, analysis of the bargaining advantage should include an examination of the authority and expertise of the players, and the budgetary contribution, as these may affect who plays, and the choice of future action channels. Examination of the bargaining advantage at this stage in the process may be difficult if, for example, the action channel currently being used is Coreper. Attempts can be made through implication analysis, but it is important to be cautious in this type of approach. If it is not possible, then this variable can be excluded from analysis without undermining the overall findings.

The decision within each particular action channel should then be analysed. The particular output may indicate the nature of 'pulling and hauling' between the players, and enable the analyst to predict the next stage in the policy process. This may also help to identify some operational characteristics of the Council. In analysing the decision, it may be useful to consider the nature of the decision (its type, importance, or whether it was a non-decision), 'speech acts', and the style of the interim decision. It is important to make the distinction between the interim decision and the final output. If the decision is not a final adoption of the particular proposal, Council negotiations on the particular proposal are not yet complete. Consequently, the action channel may change. The interim decision may have partly altered the contents of the proposal, which may have caused the actors to change, the bargaining advantage to alter, or both. This needs to be identified when analysing the decision output and the other variables already discussed.

When the decision constitutes a final adoption by the Council, the final output can be evaluated. Speech acts may indicate when this is the case. Analysis of the final output, including the time taken to adopt the proposal may indicate the nature of Council policy-making on a particular proposal. An attempt should also be made to characterize the Council by attaching the various labels of policy style. The analyst should also examine whether the style of policy-making altered during the negotiations on a particular proposal. Results can then be compared to see whether the Council's style of policy-making differs between, or within policy areas, or both.

Butler (1986: 73) argues that the various technical councils have 'slightly different personalities' but that their operational patterns are not dissimilar. The next four chapters address whether this is the case through application of the analytical framework.

# CHAPTER FIVE

# The Economic & Financial Affairs Council

The Economic & Financial Affairs Council (EcoFin) deals with most aspects of monetary and fiscal policy-making, and on occasion discusses the financial aspects of other EU policies when there is a policy overlap, or when an issue is proving difficult to resolve. However, the EcoFin Council rarely takes a final decision on such matters; it is simply a further channel of discussion. EcoFin was not officially established until 1974. From the 1960s, EcoFin Ministers used to meet quarterly in the member state holding the Presidency, but as an informal group, not as a part of the Council. Since its establishment, the EcoFin Council convenes regularly, averaging nine times per year (see Table 2.1). However, due to the implementation of the SEA and the re-emergence of EMU onto the policy agenda, the number of formal sessions has increased slightly to an average of eleven per year, as shown in Table 5.1. Consequently, EcoFin is now third in the implicit Council hierarchy.

The number of EcoFin sessions increased from the second half of 1990, due to the IGC to discuss EMU held at the beginning of EcoFin meetings. However, this analysis of the work of EcoFin between 1988 and 1992 excludes EMU as its increased importance could distort analysis and lead to conclusions about the operation of the Council that are not representative.[1]

In all EcoFin sessions, the first part of the meeting deals with monetary issues, and the second half fiscal affairs. Consequently, there is normally a change of personnel. National ministers remain the same, but advisers from the member states and officials of the General Secretariat and the Commission may change according to the particular dossier under discussion. Although Coreper II is officially charged with the work of EcoFin, over the years this has caused problems as the Coreper Ambassador was not necessarily an expert in the technical issues, and was forced to rely heavily on the advice of other members within Coreper. This also caused some conflict between EcoFin and the General Affairs Council.[2] Due to Coreper II's lack of expertise, certain member states (such as Portugal) often prefer to deal with EcoFin issues within the General Affairs Council and try to shift the proposal from one agenda to another. In addition, the knowledge and position of Finance Ministers is different in each member state, and consequently the convening of EcoFin sessions is often subject to Presidential preference. Both Germany and Spain normally send a team of three to EcoFin sessions, whereas all other member states send only one minister.[3] This has the potential to impact upon the negotiating process, and will be considered in the following two case-studies.

The cases analysed here are the proposal for the abolition of fiscal frontiers and the Directive on money laundering in the EC. EcoFin dealt with a demanding policy agenda between 1988 and 1992, addressing 84 main items (including these two cases) on its agenda.[4] These two cases offer alternative perspectives on the work of EcoFin, which satisfies the need to include different but comparable examples. The abolition of fiscal frontiers was a 'high' policy item and problematic, while the Directive on money laundering was relatively uncontentious. Furthermore, fiscal harmonization is a good example of policy overlapping. Obviously, taking only two examples means that a definitive analysis cannot be made about the operation of EcoFin. However, these contrasting cases provide some useful insights into how this Council works. These findings will be compared in Chapter 9 with those from the subsequent three chapters to identify the overall characteristics of the Council.

## The abolition of fiscal frontiers

This case-study concerns a package of proposals (hereafter referred to as 'the proposal') aimed at abolishing all fiscal frontiers within the EC by harmonizing member states' rates of Value Added Tax (VAT) and excise duties. This involved eight Directives and one Decision, although these were treated as a single package in EcoFin discussions. The abolition of fiscal frontiers clearly related to the internal market programme and the principle of the free movement of goods, services and people.[5] However, fiscal taxation is a significant means of raising revenue for all member-state governments. Therefore, due to the high political sensitivity of this issue, EcoFin rather than the Internal Market Council dealt with the proposal.

The Commission formally submitted the proposal to the Council in August 1987.[6] It was first discussed by the EcoFin Council in April 1988.

| Year | Presidency | Formal | Informal |
|------|------------|--------|----------|
| 1988/1 | Germany | 4 | 1 |
| 1988/2 | Greece | 3 | 1 |
| 1989/1 | Spain | 4 | 0 |
| 1989/2 | France | 4 | 0 |
| 1990/1 | Ireland | 4 | 1 |
| 1990/2 | Italy | 6 | 2 |
| 1991/1 | Luxembourg | 7 | 1 |
| 1991/2 | Netherlands | 6 | 1 |
| 1992/1 | Portugal | 6 | 1 |
| 1992/2 | UK | 6 | 2 |

*Note: /1 refers to the first semester of the year, /2 to the second.
Source: Compiled from Council Press Releases, Council internal documents and *Agence Europe*.

**Table 5.1  Meetings of the EcoFin Council 1988–92.**

The Council took over four years to legislate on this proposal, with final agreement in October 1992.[7] It could be argued that this case is not representative of the work of the EcoFin Council because of such an extended time-lag between proposal and adoption. However the abolition of fiscal frontiers warrants examination as it was a high priority for the EcoFin Council (and the EC as a whole), and is a good example of policy overlapping within the Council.

The first factors to consider when analysing the proposal are its subject area and objectives. Clearly, the political nature of fiscal harmonization meant that negotiations on this proposal would be difficult. The subject area encroached upon government revenue-raising capabilities in all member states. In addition, although indirect taxes accounted for only a quarter of the price disparities between member states, the abolition of fiscal frontiers was crucial in achieving the completion of the internal market. The official Commission view was that agreement would be proof of member states' commitment to the internal market programme.[8] Therefore, the nature of the proposal posed a dilemma for member-state governments. On the one hand, all member states backed the principle of completing the internal market, hoping to achieve substantial economic benefits as a result; yet, on the other hand, to fully establish such a market meant that national powers of raising revenue were threatened as member states would have to agree to common VAT rates and excise duties that might differ from individual current rates.

Employing Iklé's categories, the objective of the proposal was innovative as the proposal aimed to harmonize VAT and excise duties across all member states. There were large differences in rates of VAT and excise duties between EC member states at this time. For example, in 1991 the standard rate of VAT in Denmark was 22 per cent compared with 12 per cent in Spain. Excise duties also varied: for example Germany, Greece, Spain and Portugal levied no duty on still wine, whereas duties in Ireland and the UK were very high. The Commission recognized the radical nature of the proposal and proposed that any arrangements agreed to by the Council would be transitional until January 1997, when a definitive arrangement would be introduced after further negotiation.[9]

By July 1988, most member states (excluding Belgium, Greece and Italy) had raised political objections to the proposal. As stated, some member states were anxious about the loss of tax revenue that fiscal harmonization would incur. At the first EcoFin session to discuss this issue fully, member states also voiced their concerns about the risk of inflation, and the 'turmoil' that would arise from the standardization of taxation on such goods as petrol, cigarettes and alcohol.[10] The UK and Denmark expressed this view most clearly, arguing that the withdrawal of tax barriers would be smoother if harmonization of VAT or consumer taxes occurred afterwards. Denmark had deep reservations about the whole proposal which may have been because the Danish fiscal system was unlike any other in the EC. High indirect taxation rather than direct taxation financed high public expenditure in Denmark, and it was estimated that Denmark would lose approximately five per cent of GDP on the initial levels proposed by the Commission (Lyck, 1992: 155). Greece and Ireland were also worried that they would lose revenue due to their high rates of VAT. Portugal may also have been concerned, especially because domestic inflationary pressures increased in 1989. Luxembourg had reservations about the proposal, as fiscal harmonization would threaten its tax-haven status: VAT and excise duties there were substantially less than those being put forward by the Commission in early 1988.

The Netherlands felt that the proposed bands of excise duties were far too wide and maintained this standpoint from 1988 to 1990. France also agreed with this, but joined Germany in arguing that VAT was a consumption tax, and should be collected at the point of consumption rather than the point of origin, thus minimizing the potential loss of revenue. In addition, the Socialist government had only just been re-elected in France and was more anxious about the potential loss of revenue than it may have been at other times in the electoral cycle. In Germany's case, unification had to be financed, yet this proposal meant a potential loss of government revenue.

The UK used a familiar argument throughout the period that this proposal was under discussion, namely the threat to its national sovereignty through the loss of some tax-raising powers. Only Belgium and Italy adopted a positive stance towards the abolition of fiscal frontiers. Greece was amenable to the proposal, but this may have been because it knew that its weak economic position within the EC would necessitate special arrangements, particularly after 1990 when economic performance declined further.

Finally, it may be useful to consider the 'type' of proposal and its origin. The Commission's proposal was part of the internal market programme, and therefore member states knew that this legislation would be essential to the completion of the 1992 programme, which they had already agreed. However, unlike most measures to complete the internal market the procedure used for adoption of this proposal was Article 99 of the Treaty, which prescribes unanimity. As discussed, the abolition of fiscal frontiers involved eight Directives and one Decision. This meant that details of implementation were not set out, which had a significant bearing on the conduct of Council negotiations.

EcoFin dealt with this proposal rather than the Internal Market Council as it was primarily a fiscal matter. EcoFin Ministers are senior in rank. The German Minister for Finance, for example, occupies an extremely important position in the German cabinet, as they can veto any matter that would incur additional domestic expenditure, and Belgian representation at EcoFin sessions is exclusively reserved for a Federal Minister. EcoFin meets on a regular basis, and therefore ministers are likely to be familiar with each other. In looking at some ministerial delegations to EcoFin meetings between 1988 and 1992, there was also a high degree of continuity in terms of the personnel. For example, the Belgian Minister for Finance, Maystadt, served throughout this period, except for the first meeting in April 1988. From examining the attitudes of member states, it appeared that most of them were concerned about the possible effects of this proposal, but that each had its own different reasons for these worries. Therefore, it may have been that their individual interests came into conflict, despite their common reservations.

Negotiations on this proposal involved ten Council Presidencies. The 1991 Luxembourg Presidency made the most progress on the negotiations, and even the Council acknowledged how the Italian Presidency had given this proposal high priority during 1990, despite the predominance of EMU discussions.[11] However, the Spanish Presidency of 1989 was less successful despite earlier statements that Spain intended to use its Presidency to make progress on this proposal.[12] The Dutch Presidency was able to advance discussions on excise duties during 1991, but the most significant example of the impact of the Presidency occurred during the UK's term of office in 1992.

This proposal was also pushed up to the European Council (Strasbourg, 1989, Dublin, 1990, and Lisbon, 1992). After the Strasbourg summit, the EcoFin Council 'agreed in principle' to the harmonization of taxation which suggested that the political will did exist.[13] Later in 1989, member states agreed to keep basic VAT rates between 14 and 20 per cent, again on the basis of discussions at Strasbourg (although the UK reaffirmed the importance of zero rating).[14] The first EcoFin session after the Dublin European Council adopted further conclusions.[15] However, discussions after the Lisbon summit were less fruitful. Nevertheless, it seemed that the European Council was an important actor in the policy-making process of the EcoFin Council in this particular case. The EP and ESC were consulted in accordance with Article 99 of the Treaty.

Examination of the bargaining advantage of the actors needs to consider the authority and expertise of Council actors, and the budget contribution. The most important factor appeared to be that the majority of member states were against this proposal. This grouping involved the key EC actors, who commanded greater authority in the negotiations. However, the member states least favourable to the proposal had different reasons for their reservations. It may also have been the case that they worked out compromises between themselves in order to satisfy individual interests, or that these different interests meant that negotiations would be further complicated. Considering the time taken to adopt the proposal, the negotiations were highly problematic.

As discussed, this proposal did raise financial issues but not in terms of the budget contribution, rather the potential loss of revenue that fiscal harmonization would incur. Therefore, it was predictable that all member states (except Belgium, Greece, and Italy) would employ financial arguments in the negotiations.

Fiscal harmonization was discussed in a variety of different settings. The abolition of fiscal frontiers was on the agenda at 25 out of the 50 formal sessions held between 1988 and 1992. This is a significant amount considering that EMU was the main agenda item for most of 1990 and 1991. Restricted sessions, prolonged meetings, and the threat of supplementary sessions were also used. The French Presidency extended EcoFin meetings late into the night in November 1989, reflecting the importance that the Presidency attached to finding a solution.[16] The Luxembourg Presidency convened an extra evening session on 10 June 1991 as little progress had been made that day, despite it being a restricted session. However, even using this double tactic proved unsuccessful as this was the occasion on which the French and Belgian delegations left early.[17] Likewise, the Luxembourg Presidency's use of a working lunch failed, due to the

French refusal to attend. The Portuguese and UK Presidencies seemed to be more successful. Discussions over lunch in June 1992 brought about some progress, while the additional session convened in July 1992 resulted in a Presidency compromise being accepted.[18] However, negotiations were nearing completion by mid-1992, implying that the most difficult issues had already been resolved. Nevertheless, the final EcoFin session on this proposal did not finish until 10 p.m. Either the UK Presidency extended the meeting to ensure adoption of the proposal, or else it was the case that all delegations wanted to complete the policy-making process and avoid further meetings.

According to Council documents, two out of ten informal sessions were convened specifically to discuss this proposal. This figure may be larger, but information only exists for informal sessions held during the German and Greek Presidencies.[19] A reference is made to an informal session held during the Spanish Presidency, but this could not be corroborated.[20] The importance of these two sessions in the policy-making process is unclear. Lord Cockfield (Vice President of the Commission with responsibility for the Internal Market Portfolio 1985–9), initiated bilateral talks with member states after the 1988 informal session in Crete which resulted in the Commission amendments to the proposal.[21] However, the EcoFin meeting held after the German informal session was uneventful and makes no reference to the informal meeting.

Coreper and working parties were important Council action channels for the negotiations on this proposal. Initial discussions by the EcoFin Council in April 1988 were based on reports prepared by a Committee of Economic Policy set up by Coreper in November 1987. The work carried out by Coreper also enabled the Council to adopt some preliminary conclusions in October 1989.[22] Considering that discussions on this proposal extended over a long period, Coreper was used to find solutions that the ministers could debate at subsequent sessions. Due to the difficult nature of this proposal, the General Secretariat provided additional expertise and continuity through its Directorates-General. The General Secretariat played a part in the Presidential compromises and the referral of the proposal to the European Council.

This proposal was subject to Article 99 of the Treaty, and required EcoFin to take all decisions by unanimity. In addition, Article 99 makes reference to Article 7A which stipulates that the proposal should be adopted by 31 December 1992 (in accordance with the deadline for completion of the internal market). Given the contentious nature of fiscal harmonization, progress was bound to be slow. The requirement for unanimity may have compounded this. Had the deadline of 31 December 1992 not been in force, it may be that agreement would never have been reached.

From the available evidence, it appeared that Denmark obtained specific arrangements for quantitative restrictions on travel allowances in 1989 primarily because of the Dutch delegation's compromise.[23] This suggests that The Netherlands was able to influence the discussions, which may have satisfied its own concerns about the proposal. The Dutch Presidency was able to advance discussions on excise duties during 1991, but optimism that all problems would be solved by the end of the year was dashed by Irish objections.[24] The French delegation used its authority within the EC to influence the negotiations by leaving the June 1991 session early. Apparently France was frustrated by the UK's inflexibility over the issue of the normal rate of VAT:

> At the conclusion of the Council, several sources stated that a compromise could have been found more readily if several Ministers had not left Kirchberg at the end of the day leaving instructions with their aides considered by some to be 'contradictory' and preventing a final political arbitration on points that may only be resolved at this level.[25]

This decision to leave the meeting worked, as agreement on this issue was reached at the following session. The French Minister also refused to attend the working lunch later in June 1991. It transpired that the French wanted some concessions on the excise duty on wine and gas/oil taxation, but seemed to use British objections on the proposal to disguise its own interests.[26] The Luxembourg Presidency did put forward a compromise on the approximation of the normal rate of VAT, but Germany and the UK still maintained their reservations.[27] The UK Presidency put forward a compromise at the July 1992 session which proposed that the normal rate of VAT was to be a minimum of 15 per cent for four years, but that the Council minutes would include a declaration that this could be modified by unanimous agreement. What was interesting was that the UK had always been opposed to a standard VAT rate.[28] Therefore, the UK had made concessions on this particular matter, perhaps in exchange for a compromise by other member states elsewhere. It may also have been the case that the UK Presidency was under pressure to find a solution so that the proposal could be adopted by the 1992 deadline.

Analysis of the bargaining advantage shows that most member states were able to influence the negotiations, either as individual delegations, or as Council Presidents. This tends to confirm earlier suggestions that the diverse range of concerns about this proposal meant that the 'pulling and hauling' within the Council would be highly complex. However, those delegations represented by both Ministers for Finance and Ministers for Economic Affairs seemed to have no greater influence upon the negotiations than other delegations, despite their combined skills and expertise. The ESC and EP appeared to have little influence on this proposal, which may have been primarily a result of the consultation procedure.

There were twenty-six interim decisions during the negotiations on this proposal, but fifteen of these were non-decisions. The eleven more 'positive' interim decisions were 'agreements in principle' by the Council, and the adoption of conclusions. 'Bargaining' was the most appropriate label of the style of these decisions. The non-decisions, which were mainly referrals back to Coreper and the working party because no agreement could be reached between Ministers, indicate the difficulty in reaching agreement on this proposal. Coreper was used as a means to try to resolve problematic issues. Other examples of non-decisions include the two informal sessions convened to facilitate discussion, but not agreement.

The language employed provides a good indication of the nature of the policy-making process.[29] For example, the term 'exchange of views' implies that little of substance was agreed. This seemed to be the case in April 1988, April 1989 and June 1990.[30] When the EcoFin Council instructed Coreper or a working group, a date to report back was stipulated, demonstrating that EcoFin was keen to make progress on the proposal.[31] Adopting conclusions, such as those reached in November 1989 and December 1990, showed that some progress short of overall agreement had been made.[32] In this case-study, there was one occasion when statements by the Irish and UK delegations were added to the conclusions, a practice demonstrating that while some agreement had been reached, there was no overall consensus.[33]

A good example of the significance of the outcome was that all the EcoFin Ministers clapped when agreement finally came, which was 'an unusual event at this type of meeting'.[34] It could be argued that the decision of the EcoFin Council was only incremental as the legislation was transitional until 1997. In addition, fiscal harmonization was part of a much larger decision, namely completion of the internal market. On balance, however, the adoption of the fiscal harmonization proposal was fundamental because it affected the taxation capabilities of all member states. Using Richardson et al.'s three labels of policy style 'bargaining' is the most appropriate for this case study. The work of the EcoFin Council in relation to this proposal did not demonstrate a high level of cooperation, therefore 'problem-solving' can be excluded from the analysis. Although several member states (such as Denmark and the UK) adopted strong negotiating tactics, no EC member viewed the policy-making process as a zero-sum game, ruling out the use of 'confrontation' as the policy-style of the EcoFin Council. There were differences over the means to achieve the objectives of fiscal harmonization, but all member states agreed to the principle; in other words there were shared attitudes over this proposal. All member-state governments had previously agreed to the completion of the internal market, and all delegations had reaffirmed their commitment to fiscal harmonization at the EcoFin meeting of 18 April 1988. This corresponds to the policy-style label of 'bargaining', and as this analysis has shown, negotiations on this proposal were subject to numerous compromise agreements.

### Summary of findings

Examination of the proposal to abolish fiscal frontiers shows that it was both difficult, innovative, and part of a package – namely the completion of the internal market. Most member states raised political objections to the proposal from the outset despite the fact that they knew that it was an integral part of the 1992 programme. The highly politicized nature of the proposal also affected the actors, the bargaining advantage, and the action channel. Analysis of the actors suggested that the diverse range of concerns about this proposal may have affected the negotiations. Key member states were able to use their authority to influence the final output. The Presidency and the European Council were important actors, particularly as pushing-up discussion of fiscal harmonization to the European Council facilitated some progress in the negotiations. Analysis of the bargaining advantage, both prior to and within the negotiations, shows that the pulling and hauling would be highly complex. Most Council actors influenced the negotiations, although France and the UK had the greatest advantage.

In looking at the action channel used, there is rather mixed evidence. The use of different types of session was more successful on some occasions than others. The unanimity rule combined with the nature of the proposal meant that agreement was going to be difficult. Coreper and the various working parties played a significant part in the policy-making process because of the difficult and technical nature of the proposal. Although there is a lack of firm evidence, the skill and expertise of the General Secretariat was also important, due to Coreper II's weak command of this policy area. Distinguishing between incremental and fundamental objectives was not very helpful, as although the proposal was fundamental, it was part of a greater EC objective. However, overall the final output was fundamental because it would affect all member-states' tax-raising powers. It was possible to apply the 'bargaining' label to the style of EcoFin policy-making on this proposal. Finally, identifying non-decisions provided further insight into the negotiating process. The delays in negotiation, referrals back to Coreper, and the informal sessions indicated the difficulty of this proposal.

## Money laundering

In contrast to the previous case, adoption of the Directive on money laundering was more straightforward. The entire policy-process took just over one year. The Commission submitted the proposal on 23 March 1990, and it was first discussed by EcoFin in October 1990.[35] The Directive was finally adopted on 10 June 1991.[36] The Directive aimed to combat the laundering of capital within the EC from money gained though drug trafficking, organized crime, terrorism, etc. Measures would be introduced to prevent the use of the EC financial system to launder money gained from these examples of criminal activity. Banks, credit institutions and financial institutions would be required to identify customers who carried out financial transactions over a certain amount. In addition, a committee would be set up to coordinate information between member states.[37]

This Directive clearly related to two aspects of EC policy. First, there was an obvious connection with the programme to complete the internal market. The Directive was proposed because of the need to protect against money laundering once the free movement of capital and people had been established. Second, the EC had become increasingly involved in the fight against terrorism and drug trafficking, and the prevention of money laundering was one measure that might help in such a crackdown.

The subject area of the proposal was relatively uncontroversial. The Directive on money laundering was essentially part of the internal market programme, which member states had agreed to when they signed the SEA. In addition, there was growing concern about certain criminal activities, and all member states agreed that the EC should act collectively in an effort to combat terrorism, drug trafficking, etc. As shown in Chapter 1, the increased attention given to criminal activities resulted in expanding the remit of the Trevi Group to include judicial cooperation under the 1986 UK Presidency. Therefore, negotiations on this proposal would prove fairly simple. Leon Brittan, the UK Commissioner, stated that 'the Directive is a vital part of our strategy to develop and protect Europe's financial sector. Its rapid adoption shows the priority we give to effective action against money laundering.'[38]

The proposal was 'innovative' as it introduced new mechanisms to combat money laundering, and it was also rather sensitive since it could draw attention to a problem that has serious implications for social order and the authority of the nation-state. Yet only Germany raised objections to the proposal, and then only because it wanted the level of transactions on which banks, etc. would be asked to divulge information increased from 15,000 to 20,000 ECU.[39] This was interesting, particularly as the proposal was discussed at a time when financial movements across Europe were on the increase due to the political changes in East/Central Europe and the former Soviet Union. Other member states felt that this Directive would help them individually in the fight against criminal activity. France, Spain, and the UK had a particular interest in this Directive due to their own national government policies in this area.

The proposal took the form of a Directive, leaving details of implementation up to member states. However, the proposal was in accordance with Article 57(2), third sentence, which stipulates that the Directive should come into force by 1 January 1993. In addition, the cooperation procedure and qualified majority voting were to be used. Finally, the proposal originated out of the 1992 programme, indicating that a good deal of political will already existed on this issue.

As in the previous case-study, the first point to make is that EcoFin rather than the Internal Market Council dealt with the money laundering Directive. This was probably due to the financial element of the proposal, but it may also have been dealt with by EcoFin because it was politically sensitive. Suggestions about the status and relationship of EcoFin Ministers made in the other case-study equally apply here. There was a high degree of continuity in ministerial representation and familiarity with colleagues. Most member states favoured the proposal. France, Spain, and the UK were the most important Council actors due to their own domestic concerns about terrorism and money laundering. Germany was a crucial actor in the negotiations as it had reservations about the level of transactions to which this Directive would apply. The role of the Presidency was less important, as this Directive was only discussed during the Italian and Luxembourg Presidencies of 1990 and 1991. Both the ESC and EP were also involved in the negotiations.

From the examination of the proposal and the Council actors, France, Spain, and the UK influenced the negotiations. The proposal corresponded to their own national objectives on the fight against terrorism, and they felt that the adoption of this proposal would enhance their own domestic measures. In addition, France and the UK are key actors in the EC, which may have strengthened their authority in the discussions. Germany had slight reservations about the proposal and influenced discussions because of its importance as an EC actor. The Italian Presidency took command of the negotiations as the Italian government was keen to be seen cracking down on criminal activity at this time. The EP may have been able to affect the final output as this proposal was subject to the cooperation procedure.

Fewer types of session discussed the money laundering Directive compared to the previous case-study. Only five of the eleven formal sessions held between October 1990 and June 1992 discussed this proposal. In addition, there is no evidence that the two informal sessions held during this period discussed this matter. However, one of the five formal sessions was a special meeting (convened by the Italian Presidency in December 1990) at which overall agreement was finally reached late in the evening.[40] Finally, the proposal appeared as an 'A' point at one of the formal sessions, indicating that the EcoFin Council was making smooth progress on this issue.[41]

Due to the relative ease of discussion, Coreper played the greatest role in discussions. EcoFin Ministers only considered the dossier at five formal sessions, yet there appeared to be numerous technical and legal issues to resolve. Coreper carried out the majority of the work, exemplified by an official Council statement which said that 'the Directive was concluded within a short period despite the extent of the problems involved'.[42] There was no mention of working groups being set up to look at this proposal. Due to the political sensitivity of this proposal, Coreper II did all the preparatory work.[43] The input of the General Secretariat was only routine. It may have been behind the Italian Presidency's compromises, but it is more likely that Italian domestic objectives brought about these solutions.

The Directive on money laundering was adopted in accordance with the cooperation procedure. This meant that the EP had to be consulted twice, and that the Council's common position and final decision had to be adopted by qualified majority. However, there is no mention in any source that the Council used the qualified majority rule to adopt either the common position or the amendments made by the EP after its second reading.[44]

As with the fiscal harmonization proposal, differences in ministerial representation did not affect the negotiations, but this was primarily because the majority of the work was carried out by Coreper. Italy, in its capacity as President of the Council, influenced the negotiations. This confirms earlier suggestions that Italy may have used its Presidency for domestic reasons, but implies that France, Spain, and the UK were not such crucial actors. Furthermore, Germany actually seemed to have little negotiating strength because it did not succeed in raising the level of transactions at which banks, etc. would have to divulge customer information.

The ESC queried the legal base of the proposal, suggesting that it should be subject to the consultation rather than cooperation procedure. Essentially, the ESC felt that the issue of money laundering from drug trafficking was being ignored, and that by using either Article 100, 100A, or 235 of the Treaty of Rome, member-state governments would be able to consider this issue in more depth. However, the Council ignored the ESC's opinion due to worries that if the proposal was decided on a national basis, this would hinder completion of the single market by the prescribed deadline.

By contrast, the EP had a greater impact upon the proposal, especially on second reading.[45] Seven EP amendments had to be made to the Directive. These changes were primarily technical, amending specific words and adding two new broad articles. However, this caused difficulties for the Council as a number of declarations were added to the Directive. In particular a clause had to be drafted to introduce a review procedure to examine the success of the Directive in January 1994 (and three-yearly after that).[46]

There were two interim decisions on this proposal. The first was a non-decision as the EcoFin Council simply referred the matter back to Coreper, and the second was an agreement in principle to the Presidency's compromise. This tends to confirm earlier suggestions that Coreper, and to a lesser extent the Italian Presidency, were responsible for finding solutions to the problems on this proposal. Due to the compromise, 'bargaining' best characterizes the approach of EcoFin in these negotiations.

The language employed clearly indicated that progress was made relatively quickly, and that Coreper was an important action channel. As in the previous case study, there is similar difficulty in deciding whether the nature of the decision was incremental or fundamental in nature. On the one hand, due to the political sensitivity and innovative nature of the proposal, the adoption of the Directive on money laundering may have proved difficult. However, it was part of the internal market programme. Perhaps the relative ease of the negotiating process suggests that member states did not regard this Directive as so fundamental. The impression that negotiation was relatively uncontroversial could lead to conclusions that 'problem solving' characterizes the EcoFin policy on this occasion as there were shared attitudes about the objectives of the proposal and a good deal of cooperation in the negotiations. Yet there appeared to be differences over the means, exemplified by the need for compromises (although it is unclear what the problems were). Consequently, 'bargaining' is the most appropriate policy-style label. However, this is by no means conclusive due to the lack of detail available on this proposal.

### Summary of findings

In this analysis of the Directive on money laundering, examination of the proposal showed that the subject area was relatively straightforward in terms of reaching agreement. The proposal was part of a package rather than a single issue, and there were no real differences of opinion on the part of member states. However, firm conclusions cannot be drawn due to the surrounding political sensitivity of the proposal and its innovative objectives. As in the previous case study, analysing the origin of the proposal and its 'type' was not very helpful.

Identifying the actors proved that the proposal was politically important, as it was EcoFin that considered the matter rather than the Internal Market Council. This partly confirmed the idea that there were hidden sensitivities on this issue. The EP and the Italian Presidency were important actors in the policy process. Although analysis of the bargaining advantage prior to the negotiations suggested that France, Spain and the UK may have wanted to secure agreement on this proposal, examination of the discussions proved this not to have been the case. Analysis showed that Italy used the Council Presidency for domestic electoral advantage, and that the EP was able to influence the negotiations due to the cooperation procedure.

EcoFin made little use of other types of session in its discussions. Only one extra, extended session was convened (although this did prove a success). However, it is essential to emphasize that EcoFin only discussed this proposal at five sessions. This small number indicated that agreement did not require the use of other tactics. The most interesting conclusion from analysis of the action channel was that qualified majority voting was not used despite being prescribed, and that Coreper was an important action channel. Speech acts were a good indicator of the progress of negotiations, and in particular the input of Coreper. Again it was difficult to decide whether the EcoFin decision was incremental or fundamental in nature. In addition, although 'bargaining' appeared to be the most appropriate label for EcoFin's policy style, the lack of information prevents a definite conclusion being made.

## Characteristics of EcoFin

This section provides a preliminary assessment of both the character of the EcoFin Council and the usefulness of the analytical framework. However, these are only initial conclusions as it would be premature to offer a definitive analysis before examining other case-studies. Overall, the framework proved a useful analytical tool with which to characterize the operation of the EcoFin Council. Consideration of the proposal gave a good indication of the outcome through analysis of the subject area, its objectives, and member-state attitudes. From this, it was also possible to predict who the key actors would be in the negotiations, and consequently the bargaining advantage of the actors both before and during the negotiations. Analysis of the actors, their status and inter-relationships also showed the significance of the proposal and the probable outcome. In part, it also helped to identify the bargaining advantage and predict the likely action channels. The skill and expertise of the actors influenced the negotiations, the decision methods and the outcome. Therefore, it was also helpful to consider the bargaining advantage.

Analysis of the action channel provided some interesting observations about how the EcoFin Council preferred to operate, and the negotiating strengths of the actors; it also showed that the action channel often guided the outcome of the policy-making process. Examination of the outcome produced mixed results. The analysis of 'speech acts' was helpful in both case-studies, indicating the level of progress at each particular stage in the policy process. In addition, examination of the language used proved that the role of Coreper was important. This was especially helpful, given the lack of official information on the work of Coreper. Identification of non-decisions provided further insight into the negotiating process. Classifying the nature of the decision not only proved difficult, but indicated very little about the likely outcome of the negotiations. Finally, it was possible to characterize the policy style of the EcoFin Council through consideration of both proposals and their outcomes (though this was less certain in the case of the money laundering Directive).

Therefore, all the variables suggested by the analytical framework proved useful. However, some factors within the variables were not very helpful, including the origin of the proposal and its 'type', the budget contribution made by member states and whether the outcome was incremental or fundamental. The analytical framework did not specifically refer to the other key EC institutions. However, identifying the role and input of the EP provided useful insights into its relationship with the EcoFin Council, and the effect of the cooperation procedure, and this will be included in subsequent chapters.

Analysis of the two case-studies provides some valuable insights into the operation of the EcoFin Council. The nature of the proposal affects the entire policy-making process, although these EcoFin discussions were not influenced by the origin of the proposal or its 'type'. Member states' attitudes, and the skill and expertise of the actors involved, were the most important factors. In one case, the European Council's input was important. EcoFin uses different types of action channel, but the role of Coreper is the most significant. The General Secretariat's input was crucial when negotiations were difficult. The use of different types of session was more productive if the proposal was controversial or difficult, as were the use of non-decisions. The cooperation procedure affected EcoFin's room for manoeuvre, although qualified majority voting was not used. Finally, the style of EcoFin policy-making in these cases was that of 'bargaining'; members of EcoFin tended to agree on the objectives of proposals but often differed over the means to achieve these policy aims.

# CHAPTER SIX

# The Environment Council

The workload of the Environment Council has increased dramatically. By the end of 1992 the Council had adopted over 130 environmental Directives. The growth in environmental legislation resulted from the legal recognition given to EC action in this area by the SEA. Before 1987, environmental policy was essentially outside the Treaties. The 1972 Paris European Council promoted EC environmental action, in line with growing public awareness. Consequently, a new batch of EC policies began to emerge through the adoption of environmental action programmes. As there was no pre-existing legislation, the EC tended to face fewer difficulties in pursuing policy-making in this area. Some member states actually looked to the EC to take 'command and control' of environmental policy-making rather than pursue individual policies. This seemed logical due to the transnational nature of environmental problems.

The SEA took EC environmental policy much further. The key ideas of EC environmental policy were 'prevention at source' and 'polluters must pay', enshrined in Article 130R. The SEA stipulated the use of the cooperation procedure for most environmental proposals, although those that involved high expenditure or dealt with energy sources were still subject to unanimity (see Article 130S). The introduction of the cooperation procedure for some areas of environmental policy-making has altered Council–EP relations. The EP has used its increased influence to demand even further powers in environmental policy-making, which has tended to strain relations with the Council. The introduction of the co-decision procedure under the TEU has seen the EP pushing even harder. The President of the EP Environment Committee (Ken Collins, UK, Socialist Group at the time of writing) meets regularly with the member state holding the Council Presidency, and this has partly helped to improve relations. However, the main difficulty in their relations arises in the differentiation between Article 100A and Article 130S. A recent ECJ (European Court of Justice) ruling on the titanium dioxide case (examined in this chapter) supported the EP argument that the dividing line between its power under Article 130S and non-power under Article 100A is not always clear.

Overall, member states have been keen to adopt EU environmental legislation. Some, such as Germany and Denmark have done so out of a genuine concern for the environment; others recognize the vote-winning potential of being 'green'. However, the record of member-state implementation is uneven. Italy is the worst offender, while Spain takes a negative position on environmental policy as it affects its industrial strategy. The main problem is that implementation is hard to enforce as the EU is asking member states to impose sanctions on each other and on themselves.

As shown in Table 6.1, Environment Council sessions increased from three to five per year between 1988 and 1992, reflecting the greater attention given to policy-making in this area. Consequently, it is now a 'medium' Council in terms of the frequency of sessions, and its status in the Council hierarchy. Between 1988 and 1992, the Environment Council discussed 72 main agenda items (including the two case-studies analysed in this chapter but excluding 'A' points).[1]

Environmental policy overlaps with many other areas of EU policy activity, and especially energy. The data in Table 6.1 includes two joint sessions with the Energy Council (held during the Italian and Dutch

| Year | Presidency | Formal | Informal |
|------|------------|--------|----------|
| 1988/1 | Germany | 2 | 0 |
| 1988/2 | Greece | 1 | 0 |
| 1989/1 | Spain | 2 | 1 |
| 1989/2 | France | 2 | 0 |
| 1990/1 | Ireland | 2 | 1 |
| 1990/2 | Italy | 3 | 1 |
| 1991/1 | Luxembourg | 2 | 0 |
| 1991/2 | Netherlands | 3 | 1 |
| 1992/1 | Portugal | 3 | 1 |
| 1992/2 | UK | 2 | 1 |

*Note: /1 refers to the first semester of the year, /2 to the second.
Source: Compiled from Council Press Releases, Council internal documents and *Agence Europe*.

**Table 6.1 Meetings of the Environment Council 1988–92.**

Presidencies in 1990 and 1991 respectively) and one with the Development Council (during the Portuguese Presidency of 1992). However, as discussed in Chapter 3, one of the main problems is that member states often settle their own internal rows in joint councils. This is especially so in joint Environment Councils.

Member-state representation in Environment Councils hardly differs. Most ministers have equal status. The German Minister possibly has greater domestic status due to the high priority given to environmental policy. The fact that Spain normally sends two ministers to meetings of the Environment Council may indicate its general difficulties with EU environmental policy-making. Environment Ministers know each other fairly well and are familiar with each others' tactics. Apart from formal Council sessions, they also meet at international conferences. They often use such meetings to call their own informal EC sessions. One senior Council Secretariat official stated that close relations within the Environment Council almost make it a 'green club' in a political and diplomatic sense. However, it does not necessarily follow that it is easier to reach agreement. The equal status of Environment Ministers, together with the fact that they know each other well, may mean that no minister has a greater bargaining advantage over their counterparts in Council negotiations.

This chapter now examines two cases of the work of the Environment Council; the Regulation to establish the European Environmental Agency, and the Directive on waste from the titanium dioxide industry. Both were significant pieces of EC legislation. The primary reason for this selection is that the cases give contrasting examples of the type of legislation. As discussed in Chapter 1, Regulations are not only obligatory, but prescribe details of implementation. What needs investigating is whether this has a significant impact upon the attitudes of member states in the negotiations. Directives are the most common form of EU environmental legislation. The titanium dioxide waste Directive was selected because the legal base altered. Due to the ECJ ruling, member states had to re-negotiate this Directive. Although this was unusual, examination of this proposal will analyse the importance of the legal base, and provide indications for the future of the Environment Council's work.

## The European Environmental Agency

The European Environmental Agency proposal aimed to set up a body to collate, evaluate, and provide independent information on the state of the environment. The network would consist of the European Environmental

Agency and national centres. The information would help both the EC and member states to take the necessary and appropriate measures to protect the environment, and the public would also have access to this information.[2] The proposal was first suggested by Jacques Delors when he addressed the EP in February 1989. The Commission formally submitted its proposal on 23 June 1989.[3] The Council finally adopted the Regulation on 7 May 1990, although problems over the seat of the Agency were not resolved until the Brussels European Council of October 1993.[4]

The first factors to consider in examining the proposal are its origin, subject area and objectives. The proposal originated from the Corine programme, adopted by the Council in 1985.[5] Corine had been designed to see if there was a need for environmental information and to assess the practical difficulties in providing coordinated information; the results of this assessment were generally favourable.[6] Member states had committed themselves to the establishment of an Environmental Agency if it was shown that there was a need, and the Corine programme proved that there was such a need. However, as will be shown, some member states may have preferred the results of Corine to be less positive. The proposal was highly innovative in its objectives as it not only called for the establishment of the Environmental Agency, but also a European Environment Monitoring and Information Network.

On the basis of the nature of the proposal, member-state attitudes varied considerably. The proposal not only dealt with environmental issues, but sought a greater role for the EC in monitoring the implementation of national environmental policies. Belgium, Germany, Denmark, Luxembourg, and The Netherlands favoured this proposal because of their general positive approach to both domestic and EC environmental legislation. Conversely, Greece, Italy, Portugal, and Spain do not place environmental issues high on the domestic or EC policy agenda, and have a poor record of implementing EC environmental legislation. The costs of implementing environmental policies outweighed the perceived gains for these member states, therefore, Greece, Italy, Portugal, and Spain were less enthusiastic about the proposal. The remaining member states – France, Ireland, and the UK – tend to accept rather than welcome EC involvement in environmental policy-making. France and the UK had the most difficulty with the monitoring powers envisaged for the Agency, as it meant giving the EC the right to observe whether national environmental legislation was being implemented. Although EC environmental legislation imposes higher standards than those in Irish law, Ireland had less difficulty with the proposal due to its generally positive approach to EC policy-making. Greece, Italy, Spain, and Portugal were concerned about the potential monitoring powers proposed for the

Agency because of their general misgivings about environmental policy-making discussed above.[7] Furthermore, Spain had particular national electoral pressures in 1989, and held European elections for the first time. Greek political instability and the 1989 elections were also a factor.[8]

Finally, the Environment Council had to adopt the Regulation by unanimity, according to Article 130S. Given the divergence of member-state attitudes, it was likely that negotiations would be lengthy, and difficult. Moreover, the fact that the proposal was put forward as a draft regulation meant that the details of implementation would be prescribed. This caused further difficulties for the less enthusiastic member states. However, the proposal only took nine months to be adopted, which is relatively quick for the Council. From this examination of the proposal, there was a degree of coalition building between those member states who favoured the proposal, and those who did not. Such collective bargaining meant that the difficulties were resolved more swiftly than if member states worked alone to get the desired agreement.

Examination of the actors needs to consider not only who participated in the negotiations and their interests, but their status and relationships to each other. As discussed, Environment Ministers are fairly familiar with each other as they meet at the international as well as the EC level, and are therefore more aware of general policy positions on environmental legislation. Considering that the proposal on the European Environmental Agency was adopted fairly quickly, such familiarity helped the negotiating process in the Council. The speed of adoption was also a result of the fact that member states worked together according to their own interests. From the examination of member-state attitudes towards the proposal, there were three groups of ministerial actors. The proposal corresponded to the interests of Belgium, Germany, Denmark, Luxembourg, and The Netherlands. For France, the UK (and to a lesser extent Ireland), the proposal clashed with their interest in keeping the EC out of monitoring national legislation. The final group involves those member states who tended to take a less favourable approach to environmental legislation, at both the national and EC level, namely Greece, Italy, Portugal, and Spain. As suggested, this latter grouping were also concerned about the potential monitoring powers of the Agency. The Benelux states and Denmark felt that their positions would be strengthened by working with a key actor in the EC such as Germany, whilst the UK thought an alliance with France would boost its bargaining advantage for similar reasons. The southern member states held comparable reservations about the proposal, so a coalition amongst them may have helped their negotiating strength given their weaker economic positions as compared with other member states.

The Presidency played a less significant role in the discussions on this proposal. The French Presidency tried to keep up the momentum of the negotiations, proposing in September 1989 that final agreement should be reached by November 1989.[9] This deadline was not met, but only because the EP had not delivered its opinion. The Irish Presidency simply chaired later discussions. Although there was disagreement over whether the Agency should have its own inspectors as proposed by the EP, the Irish Presidency found that all the member states and the Commission were against this EP amendment, as it infringed upon the Commission's role as guardian of the Treaties. Both the ESC and EP were involved by giving their opinions on this proposal.

There were difficulties in agreeing the location of the Agency. Although this issue is outside the Council negotiations considered here, it did introduce new actors into the process. In addition, the Regulation could not come into force until this was decided; the issue had to be 'pushed up' to the European Council. However, it should be stressed that this was simply because all decisions on sites for EU institutions have to be approved by the European Council. It was rather ironic that *Agence Europe* had argued that the negotiations on the Regulation were demonstrating that 'the Community is capable of quick action'.[10] In December 1991, the Commission stated that 'the decision on the seat is blocked by the crossplay of vetoes and blackmail on the choice of the various seats of institutions or Community bodies'.[11] An EP Resolution was even more critical, and threatened that if no decision was taken by July 1991, it would reconsider the budgetary allocation.[12] Consequently, the Commission proposed transitional measures so that the Agency could start its work, yet the decision on the site of the Agency took a further two years.

At the first Environment Council meeting to discuss the proposal for the Agency in September 1989, most member states offered to locate it in their country.[13] The motives of some may have been that by having the Agency based in their country, they would be perceived to be more politically 'green'. As the location of EC bodies has always proved problematic, it was decided at the November 1989 meeting to refer the matter to the European Council.[14] The Dutch, Portuguese, and UK Presidencies did try to resolve the issue, but without success. Portugal held informal discussions on the fringe of the March meeting of the Environment Council, and raised the issue at the joint Environment and Energy session in May, yet found no solution.[15] The UK President, Michael Howard, proposed (by letter) that the decision on the seat should be taken by a simple majority voting procedure, but most other ministers deemed this 'inappropriate', and felt that Howard's tactic of writing to them was rather cowardly.[16]

Consequently, the Environment Council pushed up the issue to the European Council level.[17] Although the Edinburgh Council agreed on the seats of Community institutions, decisions were not taken on the location of new EC bodies such as the Environmental Agency.[18] Agreement to site the Environmental Agency in Copenhagen was finally reached at the Brussels European Council of 29 October 1993. The issue of the location of the Agency became bound up in the allocation of sites for many of the EC bodies. It is possible that Denmark was chosen not only because of its positive approach to environmental policies, but also as a means to placate the Danish public in the light of their initial rejection of the TEU.

In analysing the bargaining advantage of Council actors on this proposal before any negotiations were held, it is necessary to consider their authority and expertise. Belgium, Germany, Denmark, Luxembourg, and The Netherlands were the most favourable to the proposal. Considering that Germany is a strong actor across the range of EC policy-making activities, and that the Benelux states regularly cooperate in negotiations, this grouping exercised a significant bargaining advantage over the other member states. However, as another key EC actor, France also used its status to influence the final output. In addition, France held the Council Presidency during the majority of the negotiations, which may have enhanced its bargaining strength. As shown in Chapter 2, a member state can use its Presidency to try and steer the negotiations in a particular direction, hoping to influence the final output in a way which is beneficial to that state. Greece, Italy, Portugal, and Spain were opposed to many aspects of the proposal.

While the member states which generally favoured the proposal seemed to have a theoretical bargaining advantage over these states, poorer member states could influence the final output due to the economic costs of environmental legislation. Greece, Italy, Portugal, and Spain may have used their relatively weak economic positions to argue that the legislation would damage their interests. Faced with severe domestic difficulties, economically and electorally, Spain may also have been able to use these circumstances to gain concessions. These arguments may have influenced the negotiating positions of Belgium, Germany, Denmark, Luxembourg, and The Netherlands, particularly given the generally cooperative approach of Spain to EC policy-making. These stronger states may have been willing to make some concessions either in return for some sort of package deal on another proposal under discussion at that time in another technical council, or because they may have felt that the costs to the southern member states of establishing the European Environmental Agency would result in an even poorer record of implementation of environmental legislation by these states (which would mean further costs to the EC as the Commission would have to prosecute these states in the ECJ). Conversely, for Germany, Denmark, and the Benelux states these considerations may have been overridden by their firm commitment to both national and EC environmental policy-making.

Although the proposal was adopted through the consultation procedure, it may also be the case that the EP (and possibly the ESC) could exercise some bargaining advantage in the negotiations. As discussed earlier in this chapter, environmental policy-making is of great concern to the EP, and it is generally felt that the EP Environment Committee is well-informed, and has the necessary skills and expertise in this area.

A variety of action channels were used in the negotiations for the establishment of the European Environmental Agency. The proposal was discussed at all three Environment Council meetings held during this period: there were no informal sessions. The French Presidency allowed the first debate on this issue to take up most of the meeting, and devoted all day of the subsequent session to this proposal.[19] Other tactics proved unnecessary due to the progress made by Coreper and a working group. Moreover, the working group proposed the actual compromise.[20] The negotiations by Coreper and the working group facilitated political agreement only two months after initial discussion of the proposal. The importance of the General Secretariat is implied by the speed of negotiations on this Regulation. The General Affairs Council was also an action channel in the discussion of this proposal, because agreement on the location of the Agency had to be taken by the Foreign Ministers. However, they failed to reach an agreement, and the issue had to be further pushed up to the level of the European Council (see previous section).

The first point to note in examining the bargaining advantage within the action channels is that a working group identified the main difficulties in reaching agreement prior to the first Environment Council meeting to discuss this proposal. These problems included the monitoring role of the Agency, and the need to ensure that it did not duplicate the work carried out by other existing environmental organisations. Although it is not possible to identify which member states raised these issues, suggestions can be made by looking at the Environment Council sessions.

From the evidence available, France used its authority as a key member state, and as President of the Council to limit the monitoring role of the Agency. The French Council President may have distanced himself from his national objections, but this is unlikely given the strength of feeling held by France on this particular issue. This confirms earlier suggestions that France exercised a significant bargaining advantage in the Council. The French Presidency devoted the entire day of the November 1989 session to resolving this issue, suspending discussion of the other agenda items until the evening. Although the compromise had been reached by a working group, France (together with Greece, Italy, and Spain) ensured that its case against the monitoring powers of the Agency was put forward at the meeting. It is also possible that France used its Presidency to achieve this compromise in the working group meeting. The eventual agreement was that although the Agency would monitor the implementation of EC laws and collect information for new or revised legislation, it would not interfere in national law. The final agreement also included a provision for a review of the Agency's competences at a later date.

The opinion of the ESC was generally favourable.[21] However, the EP exerted considerable influence over the content of the Regulation, despite only having one reading (which confirms previous remarks made in this chapter).[22] A dispute broke out as the EP felt the Council tried to mislead the EP over which amendments it was accepting. Apparently, the Council did not take into account the EP's original amendments when it was considering the amended Commission proposal. MEPs were furious because the Council had reached a political agreement on the Commission's proposal without the normal EP scrutiny. The newly elected EP felt ignored and subsequently put extreme pressure upon the Council and the Commission to consider its opinion and amendments. The EP demanded a tightening of the text so that it read less ambiguously, and it won this battle. It is likely that member states responded to these demands because of the EP's expertise in this area, and the fact that they had deviated from the correct policy-making procedure and did not wish to have this exposed. In a press release, the EP spoke of how the Council had 'demonstrated that it will react favourably to sensible and reasonable approaches from Parliament'.[23]

Negotiations on this proposal involved only two decisions within the action channels analysed above, prior to the formal adoption of the Regulation. The first decision was extremely important, as it resolved all the difficulties on the proposal (although further problems arose as a result of the EP's opinion). As shown, this compromise was reached by a working group, and does constitute a non-decision by the Environment Ministers as they referred the matter to Coreper and a working group. Therefore, 'bargaining' is the most appropriate label of the Council's style of policy-making on this occasion.

The second interim decision was also a result of discussions within a working group and Coreper, and hence a previous non-decision. The Commission amended parts of the proposal after the EP had delivered its opinion. Member states agreed to compromise on whether the Agency should have its own inspectors as proposed by the EP, by agreeing that the EP could appoint two members to the management board of the Agency.

In addition, they also accepted that the role of the Agency should be reviewed after two years to see whether its work conflicted with other existing environmental bodies. This compromise meant that there were no further difficulties to the final adoption of the proposal, and can also be classified as a 'bargaining' style of policy-making.

The language employed by the Environment Council confirmed the crucial role of Coreper and the working group.[24] As discussed, the proposal was innovative in its original aims, but the negotiations altered its content. Therefore, the final output was incremental in nature as the monitoring role of the Agency was dropped; this is one possible reason why the proposal was adopted relatively quickly. The Environment Council's style of policy-making in this case-study appears to be that of 'bargaining', as both of the interim decisions were characterized by this approach. Although some member states raised key objections to this proposal, compromises were agreed, which rules out the use of the 'confrontation' label. Moreover, the negotiations did not demonstrate a high level of cooperation, ruling out the use of 'problem-solving'.

### Summary of findings

In this case-study of the work of the Environment Council, examination of the proposal showed that there were large differences in opinion between member states despite the fact that the proposal originated out of the previously-agreed Corine programme and the SEA. Consequently, it was suggested that the negotiations would prove difficult, and that there may be an element of coalition-building between the member states, especially given the innovative nature of the proposal and the unanimity rule. In addition, examination of the 'type' of proposal emphasized that objections by some member states could, in part, have arisen because this proposal was a draft Regulation. However, the proposal was adopted relatively quickly, and may have been due to the possible collective bargaining between the three groups of member states.

Analysis of the actors also suggested that the familiarity of Environment Ministers may have been a factor in the swift adoption of this proposal. Three groups of ministerial actors were identified, according to their attitudes towards environmental policy, and it was suggested that these collective groupings might have been able to influence the negotiations. The Presidency, ESC, and EP appeared to be less significant actors in the discussions on this proposal. In analysing the bargaining advantage of Council actors prior to the selection of action channels, it was suggested that France and Germany may have been able to exercise some negotiating advantage due to their authoritative positions within the EC. In addition,

France held the Presidency during the Council discussions on this proposal. However, it was also suggested that the southern member states may have been able to use their relatively weak economic positions to gain some concessions on this proposal.

Consideration of the action channels used in the negotiations for the creation of a European Environmental Agency showed that Coreper and a working group were crucial to the discussions. They made the most progress on this proposal, although negotiations on this proposal dominated the three formal Council meetings held during this period. The quick adoption of this Regulation suggests that the General Secretariat played an important role. Although outside the negotiations proper, the General Affairs Council and the European Council were also used as action channels as the matter of the location of the Agency was pushed up to these two tiers of the Council's structure.

Analysis of the bargaining advantage within the action channels seemed to confirm the earlier suggestions that France, as a key member state, and holding the Presidency of the Council, was able to exercise the most negotiating strength as the monitoring role for the Agency was dropped. However, the southern member states did not seem able to use economic arguments against the establishment of the Agency, and had to be content with the French victory on a reduced role for the Agency. Whether the southern member states' objections to this helped the French case remains unclear. The most interesting observation was the EP's considerable bargaining advantage, despite only having one reading. It is clear that the EP's input into environmental policy-making is substantial, even when proposals are not subject to the cooperation procedure.

Examination of the two interim decisions and the final output indicated that no non-decisions were used, and that the final output was rather more incremental than the original innovative proposal. This may also have been another reason for the swift adoption of this Regulation. Analysis of the 'speech acts' confirmed the importance of the working group and Coreper as action channels for the negotiations on this proposal. 'Bargaining' appears to be the most appropriate label of the Council's style of policy-making on this occasion.

## Pollution from the titanium dioxide industry

This Directive dealt with the pollution caused by waste from the titanium dioxide industry. It aimed to reduce and eliminate pollution of fresh, estuary, coastal and territorial waters, and the open sea. In addition, the proposal was designed to improve the competitiveness of the titanium dioxide industry by harmonizing the permitted levels of pollution between the member states. The Commission originally submitted this proposal in April 1983.[25] It was not adopted by the Council until June 1989. However, the Council had to re-negotiate the Directive in 1992 after the ECJ ruled that the legal base of the 1989 Directive was invalid. The Council had changed the legal base from Articles 100 and 235 to Article 130S because of the entry into force of the SEA. However, the ECJ ruled that Article 100A takes precedence where a proposal has a dual legal base – environmental action (Article 130S), and a harmonization measure aimed at the operation of the internal market (Article 100A).[26] Consequently, the Commission submitted a new proposal, and the Council finally adopted the Directive in December 1992.[27] This analysis focuses upon the period from 1988 (when the Council altered the legal base) to assess the impact of the ECJ ruling, and ensure that comparisons with other technical councils are still possible.

The proposal for this Directive originated out of an earlier EC Directive on waste from the titanium dioxide industry.[28] Therefore, according to Iklé's classifications, this proposal was redistributive in its objectives. This suggests that negotiations would not prove very difficult. Although the original proposal took six years to adopt, this was not due to difficulties with the actual contents of the proposal. Council negotiations stagnated on this Directive from 1985 as it was clear that changes brought about by the SEA would have an effect on the proposal. It seemed better to wait until after the Treaty revisions before adopting the Directive. Although the proposal dealt with a particular pollution issue (and therefore environmental policy), it also sought to harmonize the rules governing the titanium dioxide industry, and so make the industry more competitive. As stated, this falls under internal market policy-making.

Having considered the nature of the proposal, it is possible that member-state attitudes would differ considerably. The likely responses of member states can be suggested from their overall approaches to environmental, and internal market/industrial policies. As shown in the previous case-study, it is highly likely that Greece, Italy, Portugal and Spain would be the least favourable towards this proposal, whilst Germany, Denmark, and the Benelux states would probably be the most favourable, in accordance with their general policy approach towards environmental legislation. It may also have been the case that the southern member states would be reluctant to agree to this proposal due to the economic costs that their national titanium dioxide industries would have to face. In particular, Spain may have been particularly worried that this proposal would affect its national industrial strategy at that time.

The positions of the other member states are not so clear. France, Ireland, and the UK are not totally opposed to EC environmental legislation. The UK might have objected to the proposal due to the adverse effects this Directive might have on an already declining industrial base. However, Mrs Thatcher suggested a new interest in 'green' issues in late 1988, and agreement on this proposal was one possible way of proving her eco-credentials. The 'greening' of the political agenda might have also swayed France and Ireland in favour of this proposal. Although it appears that some member states were likely to have reservations about this proposal despite their commitment to the internal market, they may have felt less threatened about its effects because it was a Directive, and only redistributive in its objectives.

Environment Ministers discussed this proposal on a number of occasions. They all knew each other well and had roughly equal status but had less input than in the previous case-study. Analysis of the attitudes of member states suggests that there were probably the same three groupings of ministerial actors as in the case of the European Environmental Agency. However, from the evidence available, France, Ireland, and the UK held less reservations about this proposal. Therefore, it may have been the case that the negotiations might have involved two groupings, namely the richer (northern) member states versus the poorer (southern) countries.

In discussion of the original Directive, only one of the three Presidencies played a significant part in the negotiations. The German Presidency made every effort to try to get the Directive adopted during its Presidency. This may have been due to the high priority given to environmental issues by Germany, and that the subsequent two Presidencies (Greece and Spain) tend to be less favourable towards environmental legislation. Germany may have felt that negotiations on this proposal might stall if Greece or Spain were presiding over the Council. The ESC and EP had a role in the negotiations, although this was minimal for the EP until the ECJ ruling.

Analysis of the bargaining advantage of the Council actors before negotiations began requires consideration of their authority and expertise, and their EC budgetary contribution. As discussed, there appeared to be two groupings of ministerial actors. Denmark, France, Germany, Ireland, the UK and the Benelux states appeared to be favourable to the proposal. This group consists of a majority who support environmental action, two key EC actors – France and Germany, and a strong coalition in the Benelux states. Therefore, it may have been that this group could exercise their authority over the more reluctant member states – namely Greece, Italy, Portugal, and Spain. In addition, Germany may have been further able to use its authority in its capacity as President of the Council during the first half of 1988.

As discussed, finance may also have been an issue. Although the proposal would not incur direct costs to the EC as an institution, there would be economic costs for the titanium dioxide industry. Those member states least favourable to the proposal are also the relatively poorer EC members. Greece, Italy, Portugal, and Spain may have tried to use this economic argument to exercise some bargaining advantage over their EC partners (as in the previous case-study). The stronger states may have been willing to make some concessions in return for some sort of package deal on another proposal because they recognized that the chances of non-compliance on the part of the titanium dioxide industry in the poorer member states were high (hence litigation costs for the EC). However, the group of member states who seemed to be favourable to this proposal was fairly strong economically and politically, and generally in favour of environmental legislation. Therefore, the poorer members may not have been able to significantly influence the negotiations. Finally, it may have been the case that the EP could influence the negotiations on this proposal due to its strong commitment to EC environmental legislation, and its skills and technical expertise in this area.

The Environment Council discussed the first proposal at four out of the five formal sessions convened during this period, indicating that there were difficulties with the Directive despite its modest redistributive objectives. An informal meeting was also held during this period, but this issue was not discussed as a common position had already been reached. The Environment Council re-negotiated the Directive at three out of a possible four sessions held between March and December 1992, but simply agreed and adopted the common position and final Directive. This was because Coreper had carried out most of the re-negotiations. Indeed, Coreper and a working group were extremely important Council action channels for the discussion of this proposal. They managed to resolve the key difficulties, namely whether there should be a total ban of solid waste and high acid content waste pollution, between March and November 1988.[29] The importance of the work of the General Secretariat is implicit in the relatively short time that these key problems were solved.

The Environment Council adopted the original Directive by unanimity. After the ECJ ruling, the Council had to use the cooperation procedure. It adopted its common position and the final Directive by qualified majority voting.[30] What is unclear is whether some member states still objected to certain aspects of the proposal, or whether there were no reservations but all member states in the Environment Council thought it best to say that they had used qualified majority voting.

From the available information, both groupings of member states managed to influence the negotiations on this proposal. Those member states in favour of this Directive were led by Germany. As a key actor, and as Council President, Germany exercised a significant bargaining advantage, and although the German Presidency was unable to secure a common position on this proposal during its term of office, it did manage to reach agreement on the procedures for harmonizing pollution controls. The problem of whether pollution from solid waste and high acid content waste should be banned was reached within Coreper. The member states agreed that there should not be a total ban of these types of pollution. This shows that the more reluctant member states (Greece, Italy, Portugal, and Spain) were able to exercise some bargaining advantage, primarily using economic arguments against the proposal.

The EP had previously submitted an opinion in 1983, but this was reconsidered and delivered in May 1989 because the Council had 'modified' the legal base.[31] The EP criticized the legal base of the Directive, although this had no impact upon the Council at this time. Obviously, in the second round of negotiations on this Directive, the EP wanted to make use of its new powers, but actually proposed few alterations.[32] This was because the original Directive had taken into account EP suggestions.[33] From the evidence available, the EP had more effect on the negotiations prior to the ECJ ruling. The ESC did not resubmit its opinion on the first occasion, but welcomed the ECJ ruling in its 1992 opinion.[34]

There were three interim decisions reached within the action channels prior to the ECJ ruling, and three interim decisions afterwards. Agreement on the guidelines for harmonizing pollution controls for the titanium dioxide industry was reached within Coreper, and formally approved at the June 1988 Environment Council. A compromise was reached on this as the 'speech acts' of the March 1988 meeting implied that there were still real problems and Coreper was instructed to continue seeking solutions.[35] This referral to Coreper constitutes a non-decision by the Environment Council, as was the common position adopted in November 1988, which was a compromise that had been reached in meetings of a working group and Coreper. The Environment Council also had to amend the proposal in the light of the EP's opinion, although this made little difference to the content of the Council's negotiated proposal. In all these cases, the interim decision was the result of a compromise on the part of the member states, denoting a 'bargaining' approach to policy-making on this proposal. The three interim decisions after the ECJ ruling were more clear-cut as it was decided to retain the technical provisions of the former Directive. The interim decisions simply adopted a new common position without any real changes; there were no 'real' negotiations.

In examining the final output, the analytical framework suggests consideration of the 'speech acts', the time taken to adopt the proposal, and the nature of the decision. Consideration of the language employed by the Environment Council indicated that progress in the negotiations on this Directive was relatively quick. The final adoption prior to the ECJ ruling was delayed because of the slow delivery of the EP's opinion. 'Speech acts' also confirmed the importance of Coreper and a working group in the negotiations on this proposal.[36] The objectives of the Directive were redistributive which meant that the decision was incremental in nature, particularly because the idea of a complete ban on some pollutants was dropped. Finally, the Environment Council's style of policy-making on this proposal was one of 'bargaining', for essentially the same reasons as in the previous case study.

### Summary of findings

Analysis of the proposal showed that it was redistributive in its objectives, suggesting that discussions would be relatively easy even though there was some policy-overlapping in this proposal. There were differences between the attitudes of member states, and these fell into two broad groupings. Examination of the actors involved in the negotiations indicated that even though the Environment Ministers were familiar with each other, this did not significantly affect the discussions. This may have been because the two coalitions had clear and distinct attitudes towards the proposal. It appeared that the German Presidency was an important actor in the discussions, but the EP and ESC were the least significant of all the actors involved.

Analysis of the bargaining advantage of the Council actors prior to the actual negotiations suggested that the group of member states which were favourable to the proposal may have been able to exercise significant bargaining advantage, particularly given the prominent role of Germany. Due to this authority, the more reluctant member states may not have been so able to influence the discussions. However, this was shown not to be the case (discussed below). As in the previous case study, the Environment Council used a variety of action channels, with Coreper and a working party being the most important. The role of the General Secretariat was also implicit in this case. Both unanimity and qualified majority voting were used as decision methods, although it is unclear from the available information whether consensus was reached before the qualified majority vote was taken.

As discussed, the southern member states were able to exercise some bargaining advantage even though this might have been thought unlikely.

The richer member states accepted their economic arguments against a complete ban on some forms of pollution so that the proposal would at least be agreed in some form (as it was subject to unanimity at this point in the negotiations). The evidence also confirmed earlier suggestions that Germany was able to exercise a significant bargaining advantage, particularly in its role as Council President. The EP appeared to have very little effect upon the negotiations.

Examination of the interim decisions showed that the majority of these were the result of compromises by the member states, even though the proposal was only redistributive in its objectives. Coreper and a working party were responsible for finding the solutions: this was confirmed by analysis of the 'speech acts'. Most of the interim decisions and the final output exemplified a 'bargaining' approach to policy-making by the Environment Council on this proposal. The final output was incremental in nature.

## Conclusions

Although there was more information available for the case of the European Environmental Agency, both cases tested the framework, and provided some useful findings about the operation of the Environment Council.

Examination of the proposal was helpful. Consideration of member-state attitudes and the subject area helped to identify the key actors and the likely outcome of the negotiations in both the case-studies. Although examination of the 'type' of legislation proved that Regulations had a greater effect on discussions, it also showed that Directives do have an impact upon member-state attitudes to the proposal. Classification of the objectives of the proposal provided contrasting evidence as the redistributive Directive proved just as problematic as the innovative Regulation. Investigation of the actors involved also proved inconclusive in terms of ministerial representation and status, but did identify the importance of the Presidency and the EP. This was confirmed by looking at the bargaining advantage. Overall, actors with the greatest bargaining advantage determined the final outcome, and the size of the budgetary contribution was an important influence upon the bargaining advantage.

Consideration of the action channel showed just how important Coreper and the working parties were. Analysis of the decision rules was less helpful. 'Speech acts' confirmed the importance of Coreper and the working parties as action channels of the Council, and gave some indication of the progress made in negotiations. Distinguishing between a fundamental and incremental decision was possible in these two case-studies, but did not tally with the nature of the negotiations. By applying the analytical framework, the label of 'bargaining' seemed most appropriate for the Environment Council's style of policy-making.

The work of the Environment Council is highly influenced by member-state attitudes towards this policy area. Some member states raised objections to both proposals, according to their general line on EC environmental policy-making during this period. Consequently, whether the proposal was innovative or redistributive was partly irrelevant. Both the Regulation on the Environmental Agency and the Directive on pollution from the titanium dioxide industry proved difficult to adopt. It was also insignificant that member states had previously committed themselves to these proposals explicitly or implicitly.

The most crucial finding to emerge is the political importance attached to Regulations. Ministers negotiated more than Coreper on the Regulation, yet the reverse was true for the Directive. Therefore, the type of legislation does have an effect upon the work of the Environment Council. Coreper played an important part in the discussions on the Directive, confirming that its role as a Council action channel is crucial. Budgetary contributions tended to influence the theoretical and actual bargaining advantage of Council actors.

Another important conclusion is that the EP has a significant impact upon the work of the Environment Council even without the cooperation procedure. This confirms observations made earlier about the EP's desire to play a crucial part in environmental policy-making. The Environment Council preferred formal to informal sessions, and the only other tactics were the use of non-decisions when referring discussion to Coreper. However, no conclusions can be made about the decision rules. Finally, the Environment Council's style of policy-making is one of 'bargaining'.

# CHAPTER SEVEN

# *The Labour & Social Affairs Council*

The Labour & Social Affairs Council deals with a wide range of social policy issues. EU social policy has evolved from a number of Treaty provisions concerning worker mobility, training, education, equal opportunities, working conditions and employment rights. However, the lack of a specific legal base resulted in the slow development of EC social policy. In addition, some member states, in particular the UK, were reluctant for the EC to become involved in this area of policy-making, arguing that it should remain a national rather than a supranational concern. Consequently, most EC initiatives in the social field occurred through social action programmes. Legislation only emerged on an *ad hoc* basis and was neither innovative nor radical in nature.

The SEA changed this situation by specifically creating a legal base for greater EC social policy-making. Article 118A decrees that member states should pay particular attention to improving health and safety conditions at work. The important point to note is that this article involves the use of qualified majority voting by the Council and the cooperation procedure. Further pressures for member states to become more involved in the social dimension of the EC occurred as a result of the Social Charter. Signed by all member states (except the UK) in 1989, it provided a blueprint for future EC action. The TEU formalized the essential principles of the Social Charter, excluding the call for an EC minimum wage, in the Social Chapter, attached to the TEU, but now part of EC competences due to the UK Government's opt-in under Tony Blair. EU social policy constitutes an attempt to provide workers with certain rights, and has been slowly but continually enhanced since 1987.

Consequently, the role of the Labour & Social Affairs Council has increased in significance. It is only termed a 'small' council due to the infrequency of sessions. Between 1988 and 1992, the Labour & Social Affairs Council met on average three times per year (see Table 7.1). During the same period, it discussed 68 agenda items, including the two cases examined in this chapter but excluding 'A' points.[1] Given the infrequency of meetings, this was a considerable workload.

The increased attention given to social policy through the adoption of the Social Charter explains the higher number of formal meetings in 1989. From Table 7.1, no definite patterns emerge in relation to informal sessions; the convening of this type of session only appears to be subject to Presidential preference. As discussed in previous chapters, it may be that the status of ministers and their relationships with each other affect the conduct of negotiations. The fact that Labour & Social Affairs Ministers are of equal status could have an effect on policy discussions. Yet they meet infrequently, which means they are less familiar with each others' policy positions and tactics. However, these ministers benefit from the assistance of a working party for social affairs which meets twice a week, for a full day in total. All members of this working party know each other well and they place a high value upon the consensus approach to policy-making.

Having provided some general background information on the Labour & Social Affairs Council, this chapter will now analyse two examples of its work. Analysis will develop points made here, such as whether the input of the working party for social affairs is significant, and if ministerial

| Year | Presidency | Formal | Informal |
|------|------------|--------|----------|
| 1988/1 | Germany | 1 | 1 |
| 1988/2 | Greece | 1 | 0 |
| 1989/1 | Spain | 2 | 0 |
| 1989/2 | France | 3 | 0 |
| 1990/1 | Ireland | 1 | 2 |
| 1990/2 | Italy | 2 | 0 |
| 1991/1 | Luxembourg | 1 | 1 |
| 1991/2 | Netherlands | 2 | 1 |
| 1992/1 | Portugal | 2 | 1 |
| 1992/2 | UK | 1 | 1 |

*Note: /1 refers to the first semester of the year, /2 to the second.
Source: Compiled from Council Press Releases, Council internal documents and *Agence Europe*.

**Table 7.1 Meetings of the Labour & Social Affairs Council 1988–92.**

relationships are generally constructive despite the infrequency of Labour & Social Affairs Council meetings. The cases chosen for analysis are Directives on the health and safety of atypical workers, and the protection of workers exposed to carcinogens. In choosing these cases, it was felt that Directives required analysis as they are the most common forms of social policy legislation. In addition, both these cases reflect developments since the SEA, as they were subject to the cooperation procedure. The impact of this procedure needs investigating due to the implications this may have on the future of the Council (see Chapter 10 for further discussion of this). However, the two Directives offer some contrasting features. The Directive on atypical workers was part of the Social Action Programme, whereas the proposal for the protection of workers against carcinogens was part of a framework Directive on health and safety in the workplace. In addition, the Carcinogens Directive proved more difficult for the Labour & Social Affairs Council to adopt.

## The health and safety at work of atypical workers

This Directive aimed to improve the health and safety conditions for workers with a temporary or fixed-duration contract (atypical workers). Existing EC legislation on the health and safety of workers only covered workers in full-time permanent work. Yet there had been a significant increase in atypical employment across the EC; by the late 1980s part-time employment in the EC stood at approximately 14 million, with temporary contracted workers totalling 10 million. The fact that the Council had failed to adopt specific legislation for atypical workers in the early 1980s increased the momentum for this proposal. The Commission submitted the proposal on 29 June 1990, and it was adopted by the Labour & Social Affairs Council one year later.[2] The legislation came into force at the start of 1993.

The analytical framework suggests that the subject area, objectives, and the origin of the proposal may provide useful insights, as well as the 'type' of the proposal and member-state attitudes. The Directive on atypical workers not only related to general social policy objectives enshrined in the Social Action Programme, but linked with the completion of the internal market, as without comparable rights for part-time and temporary workers the free movement of people would be restricted. Therefore, it is possible to suggest that a certain political will by member states for EC action in this area already existed. National legislation in Belgium, Denmark, France and The Netherlands stipulates that atypical workers must be treated similarly to permanent workers. Belgium and Denmark have particularly high standards in this area. Therefore, it is possible that the proposal posed no difficulties for these member states. Italy may also have been favourable to this Directive as social rights are enshrined in the Italian Constitution. Although regional economic disparities have affected the fulfilment of such rights, it is possible to suggest that Italy would still have been willing to agree to this piece of EC legislation. Portugal may not have had difficulties with this proposal given that it had tried to reverse its national legislation to align itself with the rest of the EC countries in 1989 (Brewin and McAllister, 1989: 352). However, the UK appeared less favourable to this proposal because of its general approach to EC social policy-making. The UK had refused to sign the 1989 Social Charter, making it clear that social legislation was a suitable area for the operation of subsidiarity, and with hindsight this position has been maintained. From the above, the proposal can be termed as innovative in its objectives (according to Iklé's classifications), and may have proved difficult for the Labour & Social Affairs Council to adopt. The treaty procedure may have compounded this as it had to be adopted in accordance with Article 118A (the cooperation procedure – second reading for the EP and the use of qualified majority voting). The proposal took the form of a Directive, which meant that implementation would be left to member states.

The Labour & Social Affairs Council meets infrequently. Therefore, Social Affairs Ministers may be less familiar with each other, which could affect the negotiations. The fact that the proposal was adopted fairly quickly suggests that this relative unfamiliarity did not hinder the negotiating process. From the examination of likely member-state attitudes towards this proposal, it appeared that most member states were favourable to this proposal as it tended to complement their own national polices. However, the proposal seemed to clash with the UK's overall approach to social legislation, both at the national and EC level. Therefore, it is possible to suggest that the UK might find itself in a difficult negotiating position given the apparent consensus of the other member states on this proposal.

Both the Italian and Luxembourg Presidencies seemed to play an important role in the adoption of this Directive. The Italian Presidency was keen to see that a common position was adopted at the December 1990 meeting, while Luxembourg pushed for final adoption despite a lack of consensus between member states.[3] Both the ESC and the EP were involved, with the EP having a second reading on the proposal, due to the treaty procedure (Article 118A).

The framework suggests that the authority and expertise of Council actors, and the budgetary contribution are considered when analysing the bargaining advantage prior to the negotiations. As discussed, Belgium, Denmark,

France, Italy, The Netherlands, and Portugal seemed to be the most favourable to this proposal. Considering that France is a strong EC actor, this grouping may have been able to influence the negotiations. Furthermore, Italy was Council President for part of the time, and may have been able to use its Presidency to secure agreement on this Directive. Luxembourg held the Presidency for the latter half of the negotiations and may have used its acknowledged skills and expertise as President to finalize agreement. It is not clear whether Luxembourg favoured this proposal, but given that the Council President, Juncker, voiced his discontent at the way some member states only accept proposals that conform to their own national laws, and called for a more harmonious European approach to social legislation, it is likely that Luxembourg did want this Directive to be adopted.[4]

Finance may also have influenced the bargaining advantage, but in terms of the indirect costs to firms rather than the size of member states' contributions to the EC budget. The Directive may have incurred costs to those firms and industries which did not already give atypical workers equal rights to those of permanent staff. It may have also been the case that the economic performance of some member states might suffer as a result of firms unable to finance this additional expenditure. The UK may have used this argument, given that the effects of the recession were beginning to be felt at the time of the negotiations. Moreover, the other member states may have listened sympathetically to this argument as the 1990s recession hit them later. However, the UK may not have been able to use the economic argument to its advantage because other member states were well aware of its generally hostile view towards EC social policy-making.

All three formal sessions held during this period discussed the Directive on atypical workers. This suggests that this proposal was a priority for the Labour & Social Affairs Council despite the infrequency of meetings. The proposal may also have been discussed at the informal session held on 6 May 1991, although no reports exist about this informal meeting. Although the Council discussed this proposal at two sessions in 1990, the November meeting was only a 'general discussion'.[5] The proposal was then only discussed once more (in June 1991). Between December 1990 and June 1991, the Council had received the EP's second reading which proposed a number of amendments. From this evidence, it is possible that the working party on social affairs was important in facilitating agreement. This also implies that the General Secretariat had a significant input in the discussions, but this cannot be confirmed.

As discussed, the proposal was based on Article 118A which stipulates the use of Article 189C − in other words the cooperation procedure and qualified majority voting for the Council. This may have had an impact upon the negotiations, as the EP may have been able to influence the nature of the proposal on second reading. The common position was adopted unanimously but no definite evidence exists as to whether the final Directive was adopted by qualified majority. However, the Luxembourg Presidency's reaction to the meeting (shown above) suggests that qualified majority voting was used.

It appears that the UK influenced the outcome of discussions of the atypical workers Directive (confirming earlier suggestions). The UK proposed a compromise so that a common position could be adopted unanimously in December 1990.[6] This was particularly interesting as the common position could have been adopted by qualified majority voting. Therefore, the UK either influenced the negotiations through its economic arguments, or agreed to compromise on another proposal under discussion in the Council. The latter is more likely, as the other member states knew the UK's firm policy line on social legislation.

The Italian Presidency did not influence the negotiations as, although a common position was reached, this was the result of a compromise put forward by the UK. It may have been the case that the Italian Presidency convinced the other member states which favoured the proposal to accept the UK compromise so that the proposal would not be lost. Some reports suggest that Italy's eagerness to get the Directive through was a result of national discrepancies in its own national employment law, which implies that Italy was using the Council Presidency for domestic purposes.[7] The common position could have been adopted by qualified majority vote. Therefore, other member states accepted the UK compromise in return for a UK concession on another EC policy proposal. The Luxembourg Presidency managed to secure the final adoption of the Directive on atypical workers, but appeared to have to resort to qualified majority voting. This suggests that there were still reservations about the proposal, with the UK being the most likely candidate for reasons discussed above.

The EP had a significant effect upon this proposal as the Labour & Social Affairs Council had to amend its common position due to the EP's second reading before it could finally adopt the Directive. In particular, the EP insisted that atypical workers in areas where there was a medical risk (such as the chemical industry) would have to be given medical check-ups beyond the end of the working contract.[8] However, the ESC did not seem to exercise similar influence as it appeared that little notice was taken of its opinion.[9]

There were two interim decisions on this proposal. The general discussion of November 1990 was a non-decision in the sense that no overall agreement was sought, yet negotiations were at an early stage at this point. The second interim decision was the adoption of the common position in December

1990, and was the result of a compromise proposal submitted by the UK. This agreement was reached relatively quickly given the infrequency of meetings of the Labour & Social Affairs Council, and 'bargaining' is the most appropriate label for this interim decision.

Consideration of the 'speech acts' of the Labour & Social Affairs Council suggests that steady progress was made in the negotiations on this proposal, from a 'general discussion' in November 1990, to the agreement of a common position later in December, to the final adoption in June 1991.[10] However, due to the relative infrequency of meetings, analysis of the language employed is not as helpful as in previous chapters. The Directive on atypical workers was both incremental and fundamental in nature; it required some member states to adjust existing national legislation, but others to introduce new measures. Consequently, 'bargaining' is the most appropriate label for the style of the Labour & Social Affairs policy-making. Most member states seemed to agree upon the objectives of the atypical workers Directive, and although the UK appeared to have general reservations, it did not see the negotiating process as a 'zero-sum' game, which rules out the use of the 'confrontation' label. It could be argued that the very fact that the UK cooperated in the negotiations meant that the Labour & Social Affairs Council adopted a 'problem solving' approach. However, this label denotes a high level of cooperation, which seemed not to be the case in these negotiations. Moreover, it is likely that the UK still had reservations when it came to the final adoption of the proposal, judging by the Luxembourg Minister's comments.

### Summary of findings

Analysis of the work of the Labour & Social Affairs Council on the atypical workers Directive showed that a certain amount of political will already existed. The Directive stemmed from the Social Action Programme and was related to the internal market; member states had previously committed themselves to both. Member states were generally favourable to this proposal, with the exception of the UK. The fact that the UK did agree to the proposal might have been due to the legislative 'type' of the proposal. Analysis of the actors involved substantiated these initial observations. The status of ministers and the infrequency of Labour & Social Affairs Councils had little effect upon the negotiations.

In terms of the bargaining advantage prior to the negotiations, it appeared that the UK might be able to influence the discussions. From the evidence this was the case, as the UK obtained concessions by proposing a compromise. However, it may have been the case that the other member states gained UK concessions on another proposal somewhere else within the Council. Italy used its Presidency to pursue domestic policy objectives, but managed to get the common position adopted (with the help of the UK). Finally, analysis confirmed the heightened role and impact of the EP as a result of the cooperation procedure.

Due to the 'small' nature of the Labour & Social Affairs Council, consideration of the action channel proved less helpful. On the one hand, qualified majority voting was only used when consensus could not be reached, yet the choice of sessions was less significant due to the infrequency of meetings. This also meant that analysis of 'speech acts' and non-decisions were not very helpful. The findings of this case-study suggest that the Labour & Social Affairs Council adopted a 'bargaining' approach. The working group on social affairs was a crucial Council action channel, implying in turn that the General Secretariat had an important input in reaching a final agreement.

### The protection of workers exposed to carcinogens

The Directive on the protection of workers exposed to carcinogens at work aimed to make employers use non-carcinogenic substances. However, the Directive recognized that this might not always be possible, and therefore included proposals to ensure that the appropriate safety measures were taken.[11] The Directive was part of the overall Framework Directive on health and safety of workers at the workplace adopted by member states in June 1989, but each proposal within the Framework Directive was discussed separately by the Labour & Social Affairs Council. The Commission formally submitted the proposal on the protection of workers from carcinogens on 27 December 1987.[12] The Council finally adopted the Directive on 28 June 1990 as an 'A' point on the Telecommunication Council's agenda, and it was to be implemented from the beginning of 1993.[13]

The carcinogens Directive was part of an overall framework Directive. Although the Commission proposed the Directive, it originated from a previous Council agreement. The EC recognized that the completion of the internal market could result in some deregulation of health and safety legislation, and there was concern that excessive employment mobility might mean that employers could more easily ignore safety standards. In addition, there were large discrepancies in the level of standards between member states. This Directive had a particular objective, namely protection from carcinogens, and also overlapped with the EC's campaign against cancer adopted in 1987.[14] However, the large differences in national standards suggest that negotiations on this proposal would prove difficult, compounded by the fact that it was 'innovative' in its objectives. Even though member states had agreed in principle to the Framework Directive, the same political will was not evident in the case of this proposal; it took just under three years to adopt.

Examination of the actual negotiations on this proposal provides no precise evidence of which member states raised the most objections to it. However, from details given in the previous study, it is possible to suggest that the UK would have the most difficulty with this proposal due to its general stance on EC social policy-making. The fact that the Social Charter was drafted and agreed during this period may have caused the UK to be even more negative. In contrast, Belgium, Denmark and Portugal may have been pushing for a high standard of protection against carcinogens due to their own levels of national legislation in this area. This may have been made easier by the decision-making procedure. The Directive was proposed according to Article 118A. Consequently the Council had to employ the cooperation procedure, and could take its decision by qualified majority voting. It has been suggested that this type of legislation, namely a Directive, is less threatening to member states as details of implementation are not prescribed. However, this may not have been enough to allay UK fears considering the time taken to adopt this proposal.

The analytical framework suggests that identifying the actors may provide insights into their possible bargaining advantage, and thus the nature of the negotiations. As discussed, Labour & Social Affairs Ministers meet infrequently, and therefore may not be so familiar with each other's policy approach and negotiating tactics. This unfamiliarity may have had an effect upon the carcinogens Directive considering that negotiations were rather lengthy. In addition, there was a change of government in France (1988) and Greece (1990), and a subsequent switch of personnel which may have had an impact upon the negotiations. From the examination of member-state attitudes, it appears that only the UK would be pursuing different objectives from the other member states because of its overall attitude to EC social legislation.

The proposal was discussed during five Presidencies (Germany, Greece, Spain, France and Ireland). It may have been the case that these member states would be able to influence the negotiations, especially given that Germany and France are key EC actors. It was also the case that all these member states appeared to be generally in favour of the proposal. As stated, however, France had just experienced a change of government which may have meant that the minister was not so well-briefed on the likely difficulties of this proposal. The ESC was consulted, but the EP may have been able to play a more important role as this proposal was subject to the cooperation procedure.

Most member states had little difficulty with this proposal, except for the UK. As in the previous case-study, it may have been that the UK would be unable to influence the negotiations because it appeared to be the only objector. Furthermore, the proposal could be adopted by qualified majority voting. It may also have been the case that those member states holding the Presidency would be able to use their terms of office to their advantage, given that they all seemed to be in favour of the proposal. In particular, the German and French Council Presidents may have been the most influential due to their authority as key actors within the EC. As in the previous case study, finance may have affected the bargaining advantage of Council actors as the Directive may have incurred indirect economic consequences on those member states whose industries had to improve their safety standards. Again, the UK may have tried to use this argument to influence the other member states.

The Labour & Social Affairs Council discussed the carcinogens Directive at six out of the eight formal sessions during this period (it was not on the agenda of the two meetings convened by the Spanish Presidency). Three informal sessions were held during this period, yet there is no evidence to suggest that they were used to facilitate non-decisions. However, Coreper was the most important action channel. Despite the apparent difficulty in reaching agreement, the carcinogens Directive was finally adopted as an 'A' point, which demonstrates that there was consensus to adopt the proposal as soon as possible because negotiations had already been so prolonged. However, the final Labour & Social Affairs Council in May 1990 only 'discussed' the proposal. Therefore, there were still problems even at this late stage, and Coreper was pivotal in solving these difficulties. It is also probable that the General Secretariat assisted in the discussions, and provided some continuity over this lengthy period.

The proposal was subject to qualified majority voting and the cooperation procedure. The EP was able to alter the proposal through its second reading. Whether the Labour & Social Affairs Council adopted the common position by qualified majority vote is hard to assess. There is no evidence either way; the Council Press Release states that the Council 'approved' the common position. From discussion of the session type, it is probable that the 'A' point was simply adopted on the nod as Coreper had resolved the outstanding issues. Therefore, qualified majority voting appears not to have been used by the Labour & Social Affairs Council in relation to this Directive.

There is little evidence to suggest that any member state was able to influence the negotiations on this proposal within the formal Council. There are no details on the precise discussions because the majority of these took place within Coreper. It may have been the case that the UK was able to secure some concessions on this proposal as the other member states may have wanted to ensure that the proposal was adopted in some form. However, the aims of the original proposal were secured, suggesting that the UK's influence on the final output was slight.

None of the five Presidencies appeared to influence the negotiations on this proposal within the formal Council. The French Presidency did postpone discussion by one month in October 1989, and it is interesting that the November meeting adopted the common position. However, this was due to the preparatory work of Coreper rather than a deliberate ploy by the French Presidency that a postponement of discussions would induce agreement as the October 1989 session was dominated by discussions on the Social Charter.[15] The Spanish Presidency chose not to discuss the issue at all, but this was probably due to the lack of progress and the fact that the Labour & Social Affairs Council had to wait for the EP's and ESC's opinions. Those member states holding the Presidency may have had an influence within Coreper discussions, but again there is no available information to substantiate this.

The ESC also had little effect upon the proposal as although it argued that the Directive did not go far enough, this view was ignored by the member states.[16] By contrast, the EP influenced the negotiations. It delayed its first reading until May 1989 as it felt that the formal Council meetings had not given due consideration to the proposal.[17] The EP's second reading (of 16 May 1990) proposed 28 amendments to the Council's common position, which were nearly all accepted, except for the suggestion that young people and pregnant workers should not be exposed to carcinogens.[18]

There were four interim decisions on this proposal. Three of these were non-decisions as the discussion of the Directive was simply referred back to Coreper (at the June and December meetings of 1988, and the May 1990 session). The other interim decision was the approval of the common position in October 1989, but this had been drafted and agreed by Coreper, and therefore it is not possible to classify the policy style of the Council for this interim decision.

A number of speech acts have already been mentioned which provided useful insights into the progress on this proposal. The language employed by the Council showed that progress was slow. For example, the Council held a 'debate' in June 1988, 'an exchange of views' in December 1988, and a 'discussion' in May 1990.[19] The most important insight into this slow progress stems from statements of the Council's intention to adopt the common position at the next meeting. No such agreement came, despite such statements at each session prior to the meetings held in December 1988, April 1989 (as the Spanish Presidency did not put the proposal on the agenda), October 1990, and December 1990. 'Speech acts' also indicated that Coreper carried out most of the work on this proposal.[20]

As in the previous case-study, the Directive was both incremental and fundamental in nature, as some member states would have to adjust existing national legislation, but others would have to introduce new measures. The Labour & Social Affairs Council seemed to adopt a 'bargaining' approach in negotiations on this Directive. Most member states agreed on the objectives of the proposal, exemplified by earlier agreement to complete the internal market, and the adoption of the Framework Directive and the EC programme against cancer. No-one viewed the process as a zero-sum game, which excluded the 'confrontation' label. 'Problem-solving' can also be ruled out as a suitable label, as there were differences over the means to achieve the protection of workers from carcinogens. This is partly proved by the fact that agreement on the proposal took so long. However, the lack of information about Coreper discussions means that it is not possible to analyse the extent of these differences. Therefore, characterizing the policy style of the Labour & Social Affairs Council as that of 'bargaining' is not definitive.

### Summary of findings

Analysis of the proposal showed that the carcinogens Directive was innovative in its objectives, but related to a number of programmes already agreed by member states. Despite this apparent political will, there appeared to be differences between the UK and the other member states over this proposal. Examination of the actors suggested that the unfamiliarity of ministers may have had an effect because the negotiations were relatively slow. The EP seemed to play an important role due to the cooperation procedure, but the Presidency and the ESC had little input in the negotiations. Analysis of the bargaining advantage prior to the negotiations suggested that the UK might be able to gain some concessions. However, the majority of the negotiations were carried out by Coreper, and so there is no available information to confirm or refute this. It may have been that Coreper was used so much because of the infrequency of Labour & Social Affairs Council meetings.

It appeared that qualified majority voting was not used, which tends to confirm that this Directive was politically sensitive; this also reinforces the earlier assertion that member states prefer not to use qualified majority voting. Examination of the language used by the Labour & Social Affairs

Council was more helpful than in the previous case-study. The negotiations on the carcinogens Directive were much longer, with slower progress. Examination of the speech acts confirmed this and suggested that Coreper was the most crucial actor. Finally, the Labour & Social Affairs Council appeared to adopt a 'bargaining' approach in its work on this case-study, but this cannot be entirely proved due to the lack of information about the work of Coreper.

## Assessing the work of the Labour & Social Affairs Council

This analysis of two cases of the work of the Labour & Social Affairs Council provided some insights into the character of this technical council, and examination of most of the variables suggested by the analytical framework proved very helpful. Consideration of the proposal indicated whether the decision-making process would prove difficult or not in both case-studies. Although member states had already shown their political will to adopt both Directives through agreement on previous programmes, further analysis of member-state attitudes showed that both proposals would prove problematic. However, examination of the proposal did not help to distinguish between the level of difficulty of these two Directives. This was only achieved by looking at the time taken to adopt the proposal. Analysis of the origin of each proposal and their 'types' did not provide any useful insights.

Identification of the actors produced mixed evidence, as the unfamiliarity of ministers did affect negotiations on the carcinogens Directive, but was not a factor in the other case-study. The EP played an important part in the work of the Labour & Social Affairs Council due to the cooperation procedure. By contrast, neither the Presidency nor the ESC had a significant input. Analysis of the actors and their likely positions on the two proposals enabled suggestions to be made about their potential bargaining advantage prior to the negotiations. However, Coreper and the working group carried out most of the discussions, which made analysis of the bargaining advantage difficult. The EP was able to alter some of the content of the two Directives. Examination of the budgetary contribution indicated very little, as neither of these two Directives involved direct EC financing. There may have been indirect costs to member states if they had to alter their national legislation, but this could not be confirmed due to the lack of information.

Analysis of the action channel provided contrasting evidence. Consideration of the types of session used was helpful in the case of the more difficult carcinogens Directive. However, examination of the decision rule suggested that qualified majority voting is only used as a last resort. Finally, an assessment of the outcome of the negotiations did provide insights into the character of the Labour & Social Affairs Council, but was restricted by the amount of information available. Speech acts were again useful to analyse in the case of the more problematic carcinogens Directive, as they helped to identify the likely key actors and the nature of the negotiations.

In relation to the character of the Labour & Social Affairs Council, the nature of the proposal seems to have a direct effect upon the conduct of negotiations within this technical council. Member state attitudes at the time of each proposal appeared crucial to the policy-making process, even if previous commitments had been made. Coreper and the social affairs working group were important action channels in the negotiations on the two Directives. This is most likely to be due to the infrequency of Labour & Social Affairs Council meetings, and therefore it is probable that the General Secretariat is also significant in this respect. The EP was able to exert considerable influence on the work of the Labour & Social Affairs Council, due to Article 118A being the legal base for most EC social policy-making. The Presidency and ESC were of little importance.

There is limited evidence about the preferred action channels of the Labour & Social Affairs Council due to the infrequency of meetings. However, informal sessions were not used to facilitate agreement, nor were the tactics of restricted or prolonged formal meetings. The most important conclusion is that the Labour & Social Affairs Council avoids using qualified majority voting. The Labour & Social Affairs Council adopts a 'bargaining' approach in its work, but this final conclusion is not definitive due to the lack of information, particularly on the work of Coreper.

# CHAPTER EIGHT

## *Council activity in the sphere of education*

In contrast to the work of other councils examined, the Treaty of Rome makes no specific mention of education policy. It has developed due to the requirements of the internal market, as without some educational legislation the free movement of people and the freedom to provide services would be restricted. The EU has recognized this and aims to promote such freedoms through, for example, educational equal opportunities, the mutual recognition of qualifications, the improvement of vocational education, and the promotion of foreign language teaching and learning. The Stuttgart Declaration of 1983 gave education policy a fresh impetus since 'educational initiatives were presented as complementing Community action' (de Witte, 1989: 15). Yet it was clear that any educational programmes would have to relate to overall EC policy objectives. The SEA made no mention of education, despite references in the 1984 DTEU. Nevertheless, the EC was successful in introducing and funding a number of education programmes during the period in question, which partly ensure free movement within the EC.

Education policy is primarily intergovernmental. The Education Council convenes under the title 'meeting of the Council and the Ministers for Education meeting within the Council'. The Education Council often issues Decisions or Resolutions, but these do not have the same status as other Community legislation. Decisions are obligatory but constitute an inter-governmental rather than a supranational act; Resolutions are also intergovernmental, and non-obligatory. Until the TEU, education policy was 'brought under Community competence in a distorted way: education in this context is considered purely as a means to an economic end, and attention is focused on higher education to the exclusion of other phases'.[1]

However, the TEU makes more specific reference to education and includes an article on education that allows for some decisions to be adopted by qualified majority voting. Those working in the field of education policy welcomed this. Nevertheless, the EU cannot affect individual national education policies, due to the principle of subsidiarity.

The Education Council is also a 'small' council, precisely because of the restricted competence of the EU in education policy and the infrequency of sessions. During the period 1988–92, it met formally only once or twice per Presidency. There are far fewer issues to discuss and legislate upon – 39 main agenda items, excluding 'A' points, between 1988 and 1992 (see Table 8.1).[2] There was no formal Education Council during the Luxembourg Presidency of 1991 as little needed to be discussed. Luxembourg considered that it was not necessary to schedule a session just for the sake of doing so, although it did decide that it might be politically astute to meet informally. Portugal held an informal session jointly with the Youth Council in 1992, primarily to discuss the progress made in the Youth for Europe programme. The number of Education sessions remains low despite the TEU provisions. However, education is becoming more of an issue within other councils, such as the recognition of diplomas (which comes under the remit of the Internal Market Council), health education (which cuts across the competence of both the Education and Health Councils), and environmental education.

The Presidency often influences the number of Education Council meetings, particularly in the case of larger member states, as they are the largest budget contributors. Education programmes involve a big financial

| Year | Presidency | Formal | Informal |
|------|-----------|--------|----------|
| 1988/1 | Germany | 1 | 1 |
| 1988/2 | Greece | 1 | 0 |
| 1989/1 | Spain | 1 | 0 |
| 1989/2 | France | 2 | 0 |
| 1990/1 | Ireland | 1 | 0 |
| 1990/2 | Italy | 1 | 0 |
| 1991/1 | Luxembourg | 0 | 1 |
| 1991/2 | Netherlands | 1 | 0 |
| 1992/1 | Portugal | 1 | 1 |
| 1992/2 | UK | 1 | 0 |

*Note: /1 refers to the first semester of the year, /2 to the second.
Source: Compiled from Council Press Releases, Council internal documents and *Agence Europe*.

**Table 8.1 Meetings of the Education Council 1988–92.**

commitment, and thus larger member states want to be in control. A good example of this is the convening of two Education Councils during the French Presidency in 1989, which adopted the Jean Monnet Project.[3] The 1988 German Presidency delayed negotiations on the Youth for Europe I programme so that it could take the credit for finally adopting this scheme.

It is also possible to make some initial observations about the role and input of the other key institutions in education policy. The limited scope of EC educational initiatives restricts the Commission's power in education policy-making. It manages the various education programmes but has little scope for drafting proposals. However, as in the case of all Council committees, the Commission works with the Council in the Education Committee. According to a number of Council officials, Council–Commission relations have benefited greatly from this high level of working contact in the committee. The EP has certain powers over education policy because of its dual budgetary control. This is crucial for programmes such as Erasmus where success is partly dependent upon the EP allocating sufficient funding.

The representation at Education Councils varies considerably. The Belgian structure of government means that Ministers of the Regions or Communities attend Education Councils, as opposed to federal ministers. In the German case, the Minister will arrive at Education Councils with a pre-bargained position. The German Länder governments deal with education policy, and therefore negotiate with the Federal minister prior to Council meetings. However, several member states do not always send their leading national ministers, which according to one senior Council official epitomizes the lack of political interest in EC education policy, particularly given that the Education Council only tends to meet once per Presidency. This difference in representation can cause difficulties for the work of the Education Council, as deputies may not have the skill and expertise of their ministers. However, it is also the case that education is quite a different issue in Germany and Belgium, where education policy is devised and implemented at the regional level. Another issue is the unfamiliarity of Education Ministers with each other due to the infrequency of Education Council meetings, which could affect the operation of the Education Council, as ministers may be less aware of each other's policy positions and negotiating tactics.

It is already clear that the character of the Education Council differs from that of other technical councils. Yet it is necessary to specify these characteristics: it is insufficient to state that the Education Council is primarily intergovernmental. Although most legislative outputs occur within an intergovernmental framework, further detail is needed about the actual operation of the Education Council. The rest of this chapter examines two cases of the work of the Education Council, by applying the analytical framework set out in Figure 4.1. The two cases provide contrasting examples of the Education Council's outputs. This chapter analyses the Decision on the Lingua programme, and the Resolution on the Education Information Network in the EC (Eurydice). Both were taken within an intergovernmental framework, yet Lingua is binding upon member states, whereas Eurydice is not. Lingua is a good example of a large EC educational project in contrast to Eurydice, which had limited objectives.

## The Lingua programme

The proposal to establish the Lingua programme aimed to promote foreign-language learning throughout the EC. Exchange programmes would be set up between language-teaching establishments, and the EC would finance participants to visit partner institutions for a minimum of two weeks. Both young people and language teachers would be able to take part in the scheme.

Through these exchange programmes, it was hoped that there would be both a quantitative and qualitative improvement in foreign language communication skills across the EC. The Lingua proposal placed particular emphasis upon the least-taught EC languages such as Dutch and Flemish, which were termed 'minority' languages (but this term should not be confused with languages such as Welsh, Basque, and Catalan). Although educational establishments would be the main focus of attention, the proposal was also designed to encourage employers to promote foreign language training. However, it is important to note that Lingua only aimed to support and complement member-state policies and schemes.[4] The Education Council received the Commission's proposal in January 1989, and adopted the Decision four months later in May 1989.[5]

In considering the proposal, the first point to make is that the Lingua proposal stemmed from an earlier Resolution on the 'European Dimension in Education', adopted by the Education Council in May 1988. Through this Resolution, member states agreed that the EC should deepen its involvement in education policy. Therefore, it seemed that there was a greater political will for the EC to become further involved in educational policies when the Lingua proposal was discussed. However, some member states had been concerned that the 1988 Resolution was not sufficiently binding to enable education programmes such as Lingua to be agreed. Portugal, Spain, Italy, and The Netherlands had all expressed reservations of this kind which suggests that these member states were keen to adopt Lingua.[6] This may have been because they wanted greater EC involvement in education policy, but it may have been the case that they supported the

Lingua programme simply because it promoted their national languages. It is possible that Belgium would also have supported this proposal due to the strong linguistic cleavage in the Belgium party system, and that Ireland and Greece may have liked to have seen the promotion of their 'minority' languages in the EC.

Germany and the UK were less favourable to the Lingua proposal. This was because German and English are widely taught and they saw no benefit from agreeing to the Lingua programme. It was also the case that these member states felt that Lingua might encroach upon their own national sovereignty in education policy-making. This is a familiar, and somewhat expected, policy line of the UK. Education in Germany is a specific responsibility of the Länder, and therefore the Federal Minister has to agree policy positions with the Länder prior to Council negotiations. Germany's reservations may have resulted from domestic confrontation with the Länder over educational responsibilities resulting from the Lingua programme. It is also possible that France was less favourable to the proposal because the French language was already widely taught.

The Lingua proposal was 'innovative' (according to Iklé's classifications) as no EC foreign language exchange programme previously existed. However, this did not necessarily mean that negotiations would be difficult as member states had agreed to an earlier Resolution calling for such programmes as Lingua. Therefore, although the Commission formally submitted the proposal, its origins lay in previous Education Council agreements. The Lingua proposal also linked to the internal market programme, as the promotion of foreign language learning could help to liberalize the movement of people within the EC. Indeed, the Treaty procedure required for the Lingua proposal made specific reference to this. Article 235 allows the Council to adopt proposals unanimously if the smooth operation of the internal market requires additional action. The Lingua proposal was only subject to the consultation procedure, and the final outcome would be a Decision: in other words, an intergovernmental act by the Education Council but binding upon member states. This fact may have allayed the fears of those member states who were less favourable to the proposal, as agreement to participate in the Lingua programme would have to be unanimous.

The Lingua proposal involved fewer actors, compared with case studies examined in previous chapters. As stated in the introduction to this chapter Education Ministers tend to be less familiar with each other than, for example, EcoFin Ministers. This could affect the negotiating process, but this seemed not to be the case in the Lingua proposal. This might have been simply because the proposal was only discussed at one meeting of the Council, but the fact that this meeting resolved all the problematic issues suggests that the Education Ministers were able to work together and resolve their difficulties.

Spain held the Council Presidency during negotiations on this proposal. As discussed, it appeared that Spain was favourable towards the Lingua programme, and therefore it is possible that Spain would use the opportunity of being President of the Council to try to secure an agreement. This is confirmed by several reports which stated that the Spanish Presidency 'steamrollered it [the Lingua proposal] through the Council'. It could be argued that the European Council had been indirectly involved through conclusions on EC educational initiatives adopted at meetings prior to the Lingua proposal. However, it had no direct effect upon the negotiations. Both the ESC and the EP had to be consulted by the Council, in accordance with Article 235. The ESC delivered its opinion in March 1989, and this was generally positive.[7] The EP proposed four main amendments in its opinion, submitted in April 1989.[8] The Commission, having submitted the original proposal, was only of further significance through its work on the Education Committee (for which no precise details are known).

The framework suggests that the authority and expertise of the Council actors should be examined when analysing their bargaining advantage prior to the selection of action channels. As discussed, it appeared that Germany, France, and the UK were least favourable to this proposal. These three member states tend to command a good deal of authority within the EC, and therefore may have been able to use their positions to their own advantage in the negotiations. The member states who seemed to want to adopt the proposal have less authority in this respect. However, it is important to note that Spain held the Council Presidency. Spain was in favour of the Lingua proposal and may have been able to use its Presidency to influence the negotiations. Moreover, it may have been the case that Spain wanted to finish its first term of office as President on a positive note, by succeeding in reaching agreement on the Lingua proposal. It was also the case that elections were held in Spain at both national and European levels in 1989. Spain may have used these electoral pressures as a bargaining tool within the Education Council to secure agreement on the proposal.

The budgetary contribution was also a factor that influenced the bargaining advantage of Council actors. As shown, EC educational programmes do incur relatively large financial commitments on the part of member states. It may have been the case that those member states who appeared least favourable to the proposal (Germany, France, and the UK) were able to influence the negotiations because they are the largest contributors to the EC budget. It is interesting that the majority of member states who appeared to support the Lingua proposal are the relatively poorer countries. This may have undermined any bargaining advantage they might have had in the negotiations. There is no evidence to suggest that the EP or the ESC had any bargaining advantage in the negotiations. As discussed, this proposal was subject to the consultation procedure, which suggests that their influence would be minimal.

In examining the action channel, it is important to remember that the Education Council only meets twice per calendar year, and that informal sessions are uncommon. The Lingua proposal was discussed at one formal meeting of the Education Council in May 1989. There had been an exchange of views at the May 1988 meeting, but this was prior to the drafting of the proposal. It is significant, however, that the Lingua proposal was the only item on the agenda at the May 1989 session. Comparing the ratio of agenda items against the frequency of meetings for other technical councils, this tends to demonstrate the significance and importance of the Lingua programme. In addition, discussions lasted into the evening.

However, most of the important preparatory work had already been carried out by the Council's Education Committee, which had considered the proposal with the Commission since the adoption of the May 1988 Resolution.[9] Therefore, it appeared that the Education Committee was an important action channel, although the final compromise was reached by the ministers within the formal Council. It is likely that the progress made by the Education Committee and the Spanish Presidency on the Lingua proposal was partly due to the expertise and input of the General Secretariat, particularly because the Spanish Presidency had no previous experience of policy-making in the Council.

Analysis of the bargaining advantage of the Council actors in the negotiations tends to confirm earlier suggestions. The Spanish Presidency was responsible for the two key compromises on this proposal. Firstly, the Lingua Decision was originally two proposals but was merged into one proposal on the suggestion of the Spanish Presidency because the UK objected to the idea of teaching languages at primary-school level.[10] Secondly, the Spanish Presidency was also responsible for a compromise that Lingua grants would only be given to those between 16 and 25 years of age. The UK and Germany were worried that without a specific target group, Lingua exchange programmes would interfere with compulsory secondary schooling.

The analytical framework suggests that the authority and expertise of the actors involved can significantly affect the bargaining advantage. The case of the Spanish Presidency's effectiveness contradicts this. It may have been the case that Spain simply gave in to UK and German demands. However, the fact that most of the other member states seemed to support the Lingua programme suggests that a few compromises were preferable to the proposal being lost. Germany and the UK used their authority as key EC actors and budget contributors to gain significant concessions from other member states on the target age-range for Lingua grants.[11]

The ESC and the EP had little effect on the negotiations. Although the ESC's opinion was positive, it had suggested that foreign language training should include primary schools. However, the position of Germany and the UK meant that the ESC's view was essentially ignored. The EP proposed four amendments to the Lingua proposal which were not accepted by the Education Council. The EP wanted a budget of 300 million ECU; the final Decision only involved 200 million ECU. The EP wanted the scope of language training broadened to include non-EC languages; the Education Council agreed to include only official member-state languages. The problem in defining which languages to include was confirmed in a review of the Lingua Programme conducted by the Education Council in June 1992. As the President of the Council, Mr Coutos, stated, 'We have noted with surprise on the one hand that the programme is working well, but that, on the other, it maintains the development of the 'major languages' in Europe'.[12]

There was no interim decision on this proposal simply because it was only discussed at only one meeting of the Education Council. It could be argued that decisions were reached within the Education Committee in order that a proposal could be drafted. It is worth noting, however, that preliminary discussions on the possibility of having a foreign language learning programme occurred in May 1988. The Council held an 'exchange of views', showing that much work needed to be done before Education Ministers could fully discuss the issue.[13]

The Lingua programme was definitely fundamental in nature, yet discussion was brief, and no severe disagreements occurred between member states to necessitate the use of non-decisions. Moreover, adoption of the proposal was quick. From this, it is possible to classify the policy style of the Education Council in relation to this case study. Precisely due to the lack of conflict, 'confrontation' can be excluded from consideration. Member states demonstrated that they generally held the same attitudes towards the promotion of foreign language learning. However, due to certain objections raised by Germany and the UK, 'bargaining' as opposed to 'problem-solving' is the most suitable label of the Education Council's style of policy-making.

### Summary of findings
Analysis of the proposal to establish the Lingua programme showed that the political will already existed due to the Resolution adopted a year earlier.

This Resolution was also the origin of the proposal. The Lingua proposal was innovative in its approach, yet this previous commitment could lead one to predict that the negotiations would be fairly straightforward. Indeed, analysis of member-state attitudes showed that most appeared keen to promote EC educational initiatives. However, examination of the German and UK position suggested that they were more reluctant, which may have caused negotiating difficulties. Analysis of the legislative 'type' of this proposal was less useful due to the nature of EC education policy.

Consideration of the actors showed that the status of ministers and their familiarity with each other may have affected the negotiating process, but the evidence suggested otherwise. Again, it appears that the 'special' nature of education policy accounted for this. In addition, identification of the actors showed that while the role of the Presidency was significant, the input of the ESC and EP was negligible.

Analysis of the likely bargaining advantage of the Council actors suggested that Spain, Germany, and the UK would be the most influential in the negotiations due to their attitudes on this proposal. These suggestions tended to be confirmed by analysis of the bargaining advantage within the negotiations. The Spanish Presidency seemed to influence the negotiations, and secure compromises despite its inexperience. This may have been due to domestic electoral pressures, or the General Secretariat's advice. Examination of member-state attitudes suggested that the UK and Germany would have most difficulties with this proposal. This tended to be borne out by the negotiations. Germany and the UK were large EC budget contributors, and were able to influence the negotiations. Spain's role was also important despite its lower budgetary contribution, and is probably explained by its position as Council President and by electoral considerations. Analysis also showed that the ESC and EP have little impact upon discussions when the proposal is only subject to the consultation procedure. Although examination of the action channel showed that discussion of the Lingua programme lasted into the evening and was the only item on the agenda, this was not very significant given the infrequency of Education Council meetings. In addition, neither the use of unanimity, nor 'speech acts' were significant indications of the character of the Education Council on this proposal.

## The Eurydice Network

The Resolution on the Eurydice Network aimed to promote educational cooperation through a computerized information system. This would mean that all EC members had equal access to information on EC educational training activities. Eurydice would have its own European unit, but would cooperate with information systems of individual member states, the European Centre for the Development of Vocational Training (Cedefop) and the National Academic Recognition Information Centre (Naric). The Resolution hoped that Eurydice would become the main instrument for providing information on national and EC educational structures, systems and developments. The network would be useful in compiling comparative reports and therefore assist the EC in its educational policy-making. The proposal for this Resolution was first discussed by the Education Council in October 1989, and adopted in December 1990.[14]

The aim of the Eurydice Resolution was to create a new EC education information network. In this sense, the proposal was 'innovative' in its objectives. However, the political will already seemed to exist for the creation of Eurydice, as the Education Council had adopted a Resolution in 1976 which called for the establishment of an education information network.[15] In addition, this commitment was reaffirmed in 1980. Consequently, the proposal originated out of previous Education Council Resolutions. Member-state attitudes appeared to be generally favourable to the Eurydice proposal. There is little evidence to suggest that any one member state found difficulties with the Resolution. Firstly, the political will to establish Eurydice already existed. Secondly, the 'type' of proposal may have meant that even if member states held certain reservations, adopting the Resolution posed no threat as it was non-binding. The wording of the Resolution recognized this by appealing to member states to promote the use of Eurydice, whilst acknowledging the principle of subsidiarity.[16]

Compared with the Lingua programme, the Eurydice proposal involved even fewer Council actors. From the relative ease of discussions, it appeared that the lack of familiarity of Education Ministers with each other had little effect on the outcome of the proposal. As stated earlier, however, this was probably a result of the 'type' of proposal rather than other factors. Although discussions on Eurydice occurred during three Presidencies, neither the French, Irish, nor the Italian Presidency appeared to be important actors in the process. The ESC and EP did not participate as the Resolution was discussed outside Treaty procedures.

It is quite difficult to analyse the bargaining advantage of Council actors as it appeared that no member state had objections to the proposal. It may have been the case that the larger budget contributors would be able to influence the negotiations because of the finance that would be needed to set up the Eurydice Network. In this respect, it may have been that France would have the most influence because it is a key EC actor, and a large contributor to the EC budget.

The Eurydice Resolution was discussed at three out of a possible four formal sessions of the Education Council held during this period, although there is little to suggest that this was significant. The evidence shows that steady progress was made, and that the political will existed to adopt the Resolution. Negotiation was merely a matter of routine for the Education Council. This is partly confirmed by the fact that informal meetings were not used to facilitate agreement. The Education Committee was important in drawing up the proposal, and perhaps helped to reach agreement in its discussions once the negotiations had started. Analysis of the decision rule is unhelpful because the Resolution had emerged from previous educational commitments and was decided within an intergovernmental framework, rather than according to a Treaty procedure.

It appeared that no Council actor had a significant bargaining advantage prior to the negotiations on this proposal. Analysis of the bargaining advantage within the negotiations confirmed this. The French Presidency did put forward draft conclusions in October 1989, but these conclusions appeared not to be the result of any bargaining or compromise on the part of the Council actors.[17] Moreover, the proposal was adopted relatively smoothly, indicating that there were no substantive objections. Finance was not an issue either.

There were two interim decisions on this proposal, but there is little indication of the nature of these decisions. Conclusions were adopted by the Education Council in October 1989 and May 1990, suggesting that progress was made by the Council actors.[18] There is no evidence that these conclusions were compromise agreements, and analysis of member-state attitudes already suggests that negotiations would be relatively easy.

The analytical framework proposes that examination of 'speech acts' could provide useful insights into the work of the Council. However, as in the previous case-study in this chapter, analysis of the language employed is not very helpful. All it suggests is that the preparatory work of the Education Committee was important. Discussion of the Eurydice proposal involved no non-decisions; some agreement was reached at each stage in the policy-making process, and informal sessions were not used.

The Eurydice Resolution could be termed as a fundamental decision as it involved the establishment of a new EC information network. However, EC educational Resolutions are non-binding on member states. There was no guarantee that all member states would participate in the Eurydice Network. Therefore, to class this Resolution as fundamental may be misleading. Compared to other fundamental legislation such as the abolition of fiscal frontiers, Eurydice had a limited impact. The possible extension of

Eurydice to include EFTA states discussed in November 1992 may indicate that Eurydice proved successful.[19]

The nature of this Resolution does not significantly help analysis of the policy style of the Education Council in this case-study. 'Confrontation' can be excluded due to the fact that the Resolution was adopted in its original form. Whether 'problem-solving' is more suitable as a label than 'bargaining' is reliant on whether a high degree of cooperation arose from the limited impact that the Resolution was likely to have on member states. All member states appeared to agree on the objectives of the Eurydice Network, and there seemed to be no difficulties over the means to achieve these objectives. Therefore, 'problem solving' would appear to be the most appropriate label. However, those member states which had reservations may not have raised objections in the negotiations due to the non-obligatory nature of the Eurydice Resolution. Consequently, this restricts the usefulness of a label of policy style for the Education Council.

### Summary of findings

Analysis of the work of the Education Council in adopting the Eurydice Resolution showed that consideration of the proposal was helpful. Examination of the subject area and origins of the proposal indicated that although it was innovative, the political will already existed, and analysis of member-state attitudes suggested that this was the case. The most useful insight was gained by considering the 'type' of the proposal, as it suggested that the work of the Education Council on this proposal would be relatively easy due to the non-obligatory and intergovernmental nature of the Eurydice Resolution. Analysis of the Council actors and their bargaining advantage tended to confirm this as there was little to suggest that any member state would, or did, influence the negotiations

Consideration of the action channel provided little insight as the Eurydice Resolution was only discussed within the framework of formal sessions. There were no examples of non-decisions; progress appeared simply a matter of routine. In addition, analysis of the decision rule was unnecessary as discussion occurred outside the Treaty. 'Speech acts' tended to confirm that the negotiations were relatively easy, and that the Education Committee had an important role in the discussions. Finally, the legislative 'type' of the Eurydice proposal restricted both the analysis of the nature of the decision, and the task of characterizing the policy style of the Council. It appeared that 'problem-solving' was the most appropriate label for the Education Council in this case-study, yet objections may not have been raised by member states due to the non-obligatory nature of the Resolution.

## A developing Education Council

Overall, the framework proved a less useful analytical tool with which to characterize the operation of the Education Council, compared with other technical councils. This is primarily due to the nature of EC education policy in general. The analytical framework was more helpful in the case of the Lingua Decision because this piece of legislation was binding upon member states. However, the Eurydice Resolution was non-obligatory upon member states, which affected the usefulness of a number of variables contained in the analytical framework.

Examination of the proposal gave a good indication of the likely outcome of both the Lingua and Eurydice proposals. Analysis of the type of proposal was particularly useful for the reason given above. The origin of the proposal confirmed that the Education Council only legislates in areas that overlap with other EC policy activities. The subject area and objectives of the proposal, together with analysis of member-state attitudes, also provided some insight into the final output. From this, it was also possible to predict who the key actors would be in the negotiations, and consequently the bargaining advantage of the actors. However, analysis of the actors, their status and inter-relationships proved to be less important due to the nature of Education Council outputs. This also meant that identification of the bargaining advantage both prior to the selection of action channels and within them was not as useful compared with results from previous chapters. Examination of the action channel and the outputs were the least helpful variables. The choice of session was not an important factor because the Education Council meets so infrequently. Although examination of the speech acts confirmed the importance of the Council's sub-structure, little else could be concluded from this. In addition, analysis of the nature of the decision and the policy style of the Council could not be sufficiently carried out due to the 'special' nature of the Education Council.

Therefore, only some of the variables suggested by the analytical framework proved useful. These included the proposal, the actors and the bargaining advantage. In both case-studies, these were the most helpful variables to consider. Analysis of the final output was only possible through identification of the language used, and then only in the case of the Lingua proposal. Overall, consideration of the action channel and the outcome seems not to offer sufficient insights into the character of the Education Council.

Examination of the two case-studies did provide some indication of the character of the Education Council. The nature of the proposal appears to be significant, affecting the entire policy-making process of the Education

Council. The 'type' of proposal was important as the reaction to non-binding education policy decisions was different to the attitude of member states to obligatory legislation. Member-state attitudes towards these two cases of education policy were formed by their responses to the 'type' of proposal, the budgetary contribution, as well as domestic concerns. The Presidency tended to be of less importance (although Spain did influence the Lingua negotiations), and the ESC and EP were fairly insignificant due to the nature of the Education Council's work.

Few conclusions can be made about the preferred action channels of the Education Council due to the infrequency of meetings and the intergovernmental nature of policy-making in this area. Both the Education Committee and the General Secretariat appeared to carry out most of the work on these proposals. Characterizing the policy style of the Education Council produced mixed results. A high level of cooperation exists in the Education Council negotiations but whether 'bargaining' or 'problem-solving' is the most appropriate label is dependent upon the nature of the proposal and its legislative 'type'. Therefore, analysis of the Education Council produced rather different results due to the 'unique' nature of EC educational policy. These cases demonstrated that the reason why analysis of some of the variables was less helpful was due to the nature of the Education Council's work rather than the inapplicability of the analytical framework.

# CHAPTER NINE

# *The character of the Council*

From the results of the previous four chapters, the success of analysing the variables set out in Figure 4.1 clearly differed between councils, and between proposals. Moreover, significant differences emerge between these four technical councils that constitute part of *the* Council. Whilst these findings only provide *some* valuable insights into the operation of the Council, and are restricted by incomplete information, some conclusions can be made. They suggest that the analytical framework has some methodological value for assessing the work of the Council, and for differentiating operational charactersitics.

## The analytical tools

This section summarizes the findings of the previous four chapters. It evaluates the usefulness of each of the variables included within the analytical framework, and also shows how some variables did have an impact upon others in certain cases.

Overall, examination of the proposal was a useful tool with which to analyse the nature of the Council's operation. However, the results from analysing various factors under the heading 'proposal' varied between councils. Analysis of the subject area gave a good indication of the nature of Council negotiations in all four cases, and also helped to identify the key actors in these particular examples of Council policy-making. Consideration of the objectives of the proposal produced mixed results. In the case of the EcoFin and Labour & Social Affairs Councils, application of Iklé's three-fold classification built upon the insights gained by analysis of the subject area. In the case of the Education Council, classification of the objectives of the two proposals seemed only to confirm that the EC's education policy-making occurs in areas that overlap with other policy areas. Member states tended to have difficulties with both innovative and redistributive objectives in the case of the Environment Council, which suggests that this factor was less useful in this particular case. The objectives of the proposal appeared not to affect the choice of action channels.

Similarly, consideration of the legislative 'type' of the proposal produced conflicting results. This factor provided little insight into the work of the EcoFin and Labour & Social Affairs Councils. Identifying the legislative 'type' of proposals discussed by the Environment Council tended to confirm that Regulations have greater political significance for member states than other forms of EC legislation. However, that is not to say that the Titanium Dioxide Directive examined in Chapter 6 did not have an impact upon member-state attitudes. The 'type' of legislation provided useful insights into the work of the Education Council, but primarily because of the nature of EC education policy. The findings from analysis of the work of the Environment and Education Councils partly confirm Sloot and Verschuren's (1990) analysis that the 'type' of legislation affects the negotiating process and the time taken to adopt proposals. Yet the legislative 'type' of the proposal did not seem to affect the choice of action channel, nor the bargaining advantage. However, further examples are obviously needed to confirm these suggestions.

The analytical framework suggested that it may be useful to consider the origin of a proposal, but this proved problematic. In all cases, identifying whether the proposal originated from previous EC policy-making or not was rather ambiguous. It was possible to argue both the explicit and implicit origin of each proposal. Consequently, this provided little insight into the actors and the bargaining advantage. It may have been the Commission which submitted the proposal, yet the influences upon that proposal are difficult to prove. Examining member-state attitudes gave some indication of the key actors and the likely outcome of the negotiations. Member-state attitudes and the subject area proved the most useful factors to consider when analysing the proposal.

Investigation of the actors identified the significant players involved in Council policy-making. From the findings, the status of ministers and their relationship to each other had a discernible effect upon the conduct of Council negotiations in the case of the EcoFin and Environment Ministers. However, it would be premature to make any firmer conclusion that familiarity may have helped negotiations in these Councils without extending analysis to cover more proposals. The only case where status was important was the 'pushing up' of issues to the General Affairs Council, even though their lack of technical expertise hindered successful problem-solving.

Analysis of the proposal also gave some indication of the likely interests of the ministerial actors. It was possible to suggest who the key actors would be from examination of their attitudes towards the proposal. This also helped to identify the role of the Presidency in the negotiations. Consideration of the role and input of the ESC and the EP provided useful insights into their relationship with the Council. The findings showed that the relationship between the EP and the Council varies between the technical councils, and affects the nature of the Council's work.

Analysis of the bargaining advantage prior to the negotiations was useful. It was possible to suggest who might be able to influence the discussions from the earlier examination of the actors, and member-state attitudes. However, consideration of the bargaining advantage within the action channels only tended to confirm earlier suggestions in some of the cases, but this appeared to be because of the lack of information on the dynamics of the negotiations within Coreper. Analysis of the bargaining advantage was unhelpful in the case of the Education Council. Those actors who exerted policy-making authority were able to alter the form and content of proposals, which determined the final outcome of negotiations. Specific member states seemed to exercise significant bargaining advantage in the EcoFin Council, and in discussions on the Regulation for the European Environmental Agency.

The role of the Presidency is important in the work of EcoFin, and to a lesser extent the Education Council. Yet, in general the Presidency tends to manage rather than control the negotiations. The EP was able to influence Council negotiations on EC environmental policy and Labour & Social Affairs, even when the cooperation procedure did not apply. However, the input of the ESC was minimal. Consideration of the budgetary contribution was useful in those cases where the proposal would incur either direct or indirect financial costs to member states.

Analysis of the action channels produced mixed results. This was primarily due to the amount of information available, which restricts any assessment of the Council's work. The framework suggested that the type of session and the decision rule should be considered. The main hindrance to this was the lack of corroborative evidence about informal sessions, and whether voting had actually taken place. Examination of the Council's action channels confirmed that Coreper is crucial to the operation of the Council, and the idea that technical expertise is often essential in negotiations. In both the work of the Labour & Social Affairs and Education Councils, the role of Coreper was more important than that of the ministers.

Examination of the type of session was not useful when analysing the Education Council simply because it meets infrequently, and only proved helpful in Labour & Social Affairs Council's negotiations on the Carcinogens Directive. Analysis of the action channel used by the EcoFin Council provided the most interesting findings, showing that the action channel often guided the final output of the policy-making process. This indicates that the type of session used by the Council has a greater impact upon the negotiations when the proposal is 'difficult'. However, analysis of the action channels in the work of the Environment Council was not very helpful. It would appear then that the type of session may have a positive effect in prolonged negotiations, but this finding does not apply to the entire Council.

Consideration of the decision rule produced some interesting results regarding voting in the Council, and the effect of the cooperation procedure. The findings empirically confirmed existing academic analysis on the subject of qualified majority voting. Despite increased pressure to extend the use of voting in the Council (discussed further in Chapter 10), this method of decision is rarely used, even when prescribed by the treaties. It appears that voting is a decision method of last resort. Even though the Directive on waste from the titanium dioxide industry was adopted by qualified majority voting, this was probably due to the legal controversy surrounding this Directive, rather than the preferences of the member states to vote on this issue. The EcoFin and Labour & Social Affairs Councils avoided using qualified majority voting. Clearly, these findings exclude the work of the Education Council as it is intergovernmental in nature. However, this is a significant finding, suggesting that the Council prefers the traditional consensus approach to policy-making.

This finding is also extremely important in relation to the impact of the cooperation procedure. Despite the provision for qualified majority voting, the Council avoided using this decision method in the proposals analysed. However, the cooperation procedure has affected the Council's room for manoeuvre, as the EP has a greater input in EC policy-making. The work of the EcoFin, Environment and Labour & Social Affairs Councils has been altered by the increased participation of the EP. Moreover, it appears that the EP is able to exert greater policy-making authority in environmental policy-making even when the cooperation procedure does not apply. Obviously, this has important implications for the future role of the EP.

Analysis of the interim decisions helped to identify the nature of the negotiations, and the role of the Council actors. It was also possible to suggest the style of policy-making for the interim decisions and the final output. 'Speech acts' indicated who the actors were, and their bargaining advantage. Analysis of the language employed confirmed the key role of the

Council's sub-structure and the use of non-decisions. 'Speech acts' were particularly useful in identifying the work of Coreper, since there is no official information on Coreper. Consideration of non-decisions was valuable as it provided a good indication of the nature of the difficulties encountered by the Council, especially in cases of lengthy negotiations.

However, classifying the nature of the decision proved difficult (as was deciding the origin of the proposal). An argument could be made on both counts in some of the case studies, which produced rather ambiguous results. For example, it was possible to distinguish between an incremental and a fundamental decision in both cases of the work of the Environment Council, but this was not so easy for the two EcoFin proposals. Secondly, employing Richardson *et al.*'s three-fold classification of policy style only indicated that all the technical councils adopted a 'bargaining' style of policy-making. This may be useful as a very general label, but it says very little about the nature of Council negotiations at a particular time in the policy-making process within each of these councils. For example, fiscal harmonization caused great difficulty for the member states, despite an overall consensus that this should be achieved. To label the EcoFin Council's style of policy-making on this particular proposal as one of 'bargaining' obscures the fact that there were severe difficulties in achieving this. Moreover, it is only possible to state that 'bargaining' *seemed* the most appropriate label. Coreper played a significant part in all the Council negotiations examined, yet it is not possible to identify its approach to policy-making. Consequently, analysing the nature of the decision is unhelpful. It produces ambiguous and rather general results. If more information was available, this may be a useful factor to consider. However, it appears that only 'speech acts' were useful when analysing the outcome.

To summarize, it appears that all of the variables were useful tools for analysing the operation of the Council. In relation to the proposal, examination of the subject area and member-state attitudes were extremely useful, and should still be included. Consideration of the objectives and the legislative 'type' of a proposal did not allow confident predictions about either the choice of action channel or the outcome of negotiations. However, this factor should be included within an analytical framework, as its usefulness seems to depend upon which technical council is being examined. The only factor that did not help analysis was the origin of the proposal. There were difficulties in qualifying the origin of a proposal, and this factor did not offer any real insight even when this was possible. Therefore, this factor could be omitted from analysis. It is clearly important to identify the actors involved in Council policy-making. They affect the proposal through their attitudes, and the bargaining advantage. It is also important to include other EU institutions in analysis of the actors. Analysis of the bargaining advantage prior to and during the negotiations provides important insights into the dynamics of Council negotiations. Although it may not always be possible to clearly identify who influenced the discussions, and for what reasons, analysis should be attempted. Despite being reliant upon available information, analysis of the type of session and the decision rule (action channels) indicates the preferred working methods of the Council. This could be extremely important in future analysis of the Council, given the introduction of co-decision by the TEU and the pressures being placed on the Council to open its doors and extend the use of qualified majority voting, as discussed in the final chapter. Finally, the interim decisions and final output should be considered when analysing the Council. Examination of the nature of the decision taken by the Council at any given moment produces rather general results but does indicate the progress made in the negotiations. 'Speech acts' provide useful insights into the actors involved and non-decisions used by the Council.

The analytical framework offers a viable method of analysing the Council. It enables a much more detailed examination of the Council to be carried out than any existing approaches for analysing EU policy-making. More importantly, the analytical framework provides important insights into the relationship and interaction between the Council's component parts. Although this analytical framework is only *a* possible approach, its value is indicated by the fact that it supports conclusions obtained through other analytical methods, but provides a much broader context of analysis.

## The nature of the Council

From the outset, it must be stressed that the conclusions put forward in this section about the character of the Council are not definitive. However, the insights gained are valuable, and go some way to explain how the Council prefers to work in a number of EU policy sectors. One of the key findings was the differing operational characteristics of *all* four councils. Variations in the character of the other four technical councils were dictated by the particular proposal under discussion. However, one overall theme emerged: namely that member-state attitudes towards a proposal affected the manner in which each of these councils operated. This shows that both general views on EU policy-making, and domestic priorities of member states at any given moment, form the basis for all Council discussions; that member states are the Council. This constrains the Council's room for manoeuvre in all EU policy negotiations, even when legislation is not binding, as in the case of the non-obligatory Eurydice Resolution. Although ministers may have only attached greater importance to the Regulation to establish the European Environmental Agency due to its obligatory nature (as compared to the Directive on the titanium dioxide industry), it appears that the general attitudes of member states to EU policy-making activity, and domestic constraints, provide the foundations for their approach to Council negotiations, and consequently the character of the Council's operation.

Therefore, this may be why the consensus approach to policy-making is preferred, and will probably remain so. From the evidence of these cases, member states do not use qualified majority voting. The introduction of the cooperation procedure has affected the Council's room for manoeuvre, as seen in the case of the EcoFin, Environment, and Labour & Social Affairs Councils (discussed below). However, findings show that member states sometimes deviate from this procedure – qualified majority voting tends to be a decision method of last resort.

Another key finding was the crucial role of the Council's sub-structure. Chapter 2 discussed the various elements of the Council's composition, emphasizing their importance. The case-studies proved their significance for the effective operation of the Council and thus for EU policy-making in general. Most importantly, analysis demonstrated the influence of Coreper. All eight case-studies showed that Coreper is an integral part of the Council by playing a crucial role as a Council action channel. This was demonstrated by the progress made between formal sessions, and the use of non-decisions. In some cases, the input of Coreper was of greater significance than that of ministers, such as in the work of the Labour & Social Affairs Council. Ministers may have discussed the Regulation on the European Environmental Agency more than the Directive on the titanium dioxide industry, but Coreper was still influential in negotiations on the Regulation. Without Coreper, the Council would be less effective in its policy-making tasks. Firstly, the role of Coreper ensures that negotiations never collapse completely. Secondly, its skills and expertise are vital in cases where political or domestic pressures on ministers clash, or where ministers lack the technical knowledge. In addition, the work of the General Secretariat seems to be important. Although there is no consistent and direct evidence, the skills and expertise of the General Secretariat were possibly of most value when negotiations proved difficult, as in the case of the EcoFin Council, and in the work of the Education Council (perhaps due to the infrequency of ministerial meetings). The obvious problem, though, is the lack of information about the work of Coreper and the General Secretariat. Council documentation refers to Coreper, and as shown, it is possible to deduce the role of this body. However, as Coreper minutes are not available, and references to the General Secretariat are not made in documentation, it is not possible to provide greater substance to these conclusions. Yet it is precisely because of this lack of information that Coreper and the General Secretariat are so crucial to the operation of the Council. By knowing that details of Coreper negotiations remain confidential, member-state representatives may be able to negotiate more freely. Furthermore, the General Secretariat is trusted by all Council actors due to its impartial and invisible role. An information deficit may cause frustration to the analyst, but from the evidence, Coreper and the General Secretariat seem to be influential and powerful elements of the Council's sub-structure. Where there seems to be scope for further research is not on the importance of Coreper and the General Secretariat, but on how, when, and in what kind of issues these two elements of the Council can be most effective, and when it is the case that issues have to be referred to the appropriate ministers.

By contrast, results suggest that the office of the Presidency is of less significance than the role of Coreper. The Council Presidency allows the EU policy agenda to be managed, thus assisting the smooth operation of the Council. Conversely, member states may view the office of the Presidency as an opportunity to pursue their own national interests by manipulating the agenda, and promoting particular proposals. The evidence from analysis of the case studies is mixed. Generally, the effectiveness of a member state as President depended upon the particular proposal. For example, Italy and Luxembourg were able to secure agreement on the atypical workers, while Luxembourg and The Netherlands were relatively successful in finding solutions to problems that arose in the negotiations on the abolition of fiscal frontiers. However, it seemed that no member state presiding over discussions of the carcinogens Directive, nor the Eurydice Resolution, was effectual.

There were also some examples of member states using the Council Presidency to promote their own domestic policy priorities. The most notable were the Italian, German and Spanish Presidencies on the Directive on money laundering, waste from the titanium dioxide industry, and the Lingua Programme respectively. Whilst this Presidential influence did not have a detrimental effect upon the work of the Council on these proposals, they are clear examples of the way in which the office of the Presidency can be used to promote domestic concerns. Overall, the office of the Presidency does help to ensure the effective operation of the Council, and especially in cases of protracted negotiations. Some member states seem to use the Council Presidency to promote their own domestic policy priorities, but this is not necessarily negative and is probably a recognized and accepted practice by all member states. Again, further analysis of the Council's work would be needed to draw more definite conclusions concerning the importance of the office of the Presidency.

Another observation on the Council's sub-structure concerns the European Council. Although there was only one example of the practice of 'pushing up' issues to the European Council (EcoFin and the proposal to abolish fiscal frontiers), this shows that referrals up the Council hierarchy occur in the most politically sensitive areas. In addition, on this occasion, the European Council was able to assist the policy-making process. However, it would be wrong to make any general conclusions about this – it is simply an interesting observation.

Analysis of the operation of the Council also provided some important insights into the Council's relationship with other EU institutions. The cooperation procedure has not only increased the EP's policy-making input, but has improved Council–EP relations. Although the Council still dominates, the EP has been able to exert its influence over the Council, and there appears to be greater dialogue between these two institutions. The Labour & Social Affairs Council had to take account of EP amendments in both proposals examined, with the EP's threat of using the conciliation procedure in the case of the atypical workers Directive forcing the Council to heed EP demands. Of more significance was the fact that the EP influenced discussions on the European Environmental Agency, despite having only one reading. This may be only one example, but it appears that Council–EP relations have improved in environmental policy-making due to the existence of the cooperation procedure, even on proposals where this procedure does not apply. Clearly, this pattern may be specific to environmental policy, yet the EP has always fought against the Council in this area (as it did in this case). What may emerge is an improved dialogue between the Council and EP in all policy-making where the general legal base is the cooperation or co-decision procedure. The other institution considered was the ESC. It was clear from all the case-studies that the opinions of the ESC have little impact upon the operation of the Council. On occasions, such as in the work of the EcoFin and Labour & Social Affairs Councils, the views of the ESC were ignored. Overall, there seemed to be little Council recognition of the role of the ESC in the policy-making process.

In relation to the preferred action channels of the Council, the Council (used here collectively) seems to avoid using qualified majority voting. Chapter 3 analysed how different types of negotiating setting could affect Council discussions. The findings demonstrated that only one technical council used different types of session, namely the EcoFin Council. In the case of the money laundering Directive, one special session was convened, yet the negotiations on fiscal harmonization used a variety of tactics. Formal, informal, restricted, prolonged, and supplementary sessions were held. This was due to the difficulty surrounding this proposal, although the use of these different negotiating settings did not always prove successful. The other three technical councils only used the formal setting for their negotiations. This was either due to the work carried out by Coreper, or the relative ease of discussions. Therefore, the only pattern to emerge from this analysis is that the negotiating setting is only varied when agreement is proving extremely difficult to reach. However, such a conclusion is based on restricted information. Little documentary evidence exists, particularly on the agenda of informal sessions. In examination of the six proposals discussed by the Environment, Labour & Social Affairs, and Education Councils, there was little evidence to suggest that these proposals were considered at other types of session. By contrast, the documentation on the work of the EcoFin Council makes explicit reference to discussions within different negotiating settings. Therefore, it is possible to assume that different types of session only tend to be used in difficult policy negotiations. However, again our sample of the Council would have to be extended before making firm conclusions on this matter.

The comparative analysis of four councils that constitute the Council provide useful insights into the operation of the Council. Some conclusions about the character of the Council can be made, but they cannot be considered definitive. Most importantly, the Council (as a collective body) tends to avoid the use of qualified majority voting. Secondly, the role of the Council's sub-structure, in particular Coreper and the General Secretariat, is crucial to EU policy-making, The Presidency plays a part in Council negotiations, and even though some member states use the office of the President to promote domestic concerns, this does not necessarily have a negative impact upon the work of the Council. Thirdly, member-state attitudes and domestic constraints, rather than individual council preferences for conducting policy-making, tend to have the greatest effect upon the character of the four technical councils. The EcoFin Council used different types of session, but only because of the difficult nature of its work. Finally, Council–EP relations seem to have improved as a result of the cooperation procedure.

The Council is a multi-faceted institution. Its character is formed by member-state attitudes to the many dimensions of EU policy-making, and operational differences between the various technical councils that constitute *the* Council seem only to be a result of this. *The* Council is a unique institution. It presides over a supranational organization, is the final source of policy-making authority, yet it remains a forum in which member states 'battle out' their policy differences in relative privacy. Member states prefer the diplomatic, consensus approach to EU policy-making, and seem unwilling to alter existing practices.

# CHAPTER TEN

# The future of the Council
# of the European Union

There have been numerous developments pertaining to the work of the Council since 1992. The TEU came into force on 1 November 1993, which meant (amongst many other developments) the implementation of the co-decision procedure, and the reaffirmation of the principle of subsidiarity. The EEA (European Economic Area) was established on 1 January 1994, linking the EC with EFTA, the momentum from this resulting in a number of EFTA states joining the EU and expanding membership to fifteen with the accession of Austria, Finland, and Sweden on 1 January 1995. This enlargement required alterations to the rotation of the Presidency, and qualified majority voting thresholds. The 1996–97 IGC resulted in the Treaty of Amsterdam being signed in June 1997 (and entering into force on 1 May 1999), which extended and simplified the co-decision procedure and allowed for the appointment of a 'Ms/Mr CFSP'. Finally, further enlargement of the EU is top of the agenda, with negotiations under way for the first wave of applicants.[1] Some argue that an EU of twenty or more members cannot function under existing arrangements. This chapter examines a number of institutional issues concerning the Council, and demonstrates that despite new Treaty revisions, member states have not relinquished their final decision-making powers, and the overall character of the Council has not significantly altered.

The Council tends to be the primary target for institutional reform of the EU. For some, the Council represents all that is wrong with the EU. It lacks direct accountability, is an intergovernmental body, and acts as a brake on deeper European integration. Proposed modifications concentrate upon four main areas of the Council's operation: openness and transparency; the office of the Presidency; voting mechanisms; and the further extension of the co-decision procedure.

## Opening the Council's doors?

The Birmingham and Edinburgh European Councils agreed to a policy of greater openness and transparency for the EU, in response to calls for more accountability stemming from TEU ratification.[2] Since the public backlash to the TEU there has been growing pressure to increase public awareness about the activities of the EU. Some member states (most notably Denmark, The Netherlands, and Sweden), the EP and the Commission argue that a more transparent EU is essential, perhaps reflecting the neofunctionalist idea that this will generate a transfer of loyalties. Denmark, The Netherlands, and Sweden would like to transfer their own high standards of open government to the EU level. This may be rather optimistic, particularly in the case of the Council. It is difficult to agree with the Commission that 'the Community of regulations and directives will become a Community of people' through such piecemeal policies.[3] A greater public attachment to the EU can only occur with the determination of all member-state governments. However, such willingness is not prevalent when it comes to opening up the Council. There have been some alterations, but these have only had a very limited impact.

The Council altered its Rules of Procedure and adopted a Decision in December 1993. This Decision went some way to improving public access to Council documents and proposed to hold an open session under each Presidency. The amended Rules of Procedure include articles on openness, and access to minutes. Council Press Releases are now more readily accessible through Commission and EP databases (Rapid and Ovide/Epistel respectively), and make explicit reference to those decisions supposedly taken by qualified majority voting. This has put great pressure on the Council's press service, so much so that the despatching of press releases was suspended for four months. An almost instant (although rather slim) Annual Review of the Council's work was issued in January 1993, in line with the Edinburgh Council conclusions. However, it was written by two ghost writers, and without the usual consultation with Directors-General of the Council's Secretariat. In addition, the General Secretariat was told that it should aim to publish the Annual Review in January of each year. One Council official was rather sceptical about how this would be achieved – a doubt well-placed considering that the publication of Annual Reviews has not met this deadline.

Despite these developments, Article 4 of the 1993 Decision includes rather ambiguous criteria for public access to documents. The Council insists that consultation of its minutes is still subject to the 'obligation of professional secrecy', as set out in the Rules of Procedure. This covers Council minutes, unnumbered documents and in-house reports. In *The Guardian* newspaper's case against the Council for not implementing its policy of transparency in a request for certain minutes, the Council told the ECJ that the conclusions of the Birmingham and Edinburgh European Councils and the 1993 Decision were simply 'policy orientations'.[4] The ECJ has since ruled against the Council, stating that the ban on the disclosure of these specific Council minutes was illegal.[5] The implication is that the Council will have to agree to other requests for Council minutes. The Council pre-empted the ECJ judgement by amending its code of conduct to improve access to minutes earlier in October 1995.[6] However, it appears that the Council's amended code of conduct will protect Council minutes, despite the ECJ ruling. Member states have simply agreed to restrict the use of declarations attached to minutes. This means that any declarations will be treated as separate internal documents. Council minutes can now be accessed, but they will not contain individual positions of member states which is really what those requesting to see such documents are looking for.

Holding 'open' Council sessions began in 1993 under the Danish Presidency. The media are invited to cover these meetings, and the public can view the sessions on television screens in the press rooms of the Justus Lipsius building. However, attendance is poor. The main problem with these so-called 'open' sessions is that they do not reflect the real Council. Ministers simply read out prepared policy statements: the reality is that the key decisions are taken in private. Further proposals have been made to improve the Council's transparency. In particular, there have been calls for all legislative sessions of the Council to be opened up to the public. In theory, this would mean that it would be possible to identify the policy position of each member state on every proposal adopted. While this may address the lack of accountability of ministers to their national parliaments, it would still provide little insight into the work of the Council. These legislative sessions would be as pre-organized as the existing open sessions. Ministerial negotiations will simply get pushed even further behind closed doors.

A key point that tends to be ignored when discussing greater openness for the Council's work is that Coreper is responsible for a significant amount of Council negotiations. Proposals make no attempt to target Coreper, despite its crucial role in EU policy-making. This is probably because all member states would fight any proposal to open the doors of Coreper meetings. Therefore, attempts at improving the transparency of the Council's work can only result in superficial changes. Certain ministerial negotiations are simply pushed further behind closed doors, whilst the work of Coreper is ignored. This policy is a cosmetic exercise so that member states can be seen to be responding to demands for greater openness, knowing all the time that such a policy will never provide information about the real negotiations.

## The Council Presidency

The second area of the Council's operation under review is the office of the Presidency. Although no one disputes that the Council needs a Presidency, enlargement of the EU poses problems for the existing rotational arrangements. Yet, as shown by the results of this study, the Presidency can play a vital role in Council policy-making processes. Furthermore, the TEU enhanced the role of the European Council, and consequently the Presidency.

Reform of the Council Presidency system is a recurrent theme and every impending enlargement of the EU has generated heightened discussion on whether the office of the Council Presidency will be undermined by an increase in membership. The late 1990s is no different, although the current debate surrounding whether the Presidency matters has been given added impetus by the scale of future enlargements and the implications for effective Council policy-making.

The 1996–97 IGC and resultant Treaty of Amsterdam reflected member states' difficulties with institutional reform generally, and it was agreed to put the issue on hold until the political climate regarding enlargement was more certain. Admittedly, a new figurehead has been established for 'high' politics in the form of a Ms/Mr CFSP, yet the question of Presidency effectiveness remains.

A well-rehearsed proposal is to extend the term of office to twelve months. This would enable a greater degree of coherence, as six months is a short time in EU politics. A longer term of office could enhance the capabilities of the Presidency to cope with the demands of the future EU policy agenda, and enable 'new' members to cope with the pressures of a Presidency, given their domestic administrative structures and inexperience at the EU level. However, it could also enhance a member state's ability to manipulate the agenda and further widen the expectation-capability gap. Moreover, proponents seem to ignore the scenario of a less-capable Presidency when, for a variety of internal and external pressures, the member state is less effective, even in its role as manager of the Council agenda. A second proposal that has been made, but with fewer supporters, is to restrict the office of the Presidency to only the larger member states. This not only undermines the basic ethos of the Community that all states are equal, but runs into definitional problems as to what constitutes a large state. For example, Spain is accorded the status of a large state in its Council voting rights and number of Commissioners, yet is still seen as smaller than, say, France or Germany. Those who are worried about the accession of Central and East European countries presumably do not categorize Poland as a larger member state. A third idea is to create team Presidencies in which several member states would be grouped together, perhaps around several policy areas. This proposal appears acceptable on the surface, generating coherence and simply extending Troika principles. It was highlighted in the 1996 Reflection Group discussions. However, it could easily result in dominance by certain member states, and most particularly the larger member states. Alternatively, the Presidency could be elected. This is arguably the least viable of the alternatives as it would simply enhance sceptic arguments that there is a 'Ms/Mr Euro' presiding over and controlling European citizens. This may seem rather a simplistic view, but is nevertheless highly significant in the present political climate when it is so important for the EU as an institution to quell Euro-myths.

A final suggestion made in the past, and by degree implemented as a result of ratification of the Amsterdam Treaty, is to enhance the role of the General Secretariat. The appointment of Ms/Mr CFSP will provide a greater sense of continuity by acting as the EU spokesperson on foreign policy, and 'high' political issues. Ms/Mr CFSP may come to be viewed by EU citizens as a figure-head, thus invalidating part of the argument put forward against electing the Presidency. Yet their role will be confined to CFSP issues, and they will be appointed by unanimous agreement of the member states.

Therefore what needs to be asked is whether the disadvantages of all these options that have been put forward and debated from time to time outweigh the advantages of the existing six-month rotating Presidency. The idea of rotating the Presidency supports the learning curve argument, as it enables all member states to experience the office of the Presidency and EU policy-making processes. Maintaining such a system in an enlarged EU reduces the strength of such an argument as the term of office becomes less frequent. However, for smaller member states, it is often claimed that the Council Presidency enhances its status both within the European and international arenas. There is an element of truth in this. What is more important has been the operational trend that smaller states make more effective Council Presidencies, although there is little hard empirical evidence to back up such claims. Nevertheless, it does seem that the Council Presidency does permit smaller and new states to acquire a status within the EU, and increase their capacity against dominance by larger members. The 1998 Austrian Presidency confounded the sceptics that a new and small member to the EU would not be able to cope. Austria's leadership of the Council may not have been earth-shattering, but it exuded competence – thorough preparations and civil service secondments to partner administrations demonstrated a willingness to learn from others. Whilst the small–large dichotomy should not be over-estimated, it is worth noting that smaller states jealously guarded the Commission's right of initiative in the latest IGC, believing it to be an element of their insurance policy against domination of the policy agenda by the larger members. Another element of that insurance policy is the Council Presidency.

What also needs to be considered is whether the EU and Council of the future needs a Presidency. Ms/Mr CFSP may diminish the need for a spokesperson, which was one of the traditional roles of the Presidency. Yet there remains a most definite need for a manager for Council policy-making. Along with the continually growing policy agenda, in future the Presidency will have to operate under a darker shadow of the vote as the number of member states within the Council expands. Potentially, this could reduce the effectiveness of the Presidency, yet is also a case for having a chairperson. Moreover, member states may press even harder to maintain the existing Presidency arrangements as a result of the appointment of Ms/Mr CFSP, as they do not wish to be seen to be relinquishing power and feel compelled to demonstrate to their domestic audiences that national governments remain in control of EU policy.

The heightened debate in the face of further enlargement tends to reflect a rather negative view of new or small states. As a new member state Austria coped with holding the EU Presidency. Since 1996 some 900 Finnish officials have been involved in training programmes on EU working practices, reflecting how the Presidency enables a new member to focus upon its performance within EU institutional structures. Whilst applicant countries may have less-recent democratic experience, they need to be given the opportunity to learn about EU dynamics through the office of the Presidency. Although not an ideal situation, the EU rarely falters completely as the result of a less-capable Presidency.

Most practitioners uphold the perspective that the six-month rotation works. Most recently, Douglas Henderson stated that:

> The Presidency is an unusual institution, requiring a mix of patience, leadership and an ability to chase progress. Yet, despite all its flaws, it works and the main business gets done. There are those who advocate a change to longer terms or going for a radically different framework, but having experienced it at first hand, I would hesitate to change it. (Henderson, 1998: 572)

One wonders whether these seasoned experts are reflecting an EU truth. The Presidency performs a vital task by providing management and leadership skills, whilst at the same time permitting assimilation for new members, and allows each country the opportunity to exert at least some national influence upon the EU agenda. These skills are essential to EU policy-making efficacy, and the office of the Presidency reflects the reality of EU bargaining.

## Voting in the Council

There has been increased pressure for an extension of the use, or extended application to other kinds of issues, of qualified majority voting in the Council, due to possible enlargement and the need to speed up EC policy-making. Most of the recent research (Hosli, 1996) on this issue applies strict quantitative analysis and detracts attention from the real issues. Whilst qualified majority voting thresholds were originally based on the rough approximation of population size to the number of votes, the underlying doctrine was that 'all states are equal'. The most crucial element of this debate is that despite increasing calls for qualified majority voting to be extended, member states dislike this decision method. As shown in previous chapters, qualified majority voting appears to be less significant than originally thought.

Much criticism of the Amsterdam Treaty has been directed at the limited number of changes made to voting rules with the Council. However, such debate ignores the fact that member states prefer to avoid physically voting. The tradition of diplomacy reigns in the Council. It is the prospect that a vote could be taken which seems to be the crucial factor when analysing qualified majority voting; even the official Council view acknowledges this (Council, 1995: 16). Accurate data is hard to compile, but Council figures for the period November 1993–March 1995 state that out of 283 legislative acts, only 40 proposals were adopted with negative votes and/or abstentions, and 32 with abstentions only (Council, 1995: 53).

Therefore, it is not surprising that only 5 out of a possible 48 articles were changed from unanimity to qualified majority voting. Germany altered its policy position and led the majority of member states in resisting a blanket extension of qualified majority voting. According to Duff (1997: 145) these articles were not altered to qualified majority because of an agreement reached by the UK government under John Major. The voting arrangement may make it difficult on these occasions for the EP to negotiate with the Council, as the proposal will be subject to unanimity in the Council. However, given that it is only the knowledge that a vote could be taken that is important, these remnants of unanimity under co-decision hold negligible significance and are less of an anomaly, as previously suggested.

Sub-issues of voting discussed at Amsterdam were the threshold and future arrangements. The threshold for a qualified majority was not lowered, nor the future of majority voting resolved. Not only does this confirm that member states prefer to leave the fine-tuning of existing arrangements until enlargement negotiations are under way, but it also confirms that qualified majority voting is not a significant factor in EU policy-making processes. The stricter deadlines imposed by the Amsterdam Treaty suggest that the Presidency may have to resort to a vote more frequently in the future. However, judging by the culture of Council decision-making, there is unlikely to be a departure from existing norms. Qualified majority voting may have more status in an enlarged EU, but it takes at least five years for the bedding-down of decision-making procedures after enlargement. More member states, different policy priorities, and the enhancement of the north-south-east, and rich-poor cleavages means it will be more difficult to reach consensus, and physical voting could be increasingly required. However, for the immediate post-enlargement years, new members will have less political manoeuvrability, and the culture of EU policy-making will not significantly alter. The transition years may actually establish informal coalitions that will, in the future, circumvent formal voting practices. The Treaty of Amsterdam left this compromise intact for the time being and has the potential for member states to avoid the use of qualified majority voting even further. Unlike the Luxembourg Compromise which dictated that it could only be invoked for 'important' issues that threatened a perceived national interest, the Ioannina Compromise can be employed at any time. The Ioannina Compromise allows member states to use any pretext in opposing a decision.

Although member states know that the consensus approach is preferred even when qualified majority voting could be used in Council policy-making, they are unlikely to agree to a complete extension of qualified majority voting for an enlarged EU. Existing members may feel that the composition and political alliances of new members could threaten the consensus approach to Council policy-making. Moreover, further extension of qualified majority voting may simply enhance the already crucial role played by Coreper. To some extent, the issue of increasing voting provisions poses less threat to member states given that a significant amount of the Council's work is carried out by Coreper. Member states can use Coreper to resolve difficulties on a particular proposal so that they are not out-voted if a qualified majority vote is taken.

## Amsterdam and co-decision

Qualified majority voting is prescribed under both the cooperation and co-decision procedures for EU policy-making (introduced by the SEA and TEU respectively). As shown, the cooperation and co-decision procedures have had some effect upon the Council's internal working practices. The Amsterdam Treaty revised existing EU decision-making procedures in two key respects; by extending the scope of the co-decision procedure, and by simplifying this procedure. Member states rejected the blanket application of co-decision despite the EP flexing its political muscle and threatening to veto future enlargements. Nevertheless, the new Amsterdam Treaty has widened the scope of co-decision, thus further increasing the EP's input in formal EU policy-making processes. The co-decision procedure has also been simplified and this is decisive for the EP. In its report prepared for the 1996 Reflection Group, even the Council (1995: 18) admitted that the TEU co-decision procedure was over-complex and confrontational. What has emerged as a result of the 1996–7 negotiations, is a refined, slimlined procedure which clearly aims to increase the efficiency and effectiveness of EU policy-making. Therefore, on a formal level, the Amsterdam Treaty has placed the EP on an equal footing with the Council in a number of areas of EU policy-making activity. In this sense, the EP can be seen as a co-legislator in some policy areas, with the level of EP legislative input being increased further.

This process of narrowing the institutional division of power and responsibilities between the Council and EP has been gradual but consistently striven for through the formal treaty requirements, from the conciliation procedure established in 1975 for proposals with 'appreciable financial implications', through the SEA and TEU. Therefore, it was a natural progression for co-decision to be extended by the latest IGC. Previous experience had demonstrated that an enhanced role for the EP did not equate with a less efficient or effective policy-making process for the EU. Moreover, co-decision did not directly lead to consistent confrontation between the Council and EP. Conciliation has been a procedure of last resort, with both the Council and EP generally committed to finding a solution through negotiation, rather than having to convene the Conciliation Committee.

Co-decision has now been extended to 8 new provisions, and 15 existing articles. The Treaty of Amsterdam has also increased EP powers of assent and consultation, and enhanced its budgetary control.[7] More crucially, co-decision has been simplified by the Amsterdam Treaty in four key respects. Firstly, under the first reading, the Council can now adopt the proposal if the EP and Council are agreed, or if the EP offers no amendments; secondly, the 'intention to reject' has been dropped allowing the EP to simply reject more quickly; thirdly, the Council can no longer adopt a proposal by qualified majority if conciliation negotiations fail; and finally the Conciliation Committee must meet within six weeks (eight if necessary) and conclude within nine months. All these changes increase the speed of the co-decision procedure, and ensure greater future effectiveness. However, there is a strange anomaly whereby some proposals are subject to co-decision with unanimity in the Council.

The cooperation and co-decision procedures (and logically simplified co-decision) have affected Council–EP relations, and enhanced the role of the EP in some areas of policy-making. The Council now works more closely with the EP and results from this analysis of the Council showed that the EP seems to have an even greater input in discussions of some proposals not governed by the cooperation procedure. The informal Council–EP network is being developed to improve relations even further. Presidents of EP committees now meet regularly with Council representatives. It appears that the EP has established itself as more of a partner with the Council in certain areas of EU policy-making, although it is still not on an equal footing with the Council. Evidence also suggests that the confrontational relationship that could have arisen out of co-decision and the conciliation procedure has not occurred. The practice of co-decision has resulted in its simplification, implying that the experience of co-legislating has resulted in effective EU policy-making and should therefore be pursued. Member states would surely have resisted the Amsterdam agreement otherwise.

## Conclusions

The alterations made to the Council by the development of transparency and the ratification of the Treaty of Amsterdam will only have a superficial effect. Much of the current debate about the role and procedures of the Council, particularly in the media, is based upon ignorance of how the Council works. Consequently, discussion of the issue of Council accountability tends to be based on the notion that the Council is only a legislature. Yet, uniquely, it is also a negotiating forum for the member states of the EU. This means that the standards of direct accountability demanded by the critics are unrealistic. In any case, member states do not want to radically change the character of the Council as the present form of this body facilitates agreement with their EU partners. For some member-state governments, greater direct accountability could have adverse domestic consequences. Improving the Council's transparency ignores the fact that Coreper is responsible for a large amount of Council negotiations, and that greater openness will simply push ministerial negotiations even further behind closed doors. Reform of the rotation of the Presidency is probable but may reduce the efficiency of the Council, as the Presidency will become yet another arena of bargaining. Member states did agree to a further extension of qualified majority voting at Amsterdam. However, it appears that qualified majority voting tends not to be used that much – the consensus approach seems to dominate Council policy-making. The EP is beginning to have a greater influence in the legislative process. Undoubtedly, this will be strengthened by the new co-decision procedure. However, it is unlikely that member states will agree to a blanket coverage of co-decision. Member states may acknowledge that some alterations to Council procedures will be needed. Yet, whatever the reforms, the Council will remain the dominant institution in EU policy-making.

# Appendix 1

## The Rules of Procedure of the Council

Council Decision of 6 December 1993
(93/662/EC) (OJL 304 10.12.93), which
entered into force on 7 December 1993.
This replaced the existing Rules of
Procedure of 24 July 1979 as amended
20 July 1987.

### Article 1:

1. The Council shall meet when convened
   by its President on his own initiative or
   at the request of one of its members or
   of the Commission.
2. The President shall make known the
   dates which he envisages for meetings
   of the Council during his period of office
   as President, seven months before the
   beginning thereof.
3. In accordance with the Decision taken
   by common agreement between the
   Representatives of the Government of
   the Member States on 12 December
   1992 on the basis of the relevant Articles
   of the Treaties establishing the European
   Communities, the Council shall have its
   seat in Brussels. During the months of
   April, June and October, the Council
   shall hold its meetings in Luxembourg.
   In exceptional circumstances and for duly
   substantiated reasons, the Council, acting
   unanimously, may decide to hold a
   meeting elsewhere.

### Article 2:

1. The President shall draw up the
   provisional agenda for each meeting.
   The agenda shall be sent to the other
   members of the Council and to the
   Commission at least fourteen days before
   the beginning of the meeting.
2. The provisional agenda shall contain the
   items in respect of which a request for
   inclusion on the agenda, together with
   any documents relating thereto, has been
   received by the General Secretariat from
   a member of the Council or from the
   Commission at least sixteen days before
   the beginning of that meeting. The
   provisional agenda shall also indicate
   the items on which the Presidency,
   delegations or the Commission may
   request a vote.
3. Only items in respect of which
   the documents have been sent to the
   members of the Council and to
   the Commission at the latest by the
   date on which the provisional agenda
   is sent may be placed on that agenda.
4. The General Secretariat shall transmit
   to the members of the Council and to
   the Commission requests for the
   inclusion of items in the agenda,
   documents and indications concerning
   voting relating thereto in respect of
   which the time-limits specified above
   were not requested.
5. The agenda shall be adopted by the
   Council at the beginning of each
   meeting. The inclusion in the agenda
   of an item other than those appearing
   in the provisional agenda shall require
   unanimity in the Council. Items entered
   in this way may be put to the vote.
6. The provisional agenda shall be divided
   into Part A and Part B. Items for which
   approval of the Council is possible
   without discussion shall be included in
   Part A, but this does not exclude the
   possibility of any member of the Council
   or Commission expressing an opinion at
   the time of the approval of these items
   and having statements included in the
   minutes.
7. However, an 'A' item shall be withdrawn
   from the agenda, unless the Council
   decided otherwise, if a position on an
   'A' item might lead to further discussion

thereof or if a member of the Council or the Commission so requests.

### Article 3:

Subject to the provisions of Article 7 on the delegation of voting rights, a member of the Council who is prevented from attending a meeting may be represented.

### Article 4:

1. Meetings of the Council shall not be public except in the cases referred to in Article 6.
2. The Commission shall be invited to take part in meetings of the Council. The Council may, however, decide to deliberate without the presence of the Commission.
3. The members of the Council and of the Commission may be accompanied by officials who assist them. The number of such officials may be laid down by the Council. The names and functions of such officials shall be notified in advance to the Secretary-General.
4. Admission to meetings of the Council shall be subject to the production of a pass.

### Article 5:

1. Without prejudice to Article 7(5) and other applicable provisions, the deliberations of the Council shall be covered by the obligation of professional secrecy, except in so far as the Council decides otherwise. Where the record of a vote in Council is made public in accordance with Article 7(5), the explanation of vote made when the vote was taken shall also be made public at the request of the Council members concerned, with due regard for these Rules of Procedure, legal certainty and the interests of the Council.
2. The Council may authorise the production of a copy or an extract from its minutes for use in legal proceedings.

### Article 6:

1. The Council shall hold policy debates on the six-monthly work programme submitted by the Presidency and, if appropriate, on the Commission's annual work programme. These debates shall be the subject of public re-transmission by audio-visual means.

2. The Council may decide unanimously and on a case-by-case basis that some of its other debates are to be the subject of re-transmission by audio-visual means, in particular where they concern an important issue affecting the interests of the Union or an important new legislative proposal. To that end, it shall be for the Presidency, any member of the Council, or the Commission to propose issues or specific subjects for such a debate.

### Article 7:

1. The Council shall vote on the initiative of the President. The President shall, furthermore, be required to open proceedings on the initiative of a member of the Council or of the Commission provided that a majority of the Council's members so decides.
2. The members of the Council shall vote in the order of the Member States laid down in Article 27 of the Treaty establishing the European Coal and Steel Community (ECSC), Article 146 of the Treaty establishing the European Community (EC) and Article 116 of the Treaty establishing the European Atomic Energy Community (EAEC), beginning with the member who, according to that order, follows the member holding the office of President.
3. Delegation of the right to vote may only be made to another member of the Council.
4. The presence of six members of the Council is required to enable the Council to vote.
5. The record of the votes shall be made public:
   - when the Council is acting as legislator within the meaning of the term given in the Annex to these Rules of Procedure, unless the Council decides otherwise. This rule shall apply when the Council adopts a common position pursuant to Article 189B or 189C of the Treaty establishing the European Community;
   - when they are cast by the members of the Council or their representatives on the Conciliation Committee set up by Article 189B of the Treaty establishing the European Community;

- when the Council acts pursuant to Titles V and VI of the Treaty on European Union by a unanimous Council decision taken at the request of one of its members;
- in other cases, by Council decision taken at the request of one of its members.

### Article 8:

1. Acts of the Council on an urgent matter may be adopted by a written vote where the Council or the Committee of Permanent Representatives of the Member States (Coreper) referred to in Article 30 of the ECSC Treaty, Article 151 of the EC Treaty and Article 121 of the EAEC Treaty, unanimously decides to use that procedure. In special circumstances, the President may also propose the use of that procedure; in such a case, written votes may be used where all members of the Council agree to that procedure.

2. Furthermore, agreement by the Commission to the use of this procedure shall be required where the written vote is on a matter which the Commission has brought before the Council.

3. A summary of acts adopted by the written procedure shall be drawn up every month.

4. On the initiative of the Presidency, the Council may also act for the purpose of implementing the common foreign and security policy by means of the simplified written procedure (Coreu). In that case the proposal shall be deemed to be adopted at the end of the period laid down by the Presidency depending on the urgency of the matter, except where a member of the Council objects.

5. The General Secretariat shall establish that the written procedures have been completed.

### Article 9:

1. Minutes of each meeting shall be drawn up and, when approved, shall be signed by the President in office at the time of such approval and by the Secretary-General. The minutes shall as a general rule indicate in respect of each item on the agenda:
   - the documents submitted to the Council;

- the decisions taken or the conclusions reached by the Council;
- the statements made by the Council and those whose entry has been requested by a member of the Council or the Commission.

2. The draft minutes shall be drawn up by the General Secretariat within fifteen days and submitted to the Council for approval.

3. Prior to such approval any member of the Council, or of the Commission, may request that more details be inserted in the minutes regarding any item on the agenda.

4. The texts referred to in Article 10 shall be annexed to the minutes.

### Article 10:

1. Except as otherwise decided unanimously by the Council on grounds of urgency, the Council shall deliberate and take decisions only on the basis of documents and drafts drawn up in the languages specified in the rules in force governing languages.

2. Any member of the Council may oppose discussion if the texts of any proposed amendments are not drawn up in such of the languages referred to in paragraph 1 as he may specify.

### Article 11:

The texts of the acts adopted by the Council and that of the acts adopted jointly by the European Parliament and the Council shall be signed by the President in office at the time of their adoption and by the Secretary-General. The Secretary-General may delegate his signature to Directors-General of the General Secretariat.

### Article 12:

Regulations adopted jointly by the European Parliament and the Council as well as Council regulations shall include in their title the word 'Regulation', as followed by a serial number, by the date of their adoption and by an indication of the subject-matter.

### Article 13:

Regulations adopted jointly by the European Parliament and the Council as well as Council Regulations shall contain the following:

(a) 'The European Parliament and the Council of the European Union' or 'The Council of the European Union' as appropriate;

(b) a reference to the provisions under which the Regulation is adopted, preceded by the words 'Having regard to';

(c) a citation containing a reference to the proposals submitted and opinions obtained and to consultations held;

(d) a statement of the reasons on which the Regulation is based, introduced by the word 'Whereas';

(e) the phrase 'have adopted this Regulation' or the phrase 'has adopted this Regulation', as appropriate, followed by the body of the Regulation.

### Article 14:

1. Regulations shall be divided into Articles, if appropriate grouped into chapters and sections.

2. The last Article of a Regulation shall fix the date of entry into force, where the date is before or after the twentieth day following publication.

3. The last Article of a Regulation shall be followed by:
   - 'This Regulation shall be binding in its entirety and directly applicable in all Member States'; 'Done at............', followed by the date on which the Regulation was adopted, and in the case of:

   (a) a Regulation adopted jointly by the European Parliament and the Council, the formula:

   > 'For the European Parliament
   > The President'
   > 'For the Council
   > The President'

   followed by the name of the President of the European Parliament and of the President-in-Office of the Council when the Regulation is adopted.

   (b) a Council Regulation, the following formula:

   > 'For the Council
   > The President'

   followed by the name of the President-in-Office of the Council at the time when the Regulation is adopted.

### Article 15:

The acts referred to in Article 191(1) of the EC Treaty and the acts of the Council referred to in Article 191(2) thereof and in the first paragraph of Article 163 of the EAEC Treaty shall be published in the Official Journal by the Secretary-General. Common positions adopted by the Council in accordance with the procedures referred to in Articles 189B and 189C of the EC Treaty, and the reasons underlying those common positions, shall be published under the same conditions.

### Article 16:

- Directives and Decisions adopted jointly by the European Parliament and the Council, and Directives and Decisions of the Council shall include in their titles the word 'Directive' or 'Decision'.

- Recommendations made and opinions delivered by the Council shall include in their titles the word 'recommendation' or 'opinion'.

- The provisions relating to Regulations set out in Articles 13 and 14 shall apply *mutatis mutandis*, subject to the relevant provisions of the Treaty, to Directives and Decisions.

### Article 17:

1. Common positions within the meaning of Article J.2. and joint action within the meaning of Article J.3. of the Treaty on European Union shall bear one of the following headings, as appropriate:
   - 'Common position defined by the Council on the basis of Article J.2. of the Treaty on European Union';
   - 'Joint action adopted by the Council on the basis of Article J.3. of the Treaty on European Union'.

2. Joint positions, joint action and conventions within the meaning of Article K.3. (2) of the Treaty on European Union shall bear one of the following headings, as appropriate:
   - 'Joint position defined by the Council on the basis of Article K.3. of the Treaty on European Union';
   - 'Joint action adopted by the Council on the basis of Article K.3. of the Treaty on European Union';
   - 'Convention drawn up on the basis of Article K.3. of the Treaty on European Union'.

### Article 18:

1. The Secretary-General shall notify Council Directives other than those

referred to in Article 191(2) of the EC Treaty and Council decisions and recommendations to their addresses. He shall also notify the joint action adopted or the common positions or joint positions defined on the basis of Articles J.2, J.3 or K.3 of the Treaty on European Union. He may entrust to Directors-General of the General Secretariat the task of attending to such notification on his behalf.

2. The Secretary-General or a Director-General acting on his behalf shall send authentic copies of Directives other than those referred to in Article 191(2) of the EC Treaty and Council decisions and recommendations to the Governments of the Member States and to the Commission.

3. The decision to publish in the Official Journal the common positions and joint positions defined and the joint action adopted on the basis of Articles J.2, J.3 and K.3 of the Treaty on European Union and the measures implementing joint action and any measures implementing the conventions referred to in paragraph 4 shall in each case be taken by the Council acting unanimously when the said instruments are adopted.

4. Conventions drawn up by the Council in accordance with Article K.3(2) of the Treaty on European Union, shall be published in the Official Journal. Reference shall be made in the Official Journal to the entry into force of such conventions.

5. The Council shall decide unanimously whether the following shall be published in the Official Journal by the Secretary-General:
   – Directives other than those referred to in Article 191(1) and (2) of the EC Treaty, Council decisions and recommendations,
   – conventions signed between the Member States.

6. Where an agreement concluded between the Communities and one or more States or international organisations sets up a body vested with powers of decision, the Council shall decide, when such an agreement is concluded, whether decisions to be taken by that body should be published in the Official Journal.

### Article 19:

1. The Permanent Representatives Committee (Coreper) shall prepare the work of the Council and shall carry out the tasks assigned to it by the Council. All items on the agenda for a Council meeting shall be examined in advance by Coreper unless the Council decides otherwise. Coreper shall endeavour to reach agreement at its level to be submitted to the Council for adoption. It shall ensure adequate presentation of the dossiers to the Council. In the event of an emergency, the Council, acting unanimously, may decide to settle the matter without prior examination.

2. Committees or working parties may be set up by, or with the approval of, Coreper with a view to carrying out certain preparatory work or studies defined in advance.

3. Coreper shall be presided over, depending on the item on the agenda, by the Permanent Representative or the Deputy Permanent Representative of the Member State which holds the Presidency of the Council. Unless the Council decides otherwise, the various committees provided for in the Treaties shall also be presided over by a delegate of that Member State. The same shall apply to the committees and working parties referred to in paragraph 2, unless Coreper decides otherwise. For the preparation of meetings of Council compositions meeting once every six months and held during the first half of this period, the meetings of committees other than Coreper, and those of the working parties held during the preceding six months may be chaired by a delegate of the Member State whose turn it is to chair the said Council meetings.

### Article 20:

Notwithstanding the other provisions of these Rules of Procedure, the Presidency shall organise the meetings of the various committees and working parties so that their reports are available before the Coreper meetings at which they are to be examined.

### Article 21:

1. The Council shall be assisted by a General Secretariat under the direction

of a Secretary-General. The Secretary-General shall be appointed by the Council acting unanimously.

2. The Council shall determine the organisation of the General Secretariat. Under its authority the Secretary-General shall take all the measures necessary to ensure the smooth running of the General Secretariat.

3. The Secretary-General shall submit to the Council the draft estimate of the expenditure of the Council in sufficient time to ensure that the time-limits laid down by the financial provisions are met.

4. In accordance with the provisions of the Financial Regulation referred to in Article 78H of the ECSC Treaty, in Article 209 of the EC Treaty and in Article 183 of the EAEC Treaty, the Secretary-General shall administer the funds placed at the disposal of the Council.

### Article 22:

The detailed arrangements for public access to Council documents disclosure of which is without serious or prejudicial consequences shall be adopted by the Council.

### Article 23:

The rules on security shall be adopted by the Council.

### Article 24:

In the event of the Secretary-General of the Council being designated as depository of an agreement concluded between the Community and one or more States or international organisations, of a convention concluded between Member States or of a convention drawn up pursuant to Article K.3 of the Treaty on European Union, the acts of ratification, acceptance or approval of those agreements shall be deposited at the address of the Council. In such instances the Secretary-General shall perform all the duties of a depository of a treaty and shall also ensure that the dates of entry into force of such agreements or conventions are published in the Official Journal.

### Article 25:

1. Subject to special procedures, the Council may be represented by the Presidency or by any other of its members before the European Parliament or its committees. The Council may also be represented before those committees by its Secretary-General or by senior officials of the General Secretariat acting on instructions from the Presidency.

2. The Council may also present its views to the European Parliament by means of a written statement.

### Article 26:

Correspondence to the Council shall be sent to the President at the address of the Council.

### Annex

The Council acts as legislator within the meaning of the first indent of Article 7(5) when it adopts rules which are legally binding on or for the Member States whether by means of Regulations, Directives or Decisions on the basis of the relevant provisions of the Treaties, in particular on the basis of Article 43 of the Treaty establishing the European Community or in the framework if the procedures in Article 189B and Article 189C of that Treaty, with the exemption of discussions leading to the adoption of internal measures, administrative or budgetary acts, acts concerning inter-institutional or international relations, or non-binding acts such as conclusions, recommendations or resolutions. Votes shall not be made public in the case of discussions leading to indicative votes or the adoption of preparatory acts.

# *Appendix 2*

## Days spent on Council meetings 1958–94

| Year | Ministers | Coreper | Committees | Total |
|------|-----------|---------|------------|-------|
| 1958 | 21 | 39 | 302 | 362 |
| 1959 | 21 | 71 | 325 | 417 |
| 1960 | 44 | 97 | 505 | 646 |
| 1961 | 46 | 108 | 655 | 809 |
| 1962 | 80 | 128 | 783 | 991 |
| 1963 | 63.5 | 146.5 | 744.5 | 954.5 |
| 1964 | 102.5 | 229.5 | 1002.5 | 1334.5 |
| 1965 | 35 | 105.5 | 760.5 | 901 |
| 1966 | 70.5 | 112.5 | 952.5 | 1135.5 |
| 1967 | 75.5 | 134 | 1233 | 1442.5 |
| 1968 | 61 | 132 | 1253 | 1446 |
| 1969 | 69 | 129 | 1412.5 | 1610.5 |
| 1970 | 81 | 154 | 1403 | 1638 |
| 1971 | 75.5 | 127.5 | 1439 | 1642 |
| 1972 | 73 | 159 | 2135 | 2367 |
| 1973 | 79.5 | 148 | 1820 | 2047.5 |
| 1974 | 66 | 114.5 | 1999.5 | 2180 |
| 1975 | 67.5 | 118 | 2079.5 | 2265 |
| 1976 | 65.5 | 108.5 | 2130 | 2304 |
| 1977 | 71 | 122 | 2108.5 | 2301.5 |
| 1978 | 76.5 | 104.5 | 2090 | 2271 |
| 1979 | 59 | 107.5 | 2000 | 2166.5 |
| 1980 | 83 | 106.5 | 2078.5 | 2268 |
| 1981 | 83 | 110 | 1976 | 2169 |
| 1982 | 86 | 107 | 1885 | 2078 |
| 1983 | 121.5 | 105 | 1912.5 | 2139 |
| 1984 | 133 | 86 | 1868.5 | 2087.5 |
| 1985 | 118 | 117 | 1892 | 2127 |
| 1986 | 107 | 118.5 | 1842.5 | 2068 |
| 1987 | 123 | 120.5 | 1828 | 2071.5 |
| 1988 | 117.5 | 104 | 2000.5 | 2222 |
| 1989 | 119.5 | 100 | 1932 | 2151.5 |
| 1990 | 138 | 107 | 2021.5 | 2266.5 |
| 1991 | 115.5 | 145.5 | 2239 | 2500 |
| 1992 | 126 | 133.5 | 2147 | 2406.5 |
| 1993 | 119 | 115.5 | 2105.5 | 2340 |
| 1994 | 98 | 127 | 2662 | 2887 |

Certain observations can be made from this data. In comparing the graphs following, it is possible to observe that while meetings of ministers averaged out in the 1970s, there was a rise in meetings of Coreper and committees. Conversely, the 1980s saw an increase in ministerial Council sessions, with Coreper and committee meetings averaging out. The trend seems to indicate a rise in non-ministerial sessions for the next few years.

## Number of days spent in ministerial meetings

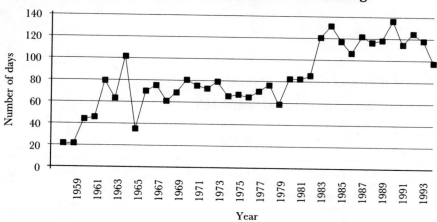

## Number of days spent on Coreper meetings

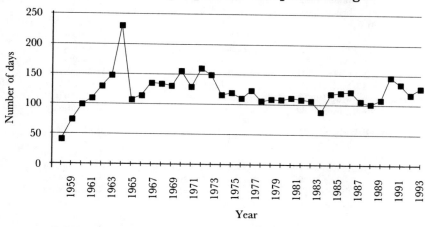

## Number of days spent on Committee meetings

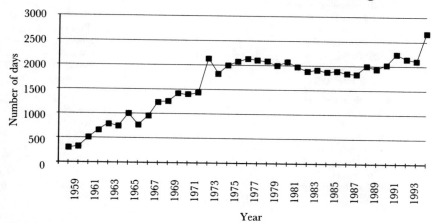

Source: *Annual Reviews of the Council's Work.*

# *Appendix 3*

## Informal sessions of the Council 1982–92

| Date | Session | Venue |
|---|---|---|
| **Presidency–Belgium** | | |
| 11 January 1982 | General | Brussels |
| 13 January 1982 | Industry | Brussels |
| 14–15 January 1982 | General | Brussels |
| 25 January 1982 | General | Brussels |
| 11 February 1982 | Textiles | Brussels |
| 25 February 1982 | Textiles | Brussels |
| 2 March 1982 | Development | Brussels |
| 5–6 April 1982 | Labour & Social | Brussels |
| 8–9 May 1982 | General | Villers |
| 10–11 May 1982 | Agriculture | Brussels |
| 17 May 1982 | EcoFin | Brussels |
| 24 May 1982 | General | Brussels |
| 20–22 June 1982 | General | Luxembourg |
| **Presidency–Denmark** | | |
| 5 July 1982 | Agriculture | Brussels |
| 9 September 1982 | General | Copenhagen |
| 27–28 September 1982 | Labour & Social | Copenhagen |
| 5 October 1982 | Development | Luxembourg |
| 11–12 October 1982 | Agriculture | Copenhagen |
| 16 October 1982 | General | Nyborg |
| 18–19 November 1982 | Industry | Elsener |
| 16 December 1982 | Coal | Copenhagen |
| **Presidency–Germany** | | |
| 21 February 1983 | Labour & Social | Bonn |
| 3 March 1983 | Development | Bonn |
| 14–15 May 1983 | General | Gymnich |
| 25–26 May 1983 | Agriculture | Brussels |
| 30–31 May 1983 | Agriculture | Oberstdorf |
| 13 June 1983 | General | Luxembourg |
| **Presidency–Greece** | | |
| 19 July 1983 | General | Brussels |
| 25 July 1983 | Steel | Brussels |
| 29–30 September 1983 | Labour & Social | Athens |
| 3 October 1983 | Environment | Athens |
| 6–7 October 1983 | Transport | Athens |
| 10 October 1983 | General | Athens |
| 22–23 October 1983 | General | Athens |
| 7 November 1983 | Labour & Social | Athens |

| | | |
|---|---|---|
| 9–12 November 1983 | General | Athens |
| 18 November 1983 | Culture | Delphi |
| 18 November 1983 | General | Brussels |
| 20 November 1983 | Tourism | Athens |

**Presidency–France**

| | | |
|---|---|---|
| 2 February 1984 | Labour & Social | Brussels |
| 14 February 1984 | Energy | Paris |
| 17–18 February 1984 | General | Paris |
| 8 March 1984 | Labour & Social | Paris |
| 9 March 1984 | Development | Grenoble |
| 2 April 1984 | Transport | Paris |
| 5 April 1984 | Labour & Social | Paris |
| 12–13 May 1984 | EcoFin | Rambouillet |
| 18 May 1984 | Industry | Brussels |
| 25–26 May 1984 | General | Marseilles |
| 28–30 May 1984 | Agriculture | Angers |

**Presidency–Ireland**

| | | |
|---|---|---|
| 11 September 1984 | General | Dublin |
| 15–16 September 1984 | EcoFin | Dromoland Castle |
| 20–21 September 1984 | Labour & Social | Dublin |
| 23–26 September 1984 | Agriculture | Killarney |
| 3–4 November 1984 | General | Dromoland Castle |

**Presidency–Italy**

| | | |
|---|---|---|
| 8 February 1985 | Labour & Social | Venice |
| 28 February–1 March 1985 | General | Brussels |
| 5 March 1985 | Transport | Tarento |
| 7 March 1985 | Labour & Social | Rome |
| 20 March 1985 | Environment | Brussels |
| 13–14 April 1985 | EcoFin | Palermo |
| 22 April 1985 | Industry | Brussels |
| 27–29 May 1985 | Agriculture | Siena |
| 8–9 June 1985 | General | Stresa |

**Presidency–Luxembourg**

| | | |
|---|---|---|
| 20 September 1985 | EcoFin | Luxembourg |
| 23–24 September 1985 | Labour & Social | Luxembourg |
| 23–24 September 1985 | Agriculture | Luxembourg |
| 23 October 1985 | Research | Luxembourg |
| 26–27 October 1985 | General | Luxembourg |

**Presidency–Netherlands**

| | | |
|---|---|---|
| 27 January 1986 | General | Brussels |
| 17–18 February 1986 | Labour & Social | Hague |
| 10–11 March 1986 | Labour & Social | Hague |
| 5–6 April 1986 | EcoFin | Ootmarsum |
| 16 April 1986 | Development | Luxembourg |
| 23–24 April 1986 | Trevi | Hague |
| 23 April 1986 | Labour & Social | Brussels |
| 16–17 May 1986 | Education | Hague |
| 7–8 June 1986 | General | Heemskerk |
| 9–10 June 1986 | Agriculture | Wageningen |
| 13 June 1986 | Culture | Hague |

**Presidency–United Kingdom**

| | | |
|---|---|---|
| 15–16 September 1986 | Energy | Worcestershire |
| 19–20 September 1986 | EcoFin | Gleneagles |

| | | |
|---|---|---|
| 22–23 September 1986 | Labour & Social | Edinburgh |
| 25 September 1986 | Trevi | London |
| 28–30 September 1986 | Agriculture | Lake District |
| 3 October 1986 | Transport | London |
| 20 October 1986 | Trevi | London |

**Presidency–Belgium**

| | | |
|---|---|---|
| 13 February 1987 | Environment | Brussels |
| 17 February 1987 | Transport | Brussels |
| 22 February 1987 | General | Brussels |
| 16–17 March 1987 | Labour & Social | Brussels |
| 3–5 April 1987 | EcoFin | Knokke |
| 27–28 April 1987 | Trevi | Brussels |
| 30 April 1987 | Labour & Social | Brussels |
| 25 May 1987 | Justice | Brussels |
| 31 May–2 June 1987 | Agriculture | Brussels |

**Presidency–Denmark**

| | | |
|---|---|---|
| 6–8 September 1987 | Agriculture | Nyborg |
| 7 September 1987 | Internal Market | Copenhagen |
| 12–13 September 1987 | EcoFin | Nyborg |
| 20–21 September 1987 | Energy | Copenhagen |
| 28–29 September 1987 | Labour & Social | Copenhagen |
| 30 September 1987 | Culture | Copenhagen |
| 3–4 October 1987 | General | Nyborg |
| 6–7 October 1987 | Education | Copenhagen |
| 10 December 1987 | Culture | Copenhagen |

**Presidency–Germany**

| | | |
|---|---|---|
| 1 February 1988 | General | Brussels |
| 18 February 1988 | Development | Bavaria |
| 25–26 February 1988 | Education | Munster |
| 25–26 February 1988 | Environment | Wildbad-Kreuth |
| 14–15 March 1988 | Labour & Social | Dortmund |
| 18 March 1988 | Trade | Constance |
| 11–12 April 1988 | Fisheries | Cuxhaven |
| 25–26 April 1988 | Transport | Hof |
| 26 April 1988 | Labour & Social | Berlin |
| 28 April 1988 | Telecommunications | Berlin |
| 5–7 May 1988 | Tourism | Gluecksburg |
| 13–15 May 1988 | EcoFin | Lubeck |
| 3 June 1988 | Trevi | Munich |
| 20–21 June 1988 | Agriculture | Wurzburg |

**Presidency–Greece**

| | | |
|---|---|---|
| 16–17 July 1988 | Youth & Sport | Athens |
| 29 July 1988 | Internal Market | Athens |
| 7–8 September 1988 | Fisheries | Athens |
| 9–10 September 1988 | Agriculture | Athens |
| 17–18 September 1988 | EcoFin | Crete |
| 19–20 September 1988 | Labour & Social | Athens |
| 24–25 September 1988 | Trevi | Athens |
| 24–25 September 1988 | Energy | Athens |
| 28 September 1988 | Culture | Delphes |
| 29–30 September 1988 | Transport | Athens |
| 1–2 October 1988 | Environment | Delphes |
| 15–16 October 1988 | General | Ioannina |

| | | |
|---|---|---|
| 21–22 October 1988 | Industry | Athens |
| 5–6 October 1988 | Telecommunications | Athens |
| 28 November 1988 | Culture | Brussels |
| 9 December 1988 | Trevi | Athens |

**Presidency–Spain**

| | | |
|---|---|---|
| 13 February 1989 | Transport | Murcia |
| 6–7 March 1989 | Labour & Social | Seville |
| 9 March 1989 | Trevi | Seville |
| 13–14 March 1989 | Culture | Toledo |
| 17–18 March 1989 | Education | Segovia |
| 30–31 March 1989 | Culture | Santiago de Compostela |
| 7–8 April 1989 | Industry | San Sebastian |
| 10–11 April 1989 | Fisheries | Toja |
| 27–28 April 1989 | Labour & Social | Toledo |
| 5–7 May 1989 | Environment | Caceres |
| 15–16 May 1989 | Agriculture | Salamanca |
| 19–21 May 1989 | EcoFin | S'Agaro-Gerona |
| 26–27 May 1989 | Justice | San Sebastian |
| 20 June 1989 | Justice | Hague |

**Presidency–France**

| | | |
|---|---|---|
| 10 July 1989 | Labour & Social | Auxerre |
| 8–10 September 1989 | EcoFin | Antibes |
| 12 September 1989 | Telecommunications | Antibes |
| 14–15 September 1989 | General | Chateau d'Esclimont |
| 29–31 September 1989 | Agriculture | Beaurie |
| 6 October 1989 | Transport | Lille |
| 14 October 1989 | Trade | Metz |
| 2 November 1989 | Culture | Blois |
| 9 November 1989 | Youth & Sport | Paris |
| 23–24 November 1989 | Regional | Nantes |
| 7 December 1989 | Fisheries | Bethurie |

**Presidency–Ireland**

| | | |
|---|---|---|
| 20 January 1990 | General | Dublin |
| 1 March 1990 | Labour & Social | Dublin |
| 10–11 March 1990 | Tourism | Ashford Castle |
| 23–24 March 1990 | Internal Market | Dromoland Castle |
| 31 March–1 April 1990 | EcoFin | Ashford Castle |
| 21 April 1990 | General | Dublin Castle |
| 21 April 1990 | Environment | Ashford Castle |
| 26 April 1990 | Labour & Social | Ashford Castle |
| 19–20 May 1990 | General | Parknasilla |
| 19 May 1990 | Trade | Dublin Castle |
| 15 June 1990 | Justice | Dublin Castle |
| 18–19 June 1990 | Agriculture | Dromoland Castle |

**Presidency–Italy**

| | | |
|---|---|---|
| 20–21 July 1990 | Health | Rome |
| 7–8 September 1990 | EcoFin | Rome |
| 18 September 1990 | Trade | Rome |
| 22–23 September 1990 | Environment | Rome |
| 30 September–2 October 1990 | Agriculture | Palermo |
| 6 October 1990 | General | Asolo |
| 12 October 1990 | Fisheries | Palermo |

| Date | Subject | Location |
|---|---|---|
| 18 October 1990 | Telecommunications | Rome |
| 18–19 October 1990 | Culture | Rome |
| 2 December 1990 | EcoFin | Milan |
| 7 December 1990 | Housing | Milan |
| 17–18 December 1990 | Youth & Sport | Rome |

**Presidency–Luxembourg**

| Date | Subject | Location |
|---|---|---|
| 8–9 March 1991 | Internal Market | Luxembourg |
| 8 March 1991 | General | Luxembourg |
| 27–28 April 1991 | General | Luxembourg |
| 6 May 1991 | Labour & Social | Luxembourg |
| 11–12 May 1991 | EcoFin | Luxembourg |
| 13 May 1991 | Labour & Social | Luxembourg |
| 2–3 June 1991 | General | Dresde |
| 2–3 June 1991 | Education | Luxembourg |
| 17 June 1991 | Agriculture | Luxembourg |
| 26 June 1991 | Trade | Luxembourg |

**Presidency–Netherlands**

| Date | Subject | Location |
|---|---|---|
| 5–6 July 1991 | Transport | Rotterdam |
| 6–7 July 1991 | Development | Apeldoorn |
| 13–14 September 1991 | Internal Market | Amsterdam |
| 21–22 September 1991 | EcoFin | Apeldoorn |
| 22–24 September 1991 | Labour & Social | Noordwijk |
| 24 September 1991 | Housing | Amsterdam |
| 29 September–1 October 1991 | Agriculture | Drachten |
| 5 October 1991 | General | Haarzuilen |
| 8–10 October 1991 | Health | Noordwijk |
| 11–12 October 1991 | Trade | Hague |
| 12–13 October 1991 | Environment | Amsterdam |
| 17–18 October 1991 | Tourism | Noordwijk |
| 18–19 October 1991 | Regional | Hague |

**Presidency–Portugal**

| Date | Subject | Location |
|---|---|---|
| 21–22 February 1992 | Environment | Estoril |
| 13–14 March 1992 | Labour & Social | Penina |
| 21 March 1992 | Industry | Lisbon |
| 10–11 April 1992 | Education/Youth | Funchal |
| 1–2 May 1992 | General | Guimaraes |
| 8–9 May 1992 | EcoFin | Porto |
| 15 May 1992 | Regional | Lisbon |
| 24–26 May 1992 | Agriculture | Curia |
| 11–12 June 1992 | Trevi | Lisbon |
| 20 June 1992 | General | Luxembourg |

**Presidency–United Kingdom**

| Date | Subject | Location |
|---|---|---|
| 16–17 July 1992 | Transport | Brocket Hall |
| 4–6 September 1992 | EcoFin | Bath |
| 7 September 1992 | Culture | London |
| 12 September 1992 | General | Brocket Hall |
| 18–20 September 1992 | Environment | Gleneagles |
| 28–29 September 1992 | Agriculture | Cambridge |
| 12–13 October 1992 | Labour & Social | Chepstow |
| 6–7 November 1992 | Trade | Brocket Hall |
| 27 November 1992 | General/EcoFin | Brussels |

Source: *Agence Europe.*

# *Appendix 4*

## Sessions of the four selected Councils 1988–92

| Session No. | Date | Council | Venue |
|---|---|---|---|
| **Presidency – Germany** | | | |
| 1221 | 09.02.88 | EcoFin | Brussels |
| Informal | 25.02.88–26.02.88 | Education | Munster |
| 1225 | 07.03.88 | EcoFin | Brussels |
| Informal | 14.03.88–15.03.88 | Labour & Social Affairs | Dortmund |
| 1228 | 21.03.88 | Environment | Brussels |
| 1233 | 18.04.88 | EcoFin | Luxembourg |
| Informal | 13.05.88–15.05.88 | EcoFin | Lubeck |
| 1241 | 24.05.88 | Education | Brussels |
| 1247 | 09.06.88 | Labour & Social Affairs | Luxembourg |
| 1248 | 13.06.88 | EcoFin | Luxembourg |
| 1251 | 16.06.88–17.06.88 and 28.06.88–29.06.88 | Environment | Luxembourg |
| **Presidency – Greece** | | | |
| 1258 | 11.07.88 | EcoFin | Brussels |
| Informal | 17.09.88–18.09.88 | EcoFin | Crete |
| 1271 | 07.11.88 | EcoFin | Brussels |
| 1278 | 23.11.88 | Education | Brussels |
| 1280 | 24.11.88–25.11.88 | Environment | Brussels |
| 1285 | 12.12.88 | EcoFin | Brussels |
| 1291 | 16.12.88–17.12.88 | Labour & Social Affairs | Brussels |
| **Presidency – Spain** | | | |
| 1296 | 13.02.89 | EcoFin | Brussels |
| 1301 | 02.03.89–03.03.89 | Environment | Brussels |
| 1304 | 13.03.89 | EcoFin | Brussels |
| Informal | 22.03.89 | Environment | Basel |
| 1310 | 05.04.89 | Labour & Social Affairs | Luxembourg |
| 1312 | 17.04.89 | EcoFin | Luxembourg |
| 1321 | 22.05.89 | Education | Brussels |
| 1328 | 08.06.89–09.06.89 | Environment | Luxembourg |
| 1330 | 12.06.89 | Labour & Social Affairs | Luxembourg |
| 1333 | 19.06.89 | EcoFin | Luxembourg |
| **Presidency – France** | | | |
| 1337 | 10.07.89 | EcoFin | Brussels |
| 1345 | 19.09.89 | Environment | Brussels |
| 1348 | 29.09.89 | Labour & Social Affairs | Brussels |
| 1350 | 06.10.89 | Education | Luxembourg |
| 1351 | 09.10.89 | EcoFin | Luxembourg |
| 1357 | 30.10.89 | Labour & Social Affairs | Brussels |

| | | | |
|---|---|---|---|
| 1362 | 13.11.89 | EcoFin | Brussels |
| 1371 | 28.11.89 | Environment | Brussels |
| 1372 | 30.11.89 | Labour & Social Affairs | Brussels |
| 1377 | 14.12.89 | Education | Brussels |
| 1379 | 18.12.89 | EcoFin | Brussels |

**Presidency – Ireland**

| | | | |
|---|---|---|---|
| 1385 | 12.02.90 | EcoFin | Brussels |
| Informal | 01.03.90 | Labour & Social Affairs | Dublin |
| 1391 | 12.03.90 | EcoFin | Brussels |
| 1393 | 22.03.90 | Environment | Brussels |
| Informal | 31.03.90–01.04.90 | EcoFin | Ashford Castle |
| Informal | 21.04.90 | Environment | Ashford Castle |
| 1398 | 23.04.90–27.04.90 | EcoFin | Brussels |
| Informal | 26.04.90 | Labour & Social Affairs | Ashford Castle |
| 1408 | 29.05.90 | Labour & Social Affairs | Brussels |
| 1409 | 31.05.90 | Education | Brussels |
| 1410 | 07.06.90–08.06.90 | Environment | Luxembourg |
| 1411 | 11.06.90–19.06.90 | EcoFin | Luxembourg |

**Presidency – Italy**

| | | | |
|---|---|---|---|
| 1421 | 23.07.90 | EcoFin | Brussels |
| Informal | 07.09.90–08.09.90 | EcoFin | Rome |
| Informal | 22.09.90–23.09.90 | Environment | Rome |
| 1427 | 08.10.90 | EcoFin | Luxembourg |
| 1434 | 29.10.90–30.10.90 | Environment | Luxembourg |
| 1436 | 29.10.90 | Energy/Environment | Luxembourg |
| 1444 | 19.11.90 | EcoFin | Brussels |
| 1449 | 26.11.90 | Labour & Social Affairs | Brussels |
| Informal | 02.12.90 | EcoFin | Milan |
| 1454 | 03.12.90 | EcoFin | Brussels |
| 1457 | 06.12.90 | Education | Brussels |
| 1459 | 10.12.90 | EcoFin | Brussels |
| 1462 | 17.12.90–19.12.90 | EcoFin | Brussels |
| 1465 | 18.12.90 | Labour & Social Affairs | Brussels |
| 1467 | 20.12.90–21.12.90 | Environment | Brussels |

**Presidency – Luxembourg**

| | | | |
|---|---|---|---|
| 1470 | 28.01.91 | EcoFin | Brussels |
| 1473 | 25.02.91–05.03.91 | EcoFin | Brussels |
| 1476 | 18.03.91 | EcoFin | Brussels |
| 1477 | 18.03.91 | Environment | Brussels |
| 1481 | 08.04.91 | EcoFin | Luxembourg |
| Informal | 06.05.91 | Labour & Social Affairs | Luxembourg |
| Informal | 11.05.91–12.05.91 & 14.05.91 | EcoFin | Luxembourg |
| Informal | 02.06.91–03.06.91 | Education | Luxembourg |
| 1494 | 03.06.91 | EcoFin | Luxembourg |
| 1496 | 10.06.91 | EcoFin | Luxembourg |
| 1497 | 13.06.91–14.06.91 | Environment | Luxembourg |
| 1503 | 24.06.91 | EcoFin | Luxembourg |
| 1504 | 25.06.91 | Labour & Social Affairs | Luxembourg |

**Presidency – Netherlands**

| | | | |
|---|---|---|---|
| 1506 | 08.07.91 | EcoFin | Brussels |
| 1512 | 09.09.91 | EcoFin | Brussels |
| Informal | 21.09.91–22.09.91 | EcoFin | Apeldoorn |

| Informal | 22.09.91–24.09.91 | Labour & Social Affairs | Noordwijk |
| 1516 | 01.10.91 | Environment | Luxembourg |
| 1517 | 07.10.91 | EcoFin | Luxembourg |
| Informal | 12.10.91–13.10.91 | Environment | Amsterdam |
| 1519 | 14.10.91 & 06.11.91 | Labour & Social Affairs | Luxembourg |
| 1530 | 11.11.91 | EcoFin | Brussels |
| 1537 | 25.11.91 | Education | Brussels |
| 1540 | 03.12.91 | EcoFin | Brussels |
| 1541 | 03.12.91 | Labour & Social Affairs | Brussels |
| 1543 | 12.12.91–13.12.91 | Environment | Brussels |
| 1544 | 13.12.91 | Environment/Energy | Brussels |
| 1546 | 16.12.91 | EcoFin | Brussels |

**Presidency – Portugal**

| 1552 | 13.01.92 | EcoFin | Brussels |
| 1555 | 10.02.92 | EcoFin | Brussels |
| Informal | 21.02.92–22.02.92 | Environment | Estoril |
| Informal | 13.03.92–14.03.92 | Labour & Social Affairs | Penina |
| 1560 | 16.03.92 | EcoFin | Brussels |
| 1561 | 23.03.92 | Environment | Brussels |
| Informal | 10.04.92–11.04.92 | Education/Youth | Funchal |
| 1570 | 30.04.92 | Labour & Social Affairs | Luxembourg |
| 1572 | 05.05.92 | Environment/Development | Brussels |
| Informal | 08.05.92–09.05.92 | EcoFin | Porto |
| 1577 | 19.05.92 | EcoFin | Brussels |
| 1581 | 26.05.92–27.05.92 | Environment | Brussels |
| 1583 | 01.06.92 | Education | Luxembourg |
| 1586 | 09.06.92–10.06.92 | EcoFin | Luxembourg |
| 1593 | 24.06.92 | Labour & Social Affairs | Luxembourg |
| 1595 | 29.06.92 | EcoFin | Luxembourg |

**Presidency – UK**

| 1597 | 13.07.92 | EcoFin | Brussels |
| 1601 | 27.07.92 | EcoFin | Brussels |
| Informal | 04.09.92–06.09.92 | EcoFin | Bath |
| Informal | 18.09.92–20.09.92 | Environment | Gleneagles |
| 1604 | 28.09.92 | EcoFin | Brussels |
| Informal | 12.10.92–13.10.92 | Labour & Social Affairs | Chepstow |
| 1607 | 19.10.92 | EcoFin | Luxembourg |
| 1609 | 20.10.92 | Environment | Luxembourg |
| 1621 | 23.11.92 | EcoFin | Brussels |
| 1624 | 27.11.92 | Education | Brussels |
| Informal | 27.11.92 | General Affairs/EcoFin | Brussels |
| 1626 | 03.12.92 | Labour & Social Affairs | Brussels |
| 1630 | 14.12.92 | EcoFin | Brussels |
| 1633 | 15.12.92–16.12.92 | Environment | Brussels |

Joint Session = /.  Data taken from *Agence Europe*.

# Notes

## Introduction

1  The Council of Ministers was referred to as the Council in Article 7 of the Treaty of Paris 1951, Article 4 of the Treaty of Rome 1957, and Article 1 of the Merger Treaty 1965. Its official title was altered by the TEU to the Council of the European Union.

2  The focus here is on both the English and French literature on the Council. However, a significant amount of work on the Council is written in German. Contact the library of the Council for details of the German literature.

3  On the role of the Presidency see for example, Edwards and Wallace (1977), O'Nuallain (ed.) (1985), de Bassompierre (1988), and Kirchner, (1992).

4  See for example Bieber and Palmer (1975), Bo Bramsen (1982), Bulmer (1985), Bulmer and Wessels (1987), Werts (1992) and Troy Johnston (1994).

5  For detailed analysis of Coreper see Noël (1967), Noël and Etienne (1971), Hayes (1984), and Hayes-Renshaw, Lequesne, and Mayor Lopez (1989).

6  For texts analysing the TEU, see for example Cafruny and Rosenthal (eds) (1993), Duff, Pinder and Pryce (eds) (1994), and Monar, Ungerer and Wessels (eds) (1993).

## Chapter 1

1  The assent and budgetary procedures are not specifically dealt with, but did confer additional decision-making input upon the EP.

2  In proposals regarding financial regulations, Article 209 requires the Council to obtain the opinion of the Court of Auditors before taking a decision in this respect.

3  The other variables that were tested include the nature of the proposal, voting procedure, input of EP and policy pressure.

4  For example, at one Question Time held during the 1992 UK Presidency, only 15 MEPs attended, and twelve of those were from the UK.

5  For example, see Kirchner (1992).

6  For detailed and useful analysis of the years in question see, for example Brewin and McAllister (1986–91), and Nugent (1993). For information on specific policy developments, but from an EU institutional perspective, consult the following: written by the Council – *Annual Review of the Council's Work.* 1982 to 1992; and for a Commission perspective see *General Report on the Activities of the European Communities* 1982 to 1992. For a less official review of this period, consult *Europe: Agence Internationale d'Information pour la Presse.* 1988–92.

7  Wallace (1994), p. 63.

8  For a rather different picture of events, see Thatcher (1993). It is interesting that Nigel Lawson (1992) makes no mention of this in his memoirs.

9  The Draft Treaty on European Union had been initiated by Spinelli. He set up the Crocodile Club, comprising of MEPs, to revise existing institutional practices, and give the EP a greater role in policy-making. The Treaty was ratified by the EP and, although not so warmly welcomed by some member states, formed the basis of the institutional agenda at the 1985 IGC.

10  The changing context of Europe meant that by the time the EEA agreement was concluded, most of the EFTA members were already seeking EC membership. The UK pushed enlargement negotiations

during its 1992 Presidency, and three EFTA states joined the EU in 1995.

11 For further details, see Spence (1991), and Westlake (1992).

## Chapter 2

1 The term General Affairs will be used, as opposed to Foreign Affairs Council, because although its membership comprises the twelve Foreign Ministers, the remit of the Council extends much further.

2 This total figure was calculated by analysing the Council Press Releases for the General Affairs Council during this five year period.

3 Data for 59 out of the 63 formal meetings showed that the General Affairs Council adopted 318 'A' points between 1988 and 1992 inclusive.

4 'The Internal Market After 1992.' *Background Report.* Commission of the European Communities (London Office) ISEC/B7/93, 4 March 1993.

5 See Appendix 2 for details of the number of days spent on Council meetings between 1958 and 1994.

6 For detailed analysis of the European Council see Bulmer (1985), Bulmer and Wessels (1987), Werts (1992), and Troy Johnston (1994).

7 Edwards and Wallace (1977), O'Nuallain (ed.) (1985), de Bassompierre (1988) and Kirchner (1992) all conclude this to be the case.

8 For detailed analysis of Coreper see Noël (1967), Noel and Etienne (1971), Hayes (1984), Hayes *et al.* (1989), and Tizzano (1991).

9 See Appendix 2 for details of the number of days spent on Coreper meetings between 1958 and 1994.

10 For a concise discussion of these committees, see Hayes-Renshaw and Wallace (1997: 70–100).

11 The Council handbook only states that there were 'over 150 on 1 January 1990'. (Council, 1991: 26).

12 See Appendix 2 for details of the number of days spent on Committee/Working Group meetings between 1958 and 1994.

13 These examples are based on the author's attendance at one Coreper meeting and two different working groups during 1993.

14 See Appendix 1, Article 2.

15 See Appendix 1.

## Chapter 3

1 The French for this is 'au sein du Conseil'.

2 It should be noted that each member state may only have one vote at joint sessions in accordance with the Treaty of Rome, which refers to the delegation by each government of 'one' of its members.

3 Points 'Agree' were introduced in 1962. See Hayes (1984: 180).

4 See Appendix 1, Article 7.

5 For a full account of the crisis, see Lambert (1966).

6 Report presented to the European Council, October 1979. For further discussion of the report see Bangemann (1980).

7 Conclusions of the Presidency 1974. See Werts (1992: 54–5) for further information on the Paris Summit.

8 These observations are based on consulting the minutes of five Council sessions held between 1961 and 1963. The average length of these minutes is approximately 50 pages – far lengthier than Council minutes taken today. The author is most grateful to the General Secretariat of the Council for granting permission to consult these documents.

9 These minutes were those of an Article 113 Committee decision to open negotiations with a third country.

## Chapter 4

1 Allison stresses that his are only initial efforts in seeking to find alternative models for decision-making and that they are not the only paradigms that could be used.

2 The position of a player shapes their perceptions of an issue. Allison and Halperin point out how important the career aspirations of players, or simply the desire to participate (in the case of junior officials, presumably to make an impression), are in shaping attitudes.

3 The term is employed within the context of the paradigm and does not imply that the EU is a government in the sense of a 'state government', but a type or form of government in the widest sense because it is a policy-maker.

4 Deniau (1984) also makes this distinction that the Council adopts decisions as a single institution.

5 For further discussion, see Weber and Wiesmeth (1991) and for a more general analysis of the issue consult Haas (1980).

6 For example, compare Iklé (1964: 3–4) with Jönsson (1983: 140) and Midgaard (1983: 152).

7 The term 'speech acts' is employed by Midgaard (1983).

**Chapter 5**

1 For further details on EC monetary affairs, see for example Tsoukalis (1993), and de Grauwe (1994). For particular consideration of the development of EMU in the late 1980s and early 1990s see Thiel, E. in Wallace (ed.) (1990: 69–88), and Sandholtz, W. in Cafruny and Rosenthal (eds) (1993: 125–44).

2 A senior Council official stated that there have been several conflictual situations between the General Affairs Council and EcoFin, but this was only one view and should be treated accordingly.

3 Germany is usually represented by the Federal Minister for Finance, and two State Secretaries – one from the Federal Ministry for Finance and the other from the Federal Ministry for Economic Affairs. The Minister for Economic Affairs, the Secretary of State for the Economy, and the Secretary of State for Finance are the Spanish representatives at EcoFin meetings.

4 This total figure was calculated by analysing the Council Press Releases for the EcoFin Council during this five year period. 'A' points are excluded here.

5 For further discussion of fiscal harmonization, see Westaway, T. in Swann (ed.) (1992: 81–105), and El -Agraa (ed.) (1994: 288–305).

6 Official Journal, C Series, 250, 18 September 1987.

7 See EC Bulletin vol. 24, no. 10, October 1991, p. 107 and Council Press Release 8404/91 Presse 159, 7 October 1991. See also Official Journal, L Series, 316, 31 October 1992. An additional two simplifying Directives were discussed in November 1992, and agreed by the EcoFin Council on 14 December 1992. Official Journal, L Series, 384, 30 December 1992, and 390, 31 December 1992. See also Council Press Release 10088/92 Presse 216, 23 November 1992.

8 Commission of the EC, *Taxation in the Single Market*. Office for the Official Publications of the European Communities. Luxembourg, June 1990, p. 30.

9 Details of the main changes that this package introduced are set out in 'Commission Guide to VAT in 1993,' *Background Report*. Commission of the European Communities ISEC/B20/92, London, July 1992.

10 *Agence Europe*, No. 4766, 18/19 April 1988 p. 5, and Council Press Release 5419/88 Presse 45, 18 April 1988.

11 Council Press Release 7003/90 Presse 89, 11 June 1990.

12 Council Press Release 10149/88 Presse 206, 12 December 1988.

13 Council Press Release 10902/89 Presse 248, 18 December 1989 and *EC Bulletin* vol. 22, no. 12, December 1989, p. 32.

14 Council Press Release 10902/89 Presse 248, 18 December 1989 and *EC Bulletin* vol. 22, no. 12, December 1989, p. 32.

15 The EcoFin session was held on 3 December 1990. See *EC Bulletin* vol. 23, no. 12, December 1990, pp. 28–9.

16 Council Press Release 9850/89 Presse 206, 13 November 1989.

17 *Agence Europe*, No. 5510, 12 June 1991. Interestingly, the Luxembourg Presidency had threatened that a special session would be convened if agreement was not reached at the previous EcoFin meeting. See Council Press Release 6571/91 Presse 80, 3 June 1991.

18 See *Agence Europe*, No. 5761, 29 June 1992, p. 10, Council Press Release 8134/92 Presse 147, 27 July 1992, *Agence Europe*, No. 5780, 27/28 July 1992, p. 6 and *Agence Europe*, No. 5783, 31 July 1992, p. 6.

19 Respectively, 13-15 May 1988 in Lübeck, and 17-18 September 1988 in Crete. See Council Press Releases 5419/88 Presse 45, 18 April 1988, and 7604/88 Presse 113, 11 July 1988.

20 Compare *Agence Europe*, No. 4998, 19 April 1989 with Council Press Release 7428/89 Presse 119, 19 June 1989.

21 Council Press Release 10149/88 Presse 206, 12 December 1988.

22 See *EC Bulletin*, vol. 22, no. 10, October 1989, p. 22.

23 See for example Council Press Release 9850/89 Presse 206, 13 November 1989.

24 *Agence Europe*, No. 5632, 18 December 1991, p. 7.
25 See *Agence Europe*, No. 5510, 12 June 1991, p. 8.
26 *Agence Europe*, No. 5519, 24/25 June 1991, p. 7.
27 *Agence Europe*, No. 5505, 5 June 1991, p. 7.
28 Council Press Release 8134/92 Presse 147, 27 July 1992, *Agence Europe*, No. 5780, 27/28 July 1992, p. 6 and *Agence Europe*, No. 5783, 31 July 1992, p. 6.
29 This was confirmed by comparing Council documentation with reports from *Agence Europe*.
30 See Council Press Release 5419/88 Presse 45, 18 April 1988, *Agence Europe*, No. 4998, 19 April 1989, p. 5, and Council Press Release 7003/90 Presse 89, 11 June 1990.
31 Compare Council Press Release 7428/89 Presse 119, 19 June 1989, *Agence Europe*, No. 5691, 18 March 1992, p. 5, Council Press Release 6542/92 Presse 88, 19 May 1992, *Agence Europe* No. 5734, 21 May 1992, p. 7, and Council Press Release 7003/90 Presse 89, 11 June 1990.
32 See Council Press Release 9850/89 Presse 206, 13 November 1989, and *EC Bulletin* vol. 23, no. 12, December 1990, pp. 29–30.
33 *Agence Europe*, No. 5732, 18/19 May 1992, p. 6.
34 *Agence Europe*, No. 5841, 21 October 1992, p. 5.
35 See Official Journal, C Series 106, 28 April 1990, and Council Press Release 8998/90 Presse 144, 8 October 1990.
36 See Council Press Release 6776/91 Presse 87, 10 June 1991, and Official Journal, L Series 166, 28 June 1991.
37 For further information, see *EC Bulletin* vol. 24, no. 6, June 1991, p. 30.
38 *Agence Europe*, No. 5509, 10/11 June 1991, p. 10.
39 See Council Press Release 10870/90 Presse 231, 17 December 1991.
40 For further details, see Council Press Release 10870/90 Presse 231, 17 December 1990.
41 This EcoFin session, held on 28 January 1991, adopted the Council's common position. See Council Press Release 4361/91 Presse 6, 28 January 1991.
42 Council Press Release 6776/91 Presse 87, 10 June 1991.

43 Council Press Release 10870/90 Presse 231, 17 December 1990.
44 For example, compare Council Press Release 10870/90 Presse 231, 17 December 1990, with Council Press Release 6776/91 Presse 87, 10 June 1991, and *Agence Europe*, No. 5509, 10/11 June 1991, p. 10.
45 The EP delivered its first reading on 22 November 1990, and its second reading on 17 April 1991. See Official Journal, C Series 324, 24 December 1990 and 129, 20 May 1991.
46 See Official Journal, L Series 166, 28 June 1991.

**Chapter 6**
1 This total figure was calculated by analysing the Council Press Releases for the Environment Council during this five year period.
2 Council Press Release 10182/89 Presse 224, 28 November 1989.
3 Official Journal, C Series 217, 23 August 1989.
4 Official Journal, L Series 120, 11 May 1990.
5 Official Journal, L Series 176, 6 July 1985.
6 For further details, see 'The European Environmental Agency.' *Background Report*. Commission of the European Communities, ISEC/B6/94, London, February 1994.
7 For further discussion, see for example Almarcha Barbado (1993), Francioni (1992), and Kazakos and Ioakimidis (1994).
8 There were further Greek elections in 1990 which resulted in a change of government, but this occurred after the proposal had been adopted.
9 Council Press Release 8501/89 Presse 156, 19 September 1989.
10 *Agence Europe*, No. 5140, 27/28 November 1989, p. 7.
11 *Agence Europe*, No. 5397, 21 December 1990, p. 5.
12 The EP adopted this Resolution on 14 June 1991. See Official Journal, C Series 183, 15 July 1991.
13 *Agence Europe*, No. 5093, 20 September 1989, p. 12.
14 *Agence Europe*, No. 5140, 27/28 November 1989, p. 7.
15 *Agence Europe*, No. 5695, 23/24 March 1992, p. 9.

16 *Agence Europe*, No. 5838, 17 October 1992, p. 10.

17 *Agence Europe*, No. 5842, 22 October 1992, p. 6, and Council Press Release 9042/92 Presse 179, 20 October 1992.

18 Council Press Release 10796/92 Presse 248, 15 December 1992.

19 See *Agence Europe*, No. 5093, 20 September 1989, p. 12 and No. 5140, 27/28 November 1989, p. 7.

20 *Agence Europe*, No. 5140, 27/28 November 1989, p. 7.

21 Official Journal, C Series 56, 7 March 1990.

22 The EP's opinion was delivered on 14 March, published in the Official Journal, C Series 96, 7 April 1990.

23 EP Press Release C/JN/26/90, Brussels, 23 March 1990.

24 For example, see Council Press Releases 8501/89 Presse 156, 19 September 1989, 10182/89 Presse 224, 28 November 1989, 5329/90 Presse 33, 22 March 1990, and *EC Bulletin* vol. 23, no. 3, March 1990, p. 26.

25 Official Journal, C Series 138, 26 May 1983. The Commission subsequently amended the proposal in June 1984 – Official Journal, C Series 167, 27 June 1984.

26 For further details see *Agence Europe*, No. 5578, 1 October 1991, p. 10, and *EC Bulletin* vol. 24, no. 10, October 1991, pp. 62–3. For the Court ruling, see Official Journal, C Series 180, 11 July 1991.

27 For the re-submitted proposal, see Official Journal, C Series 317, 7 December 1991. For the final Directive, see Official Journal, L Series 409, 31 December 1992.

28 Council Directive 78/176/EEC, Official Journal, L Series 54, 25 February 1978.

29 See *EC Bulletin* vol. 21, no. 6, June 1988, and Council Press Release 7216/88 Presse 105, 28 June 1988.

30 See Council Press Release 5032/92 Presse 39, 23 March 1992, and Council Press Release 10796/92 Presse 248, 15 December 1992.

31 Official Journal, C Series 127, 14 May 1984 and C Series 158, 26 June 1989.

32 Official Journal, C Series 94, 13 April 1992, and C Series 305, 23 November 1992.

33 *EC Bulletin* vol. 22, no. 6, June 1989.

34 Official Journal, C Series 358, 31 December 1983, and C Series 98, 21 April 1992.

35 See Council Press Release 5050/88 Presse 34, 21 March 1988.

36 Compare Council Press Release 5050/88 Presse 34, 21 March 1988, and *EC Bulletin* vol. 21, no. 6, June 1988.

## Chapter 7

1 This total figure was calculated by analysing the Council Press Releases for the Labour & Social Affairs Council during this five year period.

2 See Official Journal, C Series 224, 8 September 1990 for the Commission's proposal. The final Directive was adopted on 25 June 1991 and can be found in the Official Journal, L Series 206, 29 July 1991.

3 See *Agence Europe*, No. 5395, 19 December 1990, p. 7, and No. 5521, 27 June 1991, p. 7.

4 *Agence Europe*, No. 5521, 27 June 1991, p. 7.

5 For details of the November session, see Council Press Release 10161/90 Presse 200, 26 November 1990.

6 *Agence Europe*, No. 5395, 19 December 1990, p. 7.

7 *Agence Europe*, No. 5395, 19 December 1990, p. 7.

8 *Agence Europe*, No. 5521, 27 June 1991, p. 7. For the EP's second reading, adopted in May 1990, see Official Journal, C Series 158, 17 June 1991.

9 The ESC's opinion was adopted in September 1990, and is published in the Official Journal, C Series 332, 31 December 1990.

10 Council Press Releases 10161/90 Presse 200, 26 November 1990, 10870/90 Presse 236, 18 December 1990 and 7142/91 Presse 119, 25 June 1991.

11 See *Health and Safety at Work: A Challenge to Europe*. Commission of the European Communities. Office for Official Publications of the European Communities, Luxembourg, May 1992.

12 Official Journal, C Series 34, 8 February 1988.

13 Official Journal, L Series 196, 26 July 1990.

14 Official Journal, C Series 50, 26 February 1987.

15 Council Press Release 10309/89 Presse 228, 30 November 1989.

16 The ESC delivered its opinion on 2 June 1988, and is published in the Official Journal, C Series 208, 8 August 1988.

17 Council Press Release 10222/88 Presse 211, 16 December 1988. For the EP's first reading, see Official Journal, C Series 158, 26 June 1989.

18 Refer to Official Journal, C Series 149, 18 June 1990, and *EC Bulletin* vol. 23, no. 5, May 1990, p. 24.

19 Council Press Releases 6637/88 Presse 80, 9 June 1988, 10222/88 Presse 211, 16 December 1988, and 6711/90 Presse 70, 29 May 1990.

20 See, for example, Council Press Releases 6637/88 Presse 80, 9 June 1988, and 10222/88 Presse 211, 16 December 1988.

## Chapter 8

1 *Treaty Article on Education, Possible Implications.* Internal document. General Secretariat. Council of the European Communities, Brussels, January 1992, p. 1.

2 This total figure was calculated by analysing the Council Press Releases for the Education Council during this five-year period.

3 For further details, see Brewin and McAllister (1990: 473).

4 'For further details, see 'Community Education and Training – Achievements since 1986 and Guidelines for the Future.' *Background Report*. Commission of the European Communities. ISEC/B22/93, London, June 1993.

5 For the Commission's proposal, see Official Journal, C Series 51, 28 February 1989, and for the final Decision see Official Journal, L Series 239, 16 August 1989. Although the Education Council agreed to the Lingua programme in May 1989, it was officially adopted on 28 July 1989 after the legal text had been finalized.

6 *Agence Europe*, No. 4788, 24/25 May 1988, p. 7.

7 The ESC's opinion can be found in Official Journal, C Series 139, 5 June 1989.

8 For details of the EP's opinion, see Official Journal, C Series 120, 16 May 1989.

9 *Agence Europe*, No. 4788, 24/25 May 1988, p. 7.

10 *Agence Europe*, No. 4788, 24/25 May 1988, p. 7.

11 See *Agence Europe*, No. 5741, 1 June 1992, p. 8, and Council Press Release 6772/92 Presse 97, 1 June 1992.

12 See *Agence Europe*, No. 5741, 1 June 1992, p. 8, and Council Press Release 6772/92 Presse 97, 1 June 1992.

13 *Agence Europe*, No. 4788, 24/25 May 1988, p. 7.

14 Official Journal, C Series 329, 31 December 1990.

15 Official Journal, C Series 38, 19 February 1976.

16 See Official Journal, C Series 329, 31 December 1990.

17 See *EC Bulletin*, vol. 10, no. 10, October 1989, p. 34.

18 For further details see *EC Bulletin*, vol. 22, no. 10, October 1989, and vol. 23, no. 5, May 1990.

19 See *Agence Europe*, No. 5867, 28 November 1992, p. 8, Council Press Release 10366/92 Presse 224, 27 November 1992, and *EC Bulletin* vol. 25, no. 11, November 1992, pp. 49–50.

## Chapter 10

1 These include Poland, Hungary, Czech Republic, Slovenia, Estonia and Cyprus.

2 The Council first agreed to greater openness at a meeting with the EP in November 1993. The EP identified a loophole in The Netherlands Freedom of Information Act and tried to threaten the Council with this during EP Question Time. Although the Act is only applicable to finished Council business, Dutch MEPs argued that all Council business was ongoing.

3 'The Duty to inform about the Community'. *Target 92*. Commission of the European Communities, Brussels, March 1992.

4 *The Guardian*. 31 August 1994.

5 *The Guardian*, 20 October 1995.

6 The decision was taken by the General Affairs Council on 2 October 1995. See *The Week in Europe*. The European Commission, WE/33/95, London, October 1995, and *The Guardian*, 3 October 1995.

7 These include co-decision for the fight against fraud, second pillar costs excluding military actions, and third pillar operational costs.

# Bibliography

Allison, G. T. (1971) *Essence of Decision: Explaining the Cuban Missile Crisis.* Boston: Little, Brown and Co.

— and Halperin, M. H. (1972) 'Bureaucratic Politics: A Paradigm and Some Policy Implications', in Tanter, R. and Ullman, R. H. *Theory and Policy in International Relations.* Princeton: Princeton University Press, pp. 40–79.

Almarcha Barbado, A. (ed.) (1993) *Spain and EC Membership Evaluated.* London: Pinter.

Bachrach, P. and Baratz, M. 1962) 'Two Faces of Power.' *American Political Science Review.* 56, 947–52.

— (1963) 'Decisions and Non-Decisions: An Analytical Framework.' *American Political Science Review.* 57, 632–42.

Bangemann, M. (1980) 'Report of the Three Wise Men: A Critical Assessment.' Published Paper presented to the Conference of the European Cooperation Funds, Brussels.

Barston, R. P. (1983) 'International Negotiation: The Development of Central Concepts.' *European Journal of Political Research.* **11**, 129–38.

Beyers, J. and Dierickx, G. (1998) 'The Working Groups of the Council of the European Union: Supranational or Intergovernmental Negotiations?' *Journal of Common Market Studies.* **36**, 289–317.

Bieber, R. and Palmer, M. (1975) 'Power at the Top – the EC Council in theory and practice.' *The World Today.* 31, 310–18.

Bo Bramsen, C. (1982) 'Le conseil européen: son fonctionnement et ses resultats de 1975 à 1981.' *Revue du Marché Commun.* 262, 624–45.

Boulouis, J. (1982) 'Quelques réflexions sur le Conseil Européen.' *Administration (Paris).* 17, 25–9.

— (1989) 'La Qualité du Parlement Européen pour agir en Annulation.' *Revue du Marché Commun.* 342, 119–22.

Brams, S. J. (1985) 'New Paradoxes of Voting Power on the EC Council of Ministers.' *Electoral Studies.* 4, 135–9.

Braybrooke, D. and Lindblom, C. E. (1963) *A Strategy of Decision: Policy Evaluation as a Social Process.* New York: The Free Press.

Brewin, C. and McAllister, R. (1986) 'Annual Review of the Activities of the European Communities in 1985.' *Journal of Common Market Studies.* **24**, 313–45.

— (1987) 'Annual Review of the Activities of the European Communities in 1986.' *Journal of Common Market Studies.* **25**, 337–71.

— (1988) 'Annual Review of the Activities of the European Communities in 1987.' *Journal of Common Market Studies.* **26**, 431–67.

— (1989) 'Annual Review of the Activities of the European Communities in 1988.' *Journal of Common Market Studies.* **27**, 323–57.

— (1990) 'Annual Review of the Activities of the European Communities in 1989.' *Journal of Common Market Studies.* **28**, 451–96.

— (1991) 'Annual Review of the Activities of the European Communities in 1990.' *Journal of Common Market Studies.* **29**, 385–429.

Bulmer, S. (1983) 'Domestic Politics and European Community Policy-Making.' *Journal of Common Market Studies.* **21**, 349–63.

— (1985) 'The European Council's First Decade: Between Interdependence and Domestic Politics.' *Journal of Common Market Studies.* **24**, 89–103.

— (1991) *The Council of Ministers and the European Council: Two-Faced Institutions in a*

*Federal Order.* European Policy Research Unit Working Paper 7/91, University of Manchester.
— and Wessels, W. (1987) *The European Council.* London: Macmillan.
—, George, S. and Scott, A. (eds) (1992) *The United Kingdom and EC Membership Evaluated.* London: Pinter.
Burgess, M. (ed.) (1986) *Federalism and Federation in Western Europe.* London: Croom Helm.
Busch, S. and Puchala, D. (1976) 'Interests, influence and integration – political structure in the EC.' *Comparative Political Studies.* 9, 235–54.
Butler, M. (1986) *Europe: More Than A Continent.* London: Heinemann.
Cafruny, A. and Rosenthal, G. (eds) (1993) *The State of the European Community: The Maastricht Debates and Beyond.* Harlow: Longman.
Carrington, P. (1988) *Reflect on Things Past.* Glasgow: William Collins.
Chandernagor, C. (1982) 'La difficulté d'être au Conseil.' *Administration (Paris).* 17, 17–24.
Christodoulou, E. (1985) 'Les relations entre le Parlement et le Conseil des Ministres', in Louis, J. V. (ed.) *Le Parlement Européen dans l'évolution institutionnelle.* Bruxelles: Editions de l'Université de Bruxelles.
Corbett, R. (1989) 'Testing the New Procedures: The European Parliament's First Experiences with its new "Single Act" Powers.' *Journal of Common Market Studies.* **28**, 359–72.
— (1992) 'Increased Powers of the European Parliament.' *European Parliamentary Year Book 1992/3.* Brussels: European Parliament.
— (1993) *The Treaty of Maastricht: From Conception to Ratification: A Comprehensive Reference Guide.* Harlow: Longman.
—, Jacobs, F. and Shackleton, M. (1995) *The European Parliament.* London: Cartermill.
Commission of the European Communities (1989) *XXIInd General Report on the Activities of the European Communities 1988.* Luxembourg: Office for Official Publications of the European Communities.
— (1990a) *XXIIIrd General Report on the Activities of the European Communities 1989.* Luxembourg: Office for Official Publications of the European Communities.
— (1990b) *Taxation in the Single Market.* Luxembourg: Office for Official Publications of the European Communities, June.
— (1991) *XXIVth General Report on the Activities of the European Communities 1990.* Luxembourg: Office for Official Publications of the European Communities.
— (1992a) *XXVth General Report on the Activities of the European Communities 1991.* Luxembourg: Office for Official Publications of the European Communities.
— (1992b) 'Commission Guide to VAT in 1993.' *Background Report.* Commission of the European Communities ISEC/B20/92. London, July.
— (1992c) 'The Duty to Inform about the Community.' *Target 92.* Brussels, March.
— (1992d) *Health and Safety at Work: A Challenge to Europe.* Luxembourg: Office for Official Publications of the European Communities, May.
— (1993a) *XXVIth General Report on the Activities of the European Communities 1992.* Luxembourg: Office for Official Publications of the European Communities.
— (1993b) 'Community Education and Training Achievement since 1986 & Guidelines for the Fututre.' *Background Report.* Commission of the European Communities ISEC/B22/93. London, June.
— (1993c) 'The Internal Market after 1992.' *Background Report.* Commission of the European Communities, London Office, ISEC/B7/93, March.
— (1994) 'The European Environmental Agency.' *Background Report.* Commission of the European Communities, London Office, ISEC/B6/94, February.
— (1995) *The Week in Europe.* London Office, WE/33/95, October.
Commission General Secretariat. (1990a) *Bulletin of the European Communities.* Office for Official Publications of the European Communities, Luxembourg.
— (1992) *Treaty Article on Education: Possible Implications.* Council of the European Communities, Internal document. Brussels, January.

Council of the European Communities
(1983) *Thirtieth Review of the Council's Work.
1 January to 31 December 1982.*
Luxembourg: Office for Official
Publications of the European
Communities.
— (1984) *Thirty-First Review of the Council's
Work. 1 January to 31 December 1983.*
Luxembourg: Office for Official
Publications of the European
Communities.
— (1985) *Thirty-Second Review of the Council's
Work. 1 January to 31 December 1984.*
Luxembourg: Office for Official
Publications of the European
Communities.
— (1986) *Thirty-Third Review of the Council's
Work. 1 January to 31 December 1985.*
Luxembourg: Office for Official
Publications of the European
Communities.
— (1987) *Thirty-Fourth Review of the Council's
Work. 1 January to 31 December 1986.*
Luxembourg: Office for Official
Publications of the European
Communities.
— (1988) *Thirty-Fifth Review of the Council's
Work. 1 January to 31 December 1987.*
Luxembourg: Office for Official
Publications of the European
Communities.
— (1989) *Thirty-Sixth Review of the Council's
Work. 1 January to 31 December 1988.*
Luxembourg: Office for Official
Publications of the European
Communities.
— (1990) *Thirty-Seventh Review of the Council's
Work. 1 January to 31 December 1989.*
Luxembourg: Office for Official
Publications of the European
Communities.
— (1991a) *Thirty-Eighth Review of the Council's
Work. 1 January to 31 December 1990.*
Luxembourg: Office for Official
Publications of the European
Communities.
— (1991b) *The Council of the European
Community: An introduction to its structures and
activities 1990.* Luxembourg: Office for
Official Publications of the European
Communities.
— (1992a) *Thirty-Ninth Review of the Council's
Work. 1 January to 31 December 1991.*
Luxembourg: Office for Official

Publications of the European
Communities.
— (1992b) *Guide to the Council of the European
Communities 1992.* Luxembourg: Office for
Official Publications of the European
Communities.
— (1993) *Fortieth Review of the Council's Work.
1 January to 31 December 1992.*
Luxembourg: Office for Official
Publications of the European
Communities, 1994.
Council of the European Union (1995a)
*Progress Report from the Chairman of the
Reflection Group on the 1996 IGC.* General
Secretariat, Council of the European
Union, SN 509/1/95 REVI (REFLEX
10), Brussels, September.
— (1995b) *Report of the Council on the functioning
of the Treaty on European Union.*
Luxembourg: Office for Official
Publications of the European
Communities.
Council Press Releases. Press Service,
General Secretariat. Council of the
European Union, Brussels.
Daniels, P., Hine, D. and Nerigualdesi, M.
(1991) *Italy, the European Community and the
1990 Presidency: Policy Trends and Policy
Performance.* Occasional Paper 3,
University of Bristol: Centre for
Mediterranean Studies.
de Bassompierre, G. (1988) *Changing the Guard
in Brussels: An Insider's View of the EC
Presidency.* New York: Praeger.
de Ecotais, Y. (1973) 'Une Amélioration du
Fonctionnement du Conseil des Ministres
est-elle possible?' *Revue du Marché Commun.*
161, 1–2.
de Grauwe, P. (1994) *The Economics of
Monetary Integration.* Oxford: Oxford
University Press.
de Mesquita, B. and Stokman, F. (eds) (1994)
*European Community Decision Making: Models,
Applications and Comparisons.* London: Yale
University Press.
de Witte, B. (ed.) (1989) *European Community
Law of Education.* Baden-Baden: Nomos
Verlagsgesellschaft.
Deniau, X. (1984) 'Le vote au sein du
Conseil des Ministres des Communautés
Européennes: Théorie et Pratique.' *Revue
du Marché Commun.* 279, 316–18.
Deutsch, K. W. (1954) *Political Community at
the International Level.* USA: Archon Books.

Dewost, J. L. (1980) 'Les relations entre le Conseil et la Commission dans le processus de décision communautaire.' *Revue du Marché Commun*. 238, 289–94.

— (1982) 'Le processus de décision dans les Communautés Européennes.' *Administration (Paris)* 17, 30–8.

— (1984) 'La Présidence dans le cadre institutionnel des Communautés Européennes.' *Revue du Marché Commun*. 273, 31–4.

— (1987) 'Le vote majoritaire: simple modalité de gestion ou enjeu politique essentiel', in Amicorum, L. and Pescatore, P. (eds) *Du Droit International Au Droit De L'Intégration*. Baden-Baden: Nomos Verlagsgesellschaft, pp. 167–75.

— (1988) 'Les pouvoirs discrétionnaires du Conseil des Ministres', in Schwarze, J. (ed.) *Discretionary Powers of the Member States in the field of Economic Policies and their limits under the EEC Treaty*. Baden-Baden: Nomos Verlagsgesellschaft, pp. 165–72.

— (1989) 'Rôle et position de la Commission dans le processus législatif', in Schwarze, J. (ed.) *Legislation for Europe 1992*. Baden-Baden: Nomos Verlagsgesellschaft, pp. 85–96.

Dinan, D. (1994) *Ever Closer Union: An Introduction to the European Community*. Basingstoke: Macmillan.

Dougherty, J. E. and Pfaltzgraff, R. L. (1981) *Contending Theories of International Relations*. New York: Harper and Row.

Dreyfus, F. G., Morizet, J. and Peyrard, M. (eds) (1993) *France and EC Membership Evaluated*. London: Pinter.

Dror, Y., Lindblom, C.E., Jones, R.W., McCleery, M. and Hyderband, W. (1964) 'Government Decision-Making.' *Public Administration Review*. 24, 153–65.

Duff, A. (ed.) (1997) *The Treaty of Amsterdam. Text and Commentary*. London: Federal Trust.

— , Pinder, J. and Pryce, R. (eds) (1994) *Maastricht and Beyond: Building the European Union*. London: Routledge.

Earnshaw, D. and Judge, D. (1997) 'The Life and Times of the European Union's Cooperation Procedure.' *Journal of Common Market Studies* 35, 543–64.

Edwards, G. and Wallace, H. (1977) *The Council of Ministers of the European Community and the President-in-Office*. London: Federal Trust for Education and Research.

Edwards, G. and Spence, D. (eds) (1994) *The European Commission*. London: Cartermill.

Ehlermann, C. (1990) 'Commission lacks power in 1992 process.' *European Affairs*. 1, 65–73.

El-Agraa, A. M. (ed.) (1994) *The Economics of the European Community*. London: Harvester Wheatsheaf.

Engel, C. and Wessels, W. (eds) (1992) *From Luxembourg to Maastricht: Institutional Change in the European Community after the Single European Act*. Bonn: Institut für Europäische Politik.

Etzioni, E (1967) 'Mixed-Scanning: A "Third" Approach to Decision-Making.' *Public Administration Review*. 27, 385–92.

*Europe. Agence Internationale d'Information pour la Presse*. Bruxelles: Bulletin Quotidien Europe, 1988–92 inclusive. See Notes for specific references.

European Parliament (1997) *Working Document on the new co-decision procedure after Amsterdam*. Brussels: Committee on Institutional Affairs.

Evans, A. C. (1981) 'Participation of National Parliaments in the European Community Legislative Process.' *Public Law*. 388–98.

Federal Trust (1995) *Building the Union: Reform of the Institutions. The Intergovernmental Conference 1996*. Federal Trust Papers No.3. London: Federal Trust.

Feld, W. J. and Wildgen, J. K. (1975) 'National Administration Elites and European Integration Saboteurs at work?' *Journal of Common Market Studies*. **13**, 244–65.

Fisher, R. (1969) *Basic Negotiating Strategy*. New York: Harper and Row.

Fitzmaurice, J. (1988) 'An Analysis of the European Community's Cooperation Procedure.' *Journal of Common Market Studies*. **26**, 389–400.

Francioni, F. (ed.) (1992) *Italy and EC Membership Evaluated*. London: Pinter.

Frankel, J. (1973) *Contemporary International Theory and the Behaviour of States*. Oxford: Oxford University Press.

Frediani, C. (1992) *La politique de la CEE en matière d'éducation et de culture*. Nice: Presses d'Europe.

Garel-Jones, T. (1993) 'The UK Presidency: An Inside View.' *Journal of Common Market Studies*. **31**, 261–7.

Geoghegan-Quinn, M. (1990) 'L'Irlande et la Communauté Européenne: les priorités de la Présidence Irlandaise au premier semestre 1990.' *Revue du Marché Commun.* 333, 8–13.

González Sánchez, E. (1992) 'La Négociation des décisions communautaires par les fonctionnaires nationaux: les groupes de travail du Conseil.' *Revue française d'administration publique.* 63, 391–9.

Groom, A. J. and Taylor, P. (eds) (1975) *Functionalism: Theory and Practice in International Relations.* London: University of London.

Gustafsson, G. and Richardson, J. (1979) 'Concepts of Rationality and the Policy Process.' *European Journal of Political Research.* **7**, 415–36.

Guy Peters, B. (1992) 'Bureaucratic Politics and the Institutions of the European Community', in Sbragia, A. (ed.) *Euro-Politics: Institutions and Policymaking in the 'New' European Community.* Washington DC: The Brookings Institution, pp. 75–122.

Haas, E. B. (1958) *The Uniting of Europe.* London: Stevens and Sons.

— (1980) 'Why Collaborate? Issue Linkage and International Regimes.' *World Politics.* 32, 357–405.

Hayes, F. (1984) 'The role of Coreper in EEC decision-making.' *Administration (Dublin)* 32, 177–200.

Hayes-Renshaw, F. (1990) 'Decision-Making in the EC Council after the Single European Act.' *European Trends.* 1, 74–80.

— Lequesne, C. and Mayor Lopez, P. (1989) 'The Permanent Representations of the Member States of the European Communities.' *Journal of Common Market Studies.* **28**, 119–37.

— and Wallace, H. (1997) *The Council of Ministers.* London: Macmillan.

Henderson, D. (1998) 'The UK Presidency: An Insider's View.' *Journal of Common Market Studies.* **36**, 563–72.

Henning, A. (1992) *The European Parliament in European Community Environmental Policy.* EUI Working Paper 92/13, Florence: European University Institute.

Hoffmann, S. (1982) 'Reflections on the Nation-State in Western Europe Today.' *Journal of Common Market Studies.* **21**, 21–37.

— (1995) *The European Sisyphus: Essays on Europe 1964–1994.* Oxford: Westview Press.

Hogwood, B. W. and Gunn, L. A. (1984) *Policy Analysis for the Real World.* Oxford: Oxford University Press.

Holt, S. and Hoscheit, J. M. (1984) 'The European Council and Domestic Policy-Making', in *The European Council 1974–1984: Evaluation and Prospects.* Colloquium, Kerkrade, October. Maastricht: European Institute of Public Administration.

Hosli, M (1996) 'Coalitions and Power: Effects of Qualified Majority Voting on the Council of the European Union.' *Journal of Common Market Studies.* **34**, 255–73.

Howe, G. (1994) *Conflict of Loyalty.* London: Macmillan.

Hrbek, R. (1991) 'German Federalism and the Challenge of European Integration', in Jeffery, C. and Savigear, P. (eds) *German Federalism Today.* Leicester: Leicester University Press, pp. 84–102.

Hurwitz, L. and Lequesne, C. (eds) (1991) *The State of the European Community.* Harlow: Longman.

Iklé, F. C. (1964) *How Nations Negotiate.* New York: Harper and Row.

Jacque, J. P. (1984) 'L'Evolution du Triangle Institutionnel Communautaire depuis l'élection du Parlement Européen au Suffrage Universel Direct.' in Teitgen, P. (ed.) *Etudes de Droit des Communautés Européennes.* Paris: Pedone, pp. 183–208.

— and Simon, D. (1984) 'Le rôle constitutionnel et juridique du Conseil Européen', in *The European Council 1974–1984: Evaluation and Prospects.* Colloquium, Kerkrade, October. Maastricht: European Institute of Public Administration.

Jeffrey, C. and Sturm, R. (eds) (1992) *German Politics: Special Issue on Federalism, Unification and European Integration.* London: Frank Cass.

Jenkins, R. (1989) *European Diary 1977–1981.* London: Collins.

Jönsson, C. (1983) 'A Cognitive Approach to International Negotiation.' *European Journal of Political Research.* **11**, 139–50.

Judge, D. (ed.) (1993) *A Green Dimension for the European Community: Political Issues and Processes.* London: Frank Cass.

Kazakos, P. and Ioakimidis, P. (eds) (1994) *Greece and EC Membership Evaluated.* London: Pinter.

Keatinge, P. (ed.) (1991) *Ireland and EC Membership Evaluated.* London: Pinter.

Keohane, R. O. and Hoffmann, S. (eds) (1991) *The New European Community: Decision-Making and Institutional Change.* Oxford: Westview Press.

Kirchner, E. (1992) *Decision-Making in the European Community: The Council Presidency and European Integration.* Manchester: Manchester University Press.

Kranz, J. (1982) 'Le vote dans le pratique du Conseil des ministres des Communautés Européennes.' *Revue Trimestrielle de Droit Européen (Paris).* 3, 403–30.

Krasner, S. D. (1972) 'Are Bureaucracies Important? (or Allison Wonderland).' *Foreign Policy.* 7, 159–79.

Lambert, J. (1966) 'The Constitutional Crisis 1965–66.' *Journal of Common Market Studies.* **4**, 195–228.

Lawson, N. (1992) *The View from No.11.* London: Bantam Press.

Lequesne, C. (1991) 'Quelques considérations sur la pratique du vote au sein du Conseil des Ministres des Communautés Européennes.' *Centres de Pouvoirs Européens,* 19–23.

Lindberg, L. N. (1963) *The Political Dynamics of European Economic Integration.* Stanford: Stanford University Press.

— and Scheingold, S. (1970) *Europe's Would-Be Polity.* New Jersey: Englewood Cliffs.

Lindblom, C. E. (1959) 'The Science of Muddling Through.' *Public Administration Review.* 19, 79–88.

— (1968) *The Policy-Making Process.* New Jersey: Prentice-Hall.

— (1979) 'Still Muddling, Not Yet Through.' *Public Administration Review.* 39, 517–26.

Lyck, L. (ed.) (1992) *Denmark and EC Membership Evaluated.* London: Pinter.

MacGrew, A. G. and Wilson, M. J. (eds) (1982) *Decision-Making: Approaches and Analysis.* Manchester: Manchester University Press.

Maillet, P. (1992) 'Le double visage de Maastricht: Achèvement et nouveau départ.' *Revue du Marché Commun.* 356, 209–19.

Mangus-Martin, A. (1980) 'La participation du Comité des Représentants Permanents au processus de décision communautaire.' *Cahiers de Droit Européen.* 1, 25–53.

Marin, B. and Mayntz, R. (eds) (1991) *Policy Networks: Empirical Evidence and Theoretical Considerations.* Frankfurt am Main: Campus Verlag.

May, S. (1986) *The European Community and the task for the British Presidency in 1986.* London: Centre for Policy Studies.

Midgaard, K. (1983) 'Rules and Strategy in Negotiations: Notes on an Institutionalist and Intentionalist Approach.' *European Journal of Political Research.* **11**, 151–66.

Mitrany, D. (1965) 'The Prospect of Integration: Federal or Functional.' *Journal of Common Market Studies.* **4**, 119–49.

— (1975) *The Functional Theory of Politics.* London: Martin Robertson.

Moderne, F. (1986) 'L'administration espagnole et l'intégration européenne.' *Annuaire Européen d'Administration Publique.* 9, 137–55.

Monar, J. Ungerer, W. and Wessels, W. (eds) (1993) *The Maastricht Treaty on European Union: Legal Complexity and Political Dynamic.* Brussels: European InterUniversity Press.

Moravcsik, A. (1991) 'Negotiating the Single European Act: national interests and conventional statecraft in the European Community.' *International Organisation.* 45, 19–56.

— (1993) 'Preferences and Power in the European Community: A Liberal Intergovernmentalist Approach.' *Journal of Common Market Studies.* **31**, 473–524.

Mutimer, D. (1989) '1992 and the Political integration of Europe: Neofunctionalism reconsidered.' *Revue d'Intégration Européenne.* 1, 75–101.

Niblock, M. (1971) *The EEC: National Parliaments in Community Decision-Making.* London: Chatham House/PEP.

Nicoll, W. (1984) 'The Luxembourg Compromise.' *Journal of Common Market Studies.* **23**, 35–43.

— (1986a) 'From rejection to repudiation: EC budgetary affairs in 1985.' *Journal of Common Market Studies.* **25**, 31–49.

— (1986b) 'La procédure de concertation entre le Parlement et le Conseil.' *Revue du Marché Commun.* 293, 11–15.

— (1986c) 'Historique de la composition de la majorité qualifiée au Conseil en vertu des Traités.' *Revue du Marché Commun.* 295, 135–7.

— (1993) 'Note the Hour – and File the Minute.' *Journal of Common Market Studies.* **31**, 559–66.

— and Salmon, T. C. (1994) *Understanding the New European Community*. London: Harvester Wheatsheaf.

Noël, E. (1967) 'The Committee of Permanent Representatives.' *Journal of Common Market Studies*. **5**, 219–51.

— (1976) 'Some reflections on the preparation, development and repercussions of the meetings between Heads of Government (1974–1975).' *Government and Opposition*. 11, 20–34.

— (1984) 'Réflexions sur les processus de décision dans le Conseil des Communautés Européennes,' in Teitgen, P. (ed.) *Etudes de Droit des Communautés Européennes*. Paris: Pedone, 345–54.

— (1989) 'The Single European Act.' *Government and Opposition*. 24, 3–14.

— and Etienne, H. (1971) 'The Permanent Representatives Committee and the "Deepening" of the Communities.' *Government and Opposition*. 6, 422–47.

Nugent, N. (1994) *The Government and Politics of the European Community*. Basingstoke: Macmillan.

— (ed.) (1993) *The European Community 1992: Annual Review of Activities*. Oxford: Blackwell Publishers.

Official Journal of the European Communities, L Series. Luxembourg: Office for the Official Publications of the European Communities.

Official Journal of the European Communities, C Series. Luxembourg: Office for the Official Publications of the European Communities.

O'Nuallain, C. (ed.) (1985) *The Presidency of the European Council of Ministers*. London: Croom Helm.

Ørstrøm Moller, J. (1983) 'Danish EC Decision-Making: An Insider's View.' *Journal of Common Market Studies*. **21**, 245–60.

Parry, G. and Morris, P. (1982) 'When is a decision not a decision?', in McGrew, A. G. and Wilson, M. J. (eds) *Decision-Making: Approaches and Analysis*. Manchester: Manchester University Press, pp. 19–35.

Peirce, W. S. (1991) 'Unanimous Decisions in a Redistributive Context: The Council of Ministers of the European Communities', in Vaubel, R. and Willet, T. D. (eds) *The Political Economy of International Organisations*. Boulder, Colo.: Westview Press, pp. 267–85.

Pentland, C. (1973) *International Theory and European Integration*. London: Faber and Faber.

Peterson, J. (1995) 'Decision-Making in the European Union: Towards a Framework for Analysis.' *Journal of European Public Policy*. **2**, 69–93.

Pinder, J. (1986) 'European Community and nation-state: a case for a neo-federalism?' *International Affairs*. 62, 41–54.

Poos, J. F. (1991) 'The Priorities of the Luxembourg Presidency of the European Community,' in Clesse, A. and Vernon, R. (eds) *The European Community after 1992: A New Role in World Politics?* Baden-Baden: Nomos Verlagsgesellschaft, pp. 29–35.

Puchala, D. J. (1972) 'Of Blind Men, Elephants and International Integration.' *Journal of Common Market Studies*. **10**, 267–84.

Putnam, R. D. (1988) 'Diplomacy and Domestic Politics: The Logic of Two-Level Games.' *International Organisation*. 42, 427–60.

Richardson, J., Gustafsson, G. and Jordan, G. (1982) 'The Concept of Policy Style', in Richardson, J. (ed.) *Policy Styles in Western Europe*. London: George, Allen and Unwin, pp. 1–16.

Rosati, J. (1981) 'Developing a Systematic Decision-Making Framework: Bureaucratic Politics in Perspective.' *World Politics*. 33, 234–52.

Rosenthal, G. (1975) *The Men Behind the Decisions*. Lexington, Va.: D.C. Heath and Co.

Sandholtz, W. (1993) 'Monetary Bargains: The Treaty on EMU', in Cafruny, A. and Rosenthal, G. (eds) (1993) *The State of the European Community: The Maastricht Debates and Beyond*. Harlow: Longman, pp. 125–44.

Santer, J. (1991) 'The Luxembourg Presidency of the European Community after the first three months: The Challenge Ahead', in Clesse, A. and Vernon, R. (eds) *The European Community after 1992: A New Role in World Politics?* Baden-Baden: Nomos Verlagsgesellschaft, pp. 19–26.

Scharpf, F. W. (1988) 'The Joint-Decision Trap: Lessons from German federalism and European integration.' *Public Administration*. 66, 239–78.

— (1989) 'Decision Rules, Decision Styles and Policy Choices.' *Journal of Theoretical Politics.* **1**, 149–76.

Schelling, T. C. (1960) *The Strategy of Conflict.* Cambridge, Mass.: Harvard University Press.

Schwarze, J. (1989) 'The reform of the European Community's institutional system by the Single European Act', in Schwarze, J. (ed.) *Legislation for Europe 1992.* Baden-Baden: Nomos Verlagsgesellschaft, pp. 11–20.

Schweitzer, C. and Karsten, D. (eds) (1990) *The Federal Republic of Germany and EC Membership Evaluated.* London: Pinter.

Sidjanski, D. (1989) 'EC 1992: gouverne-ment de comités.' *Pouvoirs.* 48, 71–80.

Simon, H. (1957) *Administrative Behaviour.* New York: The Free Press.

Sloot, T. and Verschuren, P. (1990) 'Decision-Making Speed in the European Community.' *Journal of Common Market Studies.* **29**, 75–85.

Smith, G. and May, D. (1980) 'The Artificial Debate between Rationalist and Incrementalist Models of Decision Making.' *Policy and Politics.* 8, 147–61.

Soetendorp, B. (1994) 'The Evolution of the EC/EU as a Single Foreign Policy Actor', in Carlsnaes, W. and Smith, S. (eds) *European Foreign Policy: The EC and Changing Perspectives in Europe.* London: Sage, pp. 113–19.

Spence, D. (1991) 'Enlargement without accession: The EC's response to German unification', RIIA *Discussion Paper* No. 36. London: RIIA.

Spinelli, A. (1972) *The European Adventure.* London: Charles Knight and Co.

— (1978) 'Reflections on the Institutional Crisis in the European Community.' *West European Politics.*1, 77–88.

Story, J. and Grugel, J. (1991) *Spanish External Policies and the EC Presidency.* Occasional Paper No.2. University of Bristol: Centre for Mediterranean Studies.

Swann, D. (ed.) (1992) *The Single European Market and Beyond.* London: Routledge.

Swinbank, A. (1989) 'The Common Agricultural Policy and the Politics of European Decision Making.' *Journal of Common Market Studies.* **27**, 303–22.

Taylor, J. P. S. (1984) 'Relations between the European Parliament and the Council of Ministers.' *Annuaire Européen.* 32, 33–47.

Teasdale, A. L. (1993) 'The Life and Death of the Luxembourg Compromise.' *Journal of Common Market Studies.* **31**, 567–79.

Thatcher, M. (1993) *The Downing Street Years.* London: HarperCollins.

Thiel, E. (1990) 'Changing Patterns of Monetary Independence', in Wallace, W. (ed.) *The Dynamics of European Integration.* London: Pinter/Royal Institute of International Affairs, pp. 69–88.

Tizzano, A. (1991) 'The Permanent Representations of the Member States to the European Communities,' in *Public Administration and Europe 92: Proceedings of Congress and Seminars.* Roma: Editoriale Scientifica, pp. 519–48.

Tracy, M (1985) 'The Decision-Making Practice of the European Community with reference to the Common Agricultural Policy', in Pelkmans, J. (ed.) *Can the CAP be reformed?* Maastricht: European Institute of Public Administration, pp. 79–92.

Tranholm-Mikkelsen, J. (1991) 'Neo-functionalism: obstinate or obsolete?: A reappraisal in the light of the new dynam-ism of the EC.' *Millennium.* 20, 1–22.

Troy Johnston, M. (1994) *The European Council: Gatekeeper of the European Community.* Boulder, Colo.: Westview Press.

Trumpf, J. (1988) 'Reflections from three German Presidencies – high marks for the German coordination model, low marks for the Presidency system', in Wessels, W. and Regelsberger, E. (eds) *The Federal Republic of Germany and the EC: The Presidency and Beyond.* Bonn: EuropaUnion Verlag, pp. 266–75.

Tsoukalis, L. (1993) *The New European Economy.* Oxford: Oxford University Press.

Ungerer, W. (1993) 'Institutional Consequences of Broadening and Deepening the Community: The Consequences for the Decision-Making Process.' *Common Market Law Review.* 30, 71–83.

Van Meerhaeghe, M. A. G. (ed.) (1992) *Belgium and EC Membership Evaluated.* London: Pinter.

Van Raepenbusch, S. (1988) 'La coopération entre le CEE et les administrations nationales.' *Revue Française d'Administration Publique.* 48, 25–9.

Vasey, M. (1988) 'Decision-Making in the Agricultural Council and the

"Luxembourg Compromise".' *Common Market Law Review.* 25, 725–32.

Verloren van Themaat, P. (1992) 'Les Défis de Maastricht.' *Revue du Marché Commun.* 356, 203–8.

Wallace, H. (1971) 'The impact of the European Communities on National Policy-Making.' *Government and Opposition.* 6, 520–38.

— (1973) *National Governments and the European Communities.* London: Chatham House/PEP.

— (1983a) *EC Membership and the Presidency: A Comparative Perspective.* Maastricht: European Institute of Public Administration.

— (1983b) 'Negotiation, Conflict and Compromise: The Elusive Pursuit of Common Policies', in Wallace, H., Wallace, W. and Webb, C. (eds) *Policy Making in the European Community.* Chichester: John Wiley and Sons, pp. 43–80.

— (1984) 'Role and Evolution of the Presidency', in Hoscheit, J. M. (ed.) *The Impact of European Affairs on National Administrations – The Case of the Presidency.* Maastricht: European Institute of Public Administration, pp. 5–13.

— (1985) 'Negotiations and Coalition Formation in the European Community.' *Government and Opposition.* 20, 453–72.

— (1986) 'The British Presidency of the European Community's Council of Ministers: the opportunity to persuade.' *International Affairs.* 62, 583–99.

— (1989) 'The Best is the Enemy of the "Could": Bargaining in the European Community', in Tarditi, S. *et al.* (eds) *Agricultural Trade Liberalisation and the European Community.* Oxford: Oxford University Press, pp. 193–206.

— (1993) 'European Governance in Turbulent Times.' *Journal of Common Market Studies,* **31**, 293–303.

— (1994) 'The Council and the Commission on the Brink of Maastricht.' *The Annals of the American Academy of Political Social Science.* London: Sage, pp. 56–68.

Wallace, W. (1983) 'Less than a Federation, more than a Regime: the Community as a Political System', in Wallace, H., Wallace, W. and Webb, C. (eds) *Policy Making in the European Community.* Chichester: John Wiley and Sons, pp. 403–36.

— (ed.) (1990) *The Dynamics of European Integration.* London: Pinter/Royal Institute of International Affairs.

Webb, C. (1983) 'Theoretical Perspectives and Problems', in Wallace, H., Wallace, W. and Webb, C. (eds) *Policy Making in the European Community.* Chichester: John Wiley and Sons, pp. 1–41.

Weber, S. and Wiesmeth, H. (1991) 'Issue Linkage in the European Community.' *Journal of Common Market Studies.* **29**, 255–67.

Werts, J. (1992) *The European Council.* Amsterdam:Elsevier Science Publishers BV.

Wessels, W. (1984) 'The European Council. A Denaturing of the Community or Indispensable Decision-Making Body?', in *The European Council 1974–1984: Evaluation and Prospects.* Colloquium, Kerkrade, October. Maastricht: European Institute of Public Administration.

— (1987) 'Decision-Making in the European Community', in Beuter, R. and Tsakaloysnnis, P. (eds) *Experiences in Regional Cooperation.* Maastricht: European Institute of Public Administration, pp. 17–32.

— (1990) 'Administrative Interaction', in Wallace, W. (ed.) *The Dynamics of European Integration.* London: Pinter/Royal Institute of International Affairs, pp. 229–41.

— and Diedrichs, U. (1997) 'A New Kind of Legitimacy for a New Kind of Parliament – The Evolution of the European Parliament.' *European Integration On-line Papers (EIoP)* No.6.

Westaway, T. (1992) 'The Fiscal Dimension of 1992', in Swann, D. (ed.) *The Single European Market and Beyond.* London: Routledge, pp. 81–105.

Westlake, M. 'The passage through the Community's legislative system of emergency measures related to German unification.' EUI Working Paper 92/14. Florence: EUI.

Westlake, M. (1994) *A Modern Guide to the European Parliament.* London: Pinter.

— (1995) *The Council of the European Union.* London: Cartermill.

Widgren, M. (1993) 'A Nordic Coalition's Influence on the EC Council of Ministers', in Fagerberg, J. and Lundberg, L. (eds) *European Economic Integration: A Nordic Perspective.* Aldershot: Avebury.

Wolters, M. and Coffey, P. (eds) (1990) The Netherlands and EC Membership Evaluated. London: Pinter.

# Index